CITIZENSHIP AND IDENTITY IN EUROPE

For S

-LTH

In memory of Frank Polesel, John Pickering and Rudolf Wildenmann

-PM

Citizenship and Identity
in Europe

Edited by
LESLIE HOLMES
University of Melbourne
and
PHILOMENA MURRAY
University of Melbourne

Ashgate

Aldershot • Brookfield USA • Singapore • Sydney

Published by
Ashgate Publishing Ltd
Gower House
Croft Road
Aldershot
Hants GU11 3HR
England

Ashgate Publishing Company
Old Post Road
Brookfield
Vermont 05036
USA

British Library Cataloguing in Publication Data
Citizenship and identity in Europe
    1.Citizenship - Political aspects - Europe 2.Group identity
    - Political aspects - Europe 3.Nationalism - Europe
    4.Europe - Politics and government - 1989-
    I.Holmes, Leslie, 1948- II.Murray, Philomena
    323.6'094

Library of Congress Catalog Card Number: 99-72594

ISBN 1 84014 002 X

Printed and bound by Athenaeum Press, Ltd.,
Gateshead, Tyne & Wear.

Contents

About the Contributors

Stephen Castles is Research Professor of Sociology, Institute of Social Change and Critical Inquiry, University of Wollongong. He has been studying migration, ethnicity and racism for many years and has worked in Australia, Germany, Britain and Southern Africa. His books include *Immigrant Workers and Class Structure in Western Europe* (with Godula Kosack, Oxford University Press, 1973), *The Age of Migration: International Population Movements in the Modern World* (with Mark J. Miller, Macmillan, 1993) and *The Teeth are Smiling: the Persistence of Racism in Multicultural Australia* (co-edited with Ellie Vasta, Allen and Unwin, 1996).

Stephen Hall is the Director of the European Law Centre and Senior Lecturer in Law at the University of New South Wales, and was formerly Counsel at the Australian Attorney-General's Department in Sydney. He is the author of *Nationality, Migration Rights and Citizenship of the Union* (Martinus Nijhoff, 1995), and of several articles on topics such as European migration and citizenship in journals including *European Law Review* and *Lawasia*.

Linda Hancock is an Associate Professor based at the Centre for Public Policy at the University of Melbourne, and was previously Associate Professor of Public Policy at Deakin University. She is President of the Contemporary European Studies Association of Australia (CESAA) and Chair of the National Women's Justice Coalition, National Child Support Working Group Committee. Her numerous publications include *Analysing Health Policy* (Allen and Unwin, forthcoming) and a number of articles on gender and citizenship issues.

Leslie Holmes has been a Professor of Political Science at the University of Melbourne since 1988 and Director of its Contemporary Europe Research Centre since 1997. Among his single-authored publications are *The Policy Process in Communist States* (Sage, 1981), *Politics in the Communist World* (Oxford University Press, 1986), *The End of Communist Power* (Polity and Oxford University Press, 1993) and *Post-Communism* (Polity and Duke University Press, 1997). He is a past President of the Australasian Political Studies Association, and is currently a member of the ICCEES (International Council for Central and East European Studies) Executive and editor of the *ICCEES Newsletter*. He was elected a Fellow of the Academy of the Social Sciences in Australia in September 1995, and was Jean Monnet Visiting Professor at the European University Institute in Florence in March 1997.

Gisela Kaplan came to Australia from Berlin in 1968. She gained her PhD at Monash University in 1984, and became Foundation Professor in Social Sciences at Queensland University of Technology in 1992 and later Adjunct Professor in the Research Centre for Aboriginal and Multicultural Studies at the University of New England, NSW. Prof. Kaplan is a political sociologist with numerous publications on racism and gender, including *Contemporary Western European Feminism* (1992), *The Meagre Harvest: The Australian Women's Movement 1950s–1990s* (1996), *Hannah Arendt: Thinking, Judging, Freedom* (1989, jointly edited), and several concerned with fascism, nationalism and identity. Her current research concerns the influence of European political thought on the Australian polity and constitution.

Philomena Murray is a Senior Lecturer in the Department of Political Science at the University of Melbourne and founding President of the Contemporary European Studies Association of Australia (CESAA). She is co-editor of *Visions of European Unity* with Paul Rich (Colorado: Westview, 1996), *Europe in the 1990s: Australia's options* with Lilian Topic (CESAA, 1994), and *Europe: Rethinking the Boundaries* (Aldershot: Ashgate, 1998) with Leslie Holmes. She was a diplomat from 1984 to 1989 in Dublin and Paris, and has worked in European Union institutions in Brussels. She has written on European integration, major actors in the European Union, and the party groups in the European Parliament.

Aleksandar Pavkovic is an Associate Professor in Politics at Macquarie University, Sydney. He was previously a research fellow at the University of Melbourne and has lectured in philosophy at the University of Belgrade. He is the editor of *Contemporary Yugoslav Philosophy: The Analytic Approach* (1988) and a joint editor of *Nationalism and Postcommunism: A Collection of Essays* (1995). He has written *Slobodan Jovanovic: An Unsentimental Approach to Politics* (1993) and *The Fragmentation of Yugoslavia: Nationalism in a Multinational State* (1997). Apart from articles on the history of ideas and ideologies in the former Yugoslavia, he has also written on Thomas More's utopian project and on supranational European identity.

Martin Vranken is an Associate Professor at the Faculty of Law, University of Melbourne. Previously, he taught at the Catholic University of Leuven in Belgium (1979-1985) and Victoria University of Wellington, New Zealand (1985-1991). His main research interests are in the areas of comparative law, European law and labour law. Among his publications is *Fundamentals of European Civil Law and Impact of the European Community* (1997).

Preface

This book is basically the outcome of a conference that was held in Melbourne in September 1994 on the theme of 'Citizenship and National Identity in Europe'; this title was slightly amended for this volume to reflect the fact that it deals with more aspects of identity than merely national. The conference was organised by the Contemporary European Studies Association of Australia (*CESAA*), and attracted participants from all over Australia.

The book has taken longer to produce than either the editors or the other contributors would have preferred, for three main reasons. First, it had originally been intended to link the papers from the 1994 conference with those produced at the 1995 CESAA Conference. Eventually, and largely on our publisher's advice, it was decided to issue the two collections as separate volumes (the other has been published as *Europe: Rethinking the Boundaries*, ed. Philomena Murray and Leslie Holmes, 1998). But it did mean that the present volume was placed 'on hold' for more than a year. Second, one of the editors (Holmes) left Australia for almost twelve months of constant travel (work-related, of course!) just as the original version of this book was nearing completion. Unfortunately, and as the third reason, Murray was hit by a car shortly after Holmes' departure; a major outcome of this accident is that she has been unable to do more than a few minutes' writing or editorial work a day since November 1996. Only since Holmes' return has it been possible for the two editors to liaise closely with each other again on a day-to-day basis, and hence to reactivate and complete the project.

But the delay has in hindsight been advantageous. It has meant that all contributors have had an opportunity to reconsider and improve their original pieces; in one or two cases, the final version differs considerably from the original. In all events, each contributor updated his or her chapter in late-1997. Given that most topics covered are at least as significant now as they were in 1994, and in light of the updating, we believe that the present volume has not suffered because of the re-scheduling.

We would like publicly to thank Iona Annett, Annmarie Elijah, Craig Lonsdale, Carolyn O'Brien and Tim Szlachetko for the hours and effort they contributed to various aspects of the production of this book; each had an important role to play, and we are grateful to them.

We also wish to acknowledge the considerable support of various kinds provided to us by the Department of Political Science, and the financial assistance granted by the Faculty of Arts, at the University of Melbourne.

Leslie Holmes and Philomena Murray, 1998

Acronyms and Abbreviations

CDU	Christian Democratic Union (Germany)
CEE	Central and East European
CEFTA	Central European Free Trade Association
CEMR	Council of Municipalities and Regions
CESAA	Contemporary European Studies Association of Australia
CFSP	Common Foreign and Security Policy
CIS	Commonwealth of Independent States
CMEA	Council for Mutual Economic Assistance
CSU	Christian Social Union (Germany)
DG	Directorate General
EC	European Community
ECU	European Currency Unit
ECJ	European Court of Justice
ECSC	European Coal and Steel Community
EEC	European Economic Community
EECT	European Economic Community Treaty
EIU	Economist Intelligence Unit
EMU	Economic and Monetary Union
EP	European Parliament
ESF	European Social Fund
EU	European Union
EUT	European Union Treaty
FN	(National Front, France)
FSU	Former Soviet Union
GDP	Gross Domestic Product
GDR	German Democratic Republic
IGC	Intergovernmental Conference
ILO	International Labour Organisation
JHA	Justice and Home Affairs
MEP	Member of the European Parliament
MS	Member State
MTEU	Maastricht Treaty on European Union
NATO	North Atlantic Treaty Organisation

NSW	New South Wales
OECD	Organisation for Economic Cooperation and Development
OOPEC	Office for Official Publications of the European Communities
PCI	(Italian Communist Party)
PSI	(Italian Socialist Party)
SEA	Single European Act
SEM	Single European Market
SIA	(International Anti-Fascist Solidarity)
SPD	(Social Democratic Party, Germany)
TEU	Treaty on European Union
UDI	(Italian Women's Union)
UK	United Kingdom
USA	United States of America
USSR	Union of Soviet Socialist Republics
WTO	Warsaw Treaty Organisation

1 Introduction: Citizenship and Identity in Europe

LESLIE HOLMES AND PHILOMENA MURRAY

During the 1990s, the related issues of citizenship and identity have become two of the most widely debated topics in the social sciences.[1] Nowhere are they more clearly on the agenda than in Europe. Some of their ramifications apply more to Western Europe, others primarily to Central and Eastern Europe (hereafter CEE), while a third group clearly relates to both, and to the interactions of what are still, in many ways, two Europes.

There are several reasons why questions of citizenship and re-forming identity have become so salient in contemporary Europe. Some are relatively recent, others are more long-term. In the first part of this chapter, we examine some of the reasons for the re-forming and arguably strengthening of identity politics in the 1990s in so many parts of Europe. This acts as a lead-in to recent debates about, and developments in, the concept of citizenship, which constitutes the second major part of this introduction. In the third section, we consider the interaction of identity and citizenship politics, with particular reference to the current debate about group rights. The final part provides an overview of the book's chapters, and an explanation of how each fits into its general focus.

Identity Politics

There is an increasing awareness in the social sciences that everyone needs recognition, which can express itself in identity politics.[2] Unfortunately, this psychological need can manifest itself in a perceived necessity to exclude and/or dominate others, as one way of demarcating one's own identity. Raised awareness of this among analysts is a major reason for the recent substantial growth in the study of identity and identity politics. Francis Fukuyama encapsulated all of this well when he wrote in a book first published in 1992, 'The desire for recognition is the most specifically political part of the human personality because it is what drives men (*sic*) to want to assert themselves over other men'.[3] In this section, we examine a variety of ways in which some Europeans attempt to dominate and/or exclude others, and the reasons for this.

1

treats – notione
identity – ver

One of the more short-term reasons for the rise of identity politics in contemporary Europe is a ramification of the end of the Cold War. As this war drew to a close, with the collapse of communist power systems throughout Eastern Europe and the USSR from 1989 on, a number of issues that had been on hold were rapidly revitalised. According to some analysts, the widespread nationalism in CEE in the 1990s was just such an issue; tensions that had been suppressed by the largely authoritarian communist regimes since at least the 1940s, and which had not been resolved since the redrawing of European boundaries at the end of the First and Second World Wars, rapidly came to the fore. Post-communism's new freedoms, combined with its severe teething problems, provided an ideal arena and context for the exposure and exacerbation of inter-ethnic conflict. Precisely these conflicts, new freedoms (notably to travel), and serious economic and other difficulties encouraged many CEE citizens to flee their traditional homelands and seek refuge in more stable and affluent parts of Europe.

Unfortunately, these migrants—including asylum seekers and refugees—often discovered that they were less welcome in the West than they had hoped and expected. In many West European towns and cities, racists of various kinds made life a misery for people who had believed they at last had an opportunity to make something of their lives. Indeed, the lives of some new migrants were not merely miserable but sometimes even taken; violent and occasionally fatal racist attacks occurred in many parts of Western Europe, including Germany and the UK.[4]

Hence our first explanation focuses on the notion that some citizens of Western states believed their national identity was being threatened by the influx of newcomers.[5] Here, then, the 'defence' of national identity was an inherently conservative or reactionary phenomenon, since it represented attempts to avoid major change in society or even to return to an essentially mythical golden age of intact identity and national cohesion. It is important to bear in mind that the concept of identity, particularly national identity, emphasises both myth and memory as part of its imagination of political community.

A second reason for this aggressive form of identity politics is that Western Europe itself was undergoing major change, partly as a result of the Cold War, which acted as a destabilising force for some. In particular, the European Union[6] was undergoing a dual process of widening and deepening. Regarding the former, the EU was in the early-1990s preparing for the admission of up to four new members (Austria, Finland, Norway and Sweden); although Norway eventually opted not to join the EU, the latter grew from a 12-member into a 15-member organisation in January 1995. This particular widening was perceived by the existing members of the EU as far less threatening or destabilising than was the potential future membership of CEE countries, however. Since the latter would have been inconceivable prior to 1990, it becomes obvious why this was a ramification of the end of the Cold War. In many ways even more significant was the marked deepening of the integration process, symbolised primarily by the 1992 Maastricht Treaty on European Union. While enthusiasts for the further integration of Europe sought to placate those with reservations by emphasising concepts such as subsidiarity, the fact was that both citizens and politicians in some member-states of the EU, including the UK and Denmark, were deeply concerned that moves were afoot to transform the EU into a federalised super-state.[7] Many opponents of the Maastricht Treaty believed that existing 'nation-states'[8] were being marginalised and encouraged to renounce so many sovereign rights that there was a real danger that they (existing states) would in time disappear, to be replaced by bureaucratic centralization in Brussels. The more the EU sought to introduce or develop a common currency, a European Central Bank, and a Common Foreign and Security Policy, the more this fear was fuelled that long-established nations and states would disappear. This apprehensiveness was further exacerbated by the introduction of a common EU citizenship in 1993.

Had the EU proved capable of overcoming many of the problems individual nation-states had faced in recent years, some of these fears might have been allayed. But the EU was proving to be no better at overcoming profound socio-economic problems, such as high levels of unemployment and even recession, than were the individual nation-states. Hence, it was far from obvious that deepening integration would represent any real improvement on the *status quo*; yet it increased fears for the nation-state, national identity and sovereignty. These fears were reflected both in opinion polls and in the less than overwhelming support for the Maastricht and Amsterdam treaties in the referenda held on them in 1992–3 and 1998.[9]

In addition to fears about identity, there were related ones concerning the manner in which decisions were made within the EU, particularly by ministers and appointed officials. These fears led to calls for increased transparency of decision-making, and to a growing realisation among EU officials that the so-called permissive consensus on elite decision-making on EU issues had eroded quite considerably in the 1990s.[10]

A third, longer-term reason for the focus on changing forms of collective identity is that voting patterns and opinion-surveys endorse the notion that class has become less salient as a form of identification.[11] With the moves to post-industrial society and its effects on the division of labour, plus the expansion of higher education, traditional affiliations to the working class or even the more amorphous middle class have been weakened.[12] In one sense, this is ironic in the context of the West. With the spread of Thatcherism and

4 Citizenship and Identity in Europe

economic rationalism (neo-liberalism), it could be argued that the need for collective identities to defend working people is as high as it was in the past. Yet by the early-1990s, trade unions in many countries had become weaker than they had been for decades, while their membership in some countries was also declining markedly.[13] One reason for this is both the phenomenon and the quasi-ideology of globalisation, which has led many to conclude that nationally-based trade unions are helpless in the face of international capital. Corporations that consider they have too many difficulties with their workforces in Germany or France or the UK, whether this be in the form of strikes or the often related issue of demands for better conditions, have often transferred production to parts of the world where labour is cheaper and/or is perceived to be less prone to strike.[14]

This is not the place to examine the political economy or ideology of globalisation in any detail. However, this brief overview, together with the references to post-industrialism, help to explain why one traditional identity, class, has been in decline. Like Europeanisation, globalisation is often regarded as a threat to national identity (as well as to national economies and boundaries) and to traditional class identities, given its own putative classless and stateless nature.[15] Moreover, multi- and transnational corporations and world market forces are characterised by even more of a democratic legitimacy deficit than is the EU.[16]

While national and class identities have in general been perceived to be either under threat or else declining in Western Europe, there has been increased debate regarding sexual identity, as well as a greater awareness, and arguably tolerance, of sexual diversity. Where homosexuals, bi-sexuals and transsexuals were once typically secretive about their sexualities, 'coming out' has in many European societies become a political statement. Although most heterosexuals have reacted either positively or indifferently to this development, many homophobes possess their anti-homosexual attitudes partly because they fear losing their own identities. Rather than exhibit tolerance or acceptance, they see the assertion of 'other' sexual identities as a zero-sum game, in which their own identities will be increasingly threatened and marginalised if they do not defend their turf. This is another dimension of the 'search for identity'— which is in many cases a reassertion of pre-existing identities—that is so salient a feature of contemporary Europe, and that helps to explain many of its more unsavoury developments of recent years.

Just as sexuality has become a more salient issue in recent times, so too has there been a marked increase within Europe in awareness of, and debate on, gender.[17] Feminism has moved through various stages since the late-1960s, and some men have felt increasingly threatened by it. This has resulted in various forms of backlash,[18] including a growing tendency among some men to form groups and even develop masculinist theories.[19] There is a marked masculine orientation to much of the racist violence referred to above; while this violence represents only an extreme fringe of the reassertion of male identity, no attempt at a comprehensive explanation of identity politics in today's Europe would be complete without reference to it.

Another reorientation of identity to have become more obvious recently is the focus on regions, often more or less equating with local ethnic groups. For most citizens and many politicians, this identification with a region means primarily micro-regions (i.e. sub-national units within existing states), while for a few 'Europeanists' it refers much more to macro-regions, notably the EU.[20] The focus on and demand for smaller units in CEE has already resulted in the break-up of three states (Czecho-Slovakia, the USSR, and the former Yugoslavia), and may yet bring about further disintegration (e.g. of rump Yugoslavia, possibly of Russia). In Western Europe, Belgium became a federal state in July 1993, and could divide, primarily along ethnic lines, into two states in the future. Within the EU itself, there has been growing recognition of the significance of the politics of the so-called third level; that more and more micro-regions have claimed a distinctive identity and culture within the 'nation-state' has been recognised by the EU, under the terms of the Maastricht Treaty, through the creation of the Committee of Regions. While the powers, structures and self-perceptions of such micro-regions vary considerably— and nowhere is a region adequately defined, despite the significant and obvious differences between them—their emergence and development constitute another important component of changing identity politics.[21]

In several countries, ethnic identity has become more salient again partly as a way, for some, of coping with major societal change and the rise or influx of new identities.[22] While this is perhaps most obvious in CEE, there continue to be many forms of ethnic and nationalist politics in Western Europe, too. In addition to the ethnic-based regionalisms just analysed, these forms include aggressive nationalism, racism, separatism (as in the cases of the Basques, the Corsicans, the Northern League in Italy, the Scots and Welsh, etc.), irredentism (as in Northern Irish republicanism), and demands on the part of some member-states for greater autonomy within the EU.

It would be a serious oversight in any analysis of the issue of identity politics (and subsequently citizenship) in Europe during the 1990s not to refer to the severe economic problems that emerged in the Anglo-American world at the end of the 1980s and then spread to Continental Europe in the early-1990s, as well as to the long term implications of the economic crises and recession of the 1970s. In the past quarter of a century, the welfare state has been under increasing pressure to provide services and programs, at a time when most governments have been anxious to reduce spending. The perceived growing gap between popular expectations and governments' willingness and capacity to meet these leads to a decline in the state's legitimacy. In addition, the unemployment and insecurity that recessions typically engender, combined with the more general insecurity associated with the economic rationalism of this era (for instance because of downsizing), is unquestionably another factor explaining the rise of identity-related politics. A situation in which some retain their jobs, while others lose theirs, have to transfer to part-time work or cannot even commence employment once they have finished school, can have a divisive effect. Those with jobs seek to retain them, those without can become resentful. The situation is further exacerbated if people cannot be confident that the state will look after them in such circumstances. This is fertile soil for exclusionary forms of identity. Those who have become unemployed may feel they have lost an important part of their identity and seek to replace this by reference to other parts of their identity, such as ethnicity or gender. This can in turn lead to scapegoating for one's own problems, blaming others for 'taking' one's employment or for adding to the pressure on the welfare state. Even when unemployment does not rise substantially, the uncertainties associated with and encouraged by the ideologies or quasi-ideologies of neo-liberalism and globalisation can foster a psychological need for an enhanced sense of security through closer identification with a particular group.

Yet another explanation for the new salience of identity politics and the rise of racism can on one level be seen as a further ramification of the spread of economic rationalism and the (often closely related) effects of globalisation. That factor is the state's effectiveness in dealing with crime and state security. As states have sought to reduce their spending in most areas, so policing has sometimes suffered or has been perceived to have done.[23] This has been associated in some people's minds with sometimes quite marked increases in the number of reported crimes in one or two EU countries, notably the UK, and in CEE countries that have found it difficult to cope with the serious economic problems of early post-communist transition. Public perception that crime is on the rise has often linked such increases with immigrants and other 'outsiders', such as Romanies, who might in fact have been living for generations in a given country. Such perceptions can be encouraged by the manner in which some states present crime statistics. Germany, for example, identifies the percentage of non-Germans found guilty each year of crimes.[24] While such data are presumably accurate, the way in which they are presented can fuel the perception that 'foreigners' are particularly prone to criminal acts. In fact, some of the 'criminal' activity is of a relatively minor nature, such as infringements of immigration rules and traffic offenses. But even though 'foreigners' are, at least according to German statistics, also more prone than 'natives' to serious crime,[25] the primary explanation for this might be much less related to their 'foreignness' than to the fact that, in various ways, they are treated as outsiders. Unemployment levels, for instance, are typically higher among most 'outsider' groups—and unemployment can encourage various forms of anomic behaviour. In short, there is an important 'chicken and egg' question here, and the state's conscious or unconscious privileging or recognition of unidirectional causal explanations can encourage racism and other forms of exclusion.

In sum, there has in recent years been a tendency for people in Europe to reconsider their identities. While many have been moving away from traditional identities relating to their class position and towards those relating to gender and sexuality, others have felt threatened by these changes and have sought to reassert older identities, typically focusing on ethnicity and/or the 'nation-state' and/or micro-regions. At the same time, members of both groups can be subject to increasing fears—of unemployment; of greater competition for already scarce resources such as housing and social security benefits; of the accelerating pace and implications of globalisation and the technology and information revolutions; of growing centralisation to the EU; and many other factors. In some cases, the desire for recognition of one's individual or group identity has led to no more than a push for increased representation, and active lobbying by interest groups organised around issues and identities as diverse as agriculture, ethnically oriented regions, and minority languages. These groups frequently have an active program of political lobbying not only at the nation-state but also at the EU level.[26] But in many other cases, people have felt increasingly alienated from the formal institutions of power, and have addressed all these changes and conflicting identities by other means. Unfortunately, many have attempted to confront their own fears and confusion through rather primitive (violent) assertions of self or selves vis-à-vis others. Moreover, the mass media have sometimes played on such fears. For example, many have emphasised the negative impact of increased migration flows in recent decades, instead of stressing the positive aspects of both immigration and multiculturalism.

Although the trend away from class identification and towards gender and/or sexual and/or even ethnic identity might be described by some as a move towards post-modern politics, the fact that such moves are often accompanied by increased rejection of others is clear evidence that the greater tolerance of 'other'—indeed the deconstruction of the very concepts of 'them' and 'us'—that is often taken as a key dimension of post-modern societies is much less salient a feature of today's Europe than some claim and hope for. The rise of the far right is also indicative of this lack of tolerance. The most that might be argued is that there are *some* signs of moves towards a post-modern condition,[27] but that even these are currently under threat.[28]

It is appropriate to finish this section by raising the matter of European identity. This concept is highly contentious, partly because there is a major question of whether or not a European identity can be compatible with the maintenance of national and regional identities. As shall be argued in the next section, on citizenship, the concept of multiple identities has become increasingly pertinent at the end of the 20th century.

Citizenship

So far in this discussion, the principal focus has been on identity. One way in which some individuals and groups can seek to enhance their own identity and self-demarcation is through more exclusive conceptions of citizenship. Paradoxically, other individuals and groups can seek to enhance *their* own identity through more inclusive conceptions of citizenship. In today's Europe, pressure in both directions is clearly visible. On the one hand, racist and exclusionary citizens and politicians (the latter include France's Jean-Marie Le Pen, Hungary's Istvan Csurka, or, in the early-to-mid-1990s, Germany's Franz Schönhuber and Estonia's Jüri Toomepuu) have sought to tighten laws on citizenship so as to exclude those they believe should not be entitled to the rights conferred by their particular country's citizenship.[29] On the other hand, many—including some women's groups and members of ethnic minorities—are seeking more inclusive and comprehensive conceptions of citizenship, as part of their demands for more equal and comprehensive human and civil rights.

The issue of citizenship is currently being widely debated, often in the context of identity politics and conceptions of self and other. Within the European context, the most important debate is on what rights and responsibilities citizenship should confer. In the classical—Greek city-state—conception of citizenship, the term connoted primarily a right to participate in the *polis'* decision-making processes (although even this right was granted exclusively to male property-owners). While this limited conception has spread in twentieth century Europe to a broader group, including women, far more comprehensive interpretations of what citizenship should entail were on the agenda in the period immediately following the Second World War. The best-known exponent and proponent of this broader conception was T. H. Marshall. In addition to the political participatory elements of citizenship, Marshall argued for both civil and social elements. By the former he meant that full citizenship should confer 'the rights necessary for individual freedom—liberty of the person, freedom of speech, thought and faith, the right to own property and to conclude valid contracts, and the right to justice'.[30] While most European states now recognise these civil elements, Marshall's 'social element' has in recent years been increasingly questioned, if often implicitly.[31] One reason for this questioning is that, as mentioned above, many states in both Eastern and Western Europe have experienced serious economic problems, including fiscal ones, and have typically sought to overcome or reduce these by limiting the state's responsibilities and attempting to shift the onus for welfare and other functions onto civil society. Since Marshall's 'social element' includes rights to 'a modicum of economic welfare and security', education and social services,[32] it is not surprising that the fiscal difficulties faced by so many states have led to its questioning. Thus the broad conception of citizenship rights has been under attack.[33]

Ironically, the state's attempts to transfer welfare and other responsibilities to 'civil society' have often backfired, at least in terms of the state's own legitimacy. Many citizens have with justification argued that there is a power gap between individuals and those in control of rights, and that responsibilities have often been foisted on citizens with far too little discussion.[34] The rise of new social movements has been accompanied by what Newman refers to as the rediscovery of citizenship; by this he means that movements have sought a broader means of political participation, and have questioned narrow definitions of rights and citizenship.[35] However, many of these demands have gone largely unheeded, and the state has often attempted to transfer tasks without increasing overall rights. There is an important distinction between a top-down and a bottom-up push for society to assume many responsibilities that states were until recently expected to shoulder. Expressing this another way, there is a significant difference between a situation in which civil society *chooses* to assume tasks hitherto performed by the state, and one in which well-heeled elites attempt on their own accord to shift responsibility to non-state agencies that are ill-equipped to implement social policies, and inexperienced at doing so.

In the particular case of the CEE countries, the fact that 22 of the 27 post-communist states of former Eastern Europe and the Former Soviet Union are 'newly' sovereign (in the sense of not having been sovereign in recent decades) has meant, *inter alia*, that they have had to address the issue of what citizenship entails in a newly independent and sovereign country. Since these countries have had so many other problems to deal with in what have been multiple simultaneous transitions,[36] it is hardly surprising that there has been confusion over just what citizenship can and should mean.

Most people accept that citizens must abide by laws and pay taxes. But should they also be required to perform military duties, and can they justifiably expect a welfare state? If they *can* expect the latter, how extensive should it be? While few would contest the notion that citizens in a democratic state should have the right to vote, what is the nature of this right? Is it to be assumed that citizens should have the right to elect the head of state, and, if so, must popular monarchies be dismantled? There are clearly a number of significant aspects of citizenship that still need to be addressed and resolved.

At the same time as there exist so many unresolved issues within individual states, the EU has introduced a brand new type of citizenship which, as demonstrated elsewhere in this book, could be seen to challenge traditional notions of citizenship. This new concept currently suffers from a number of fundamental flaws. One is that citizenship has traditionally been associated with a particular state, which is answerable to its citizenry; since the EU is not a state, and is widely recognised to suffer from a serious democratic deficit, there are several basic issues to be resolved before EU citizenship becomes a legitimate concept. One of these relates to the rights of political participation, including even the most minimal dimension of this, voting rights. Brewin suggests that the right to vote should be based on residency rather than national citizenship. He further argues that the EU should be a single constituency with a proportional representational form of voting; this would undermine national control of voting and hence of citizenship, and would thus weaken the traditional linkage and identification with the 'nation-state'.[37] Yet such a putative weakening could also be viewed as a means of encouraging recognition of the legitimacy of multiple identities, precisely by recognising two levels of citizenship.

The notion of a new type of dual citizenship—not of two states, but of a state and a macro-region—has led analysts such as Elizabeth Meehan to discuss whether or not it is possible to be both a European and a national citizen. She suggests that, 'a new understanding of citizenship is emerging that is neither national nor cosmopolitan'. This citizenship is multiple, in the sense that the identities, rights and obligations that Derek Heater has associated with citizenship[38] are expressed through an increasingly complex configuration of EU 'institutions, states, national and transnational voluntary associations, regions and alliances of regions'.[39] Meehan further argues that future developments are likely to be in one of two directions, or that reality will lurch between these. The first scenario is one in which citizenship will remain primarily associated with the individual 'nation-state', but will be enriched through a European dimension as a sort of 'add-on'. The second is that citizenship will approximate more to the situation in the Roman Empire, in the sense that citizens will be able to appeal to more than one jurisdiction when claiming their rights.[40] With considerable justification, she sees this capacity to appeal to a plurality of institutions as an enhancement of citizen rights; after all, so many conceptions of liberal democracy focus on the significance of pluralism in its many guises that adding a new dimension to it should be seen as inherently democratic.

Considering these developments in the concept of citizenship from a more radical perspective, we need to address the thorny issue of its dynamic in the context of the changing nature and role of the state. If the state itself is being transformed or even rendered redundant by the development of both micro- and macro-regionalisms, then surely the concept of citizenship as presently understood must also be transformed and may eventually become redundant. If the latter occurs, what will and/or should replace citizenship—assuming *anything* should replace it? If it does disappear, will this exert positive or negative pressures on identity politics? Is it time for political theorists to acknowledge that democracy is an unobtainable ideal that is increasingly irrelevant in an era of globalisation, technological standardisation and the Internet? Conversely, does the growth of interactive technology increase the realistic possibilities for much more meaningful citizenship participation in both discussions and decision-making? If this can operate at the level of existing states, can it also apply at the higher level of supra-national organisations? Within an organisation such as the EU, does the cultural and linguistic diversity render such participation much less feasible than might be the case in a large but culturally and linguistically more homogeneous political organisation such as the USA? These are large and complex questions, and it would be unrealistic to expect to be able to answer them all satisfactorily. But it is important to identify and problematise these issues, as a step towards a more adequate conceptualisation of citizenship and its dynamism.

One way in which the concept of citizenship, especially as a multi-layered phenomenon, could be more clearly articulated and developed would be through debate on and eventual adoption of an EU constitution. As Ulrich Preuss points out, such a constitution would have to be different from the constitutions of nation-states, since the EU is not a state.[41] But in clarifying and standardising approaches to major political issues such as citizenship, the state, and new conceptions of federalism, such a document could play a positive role in the construction of new interpretations more attuned to the realities of Europe in the twenty first century.

In a sense, the country often seen nowadays as the powerhouse and centre of Europe—Germany—serves as a microcosm of many of the kinds of pressures on both identity and citizenship that can be observed in contemporary Europe. Like Europe generally, Germany experienced an enormous sense of excitement when communist power collapsed; indeed, the fall of the Berlin Wall in November 1989 was for many the ultimate symbol of the new world. As in Europe generally, this initial euphoria was soon superseded by an awareness of the enormous magnitude of the task of rebuilding and developing the former communist part. Furthermore, both the Westerners and the Easterners have mixed feelings about each other and their own pasts. Many east Germans have begun to forget the worst aspects of their experiences of communism— their lack of freedom of speech and to travel, the shortages of consumer goods, the deaths of fellow citizens who tried to escape from the GDR—and yearn for the security and relatively stable prices of the 'good old days'; this is not so dissimilar from the kinds of perceptions and emotions that brought communist successor parties to power in Lithuania, Poland and Hungary in the early-to-mid-1990s. This *Ostalgie* may reflect on one level the selective memory of many Germans. This selectivity is part of the problem of identity in the modern world, in that many people consciously and sub-consciously choose what it suits them to choose from historical memory and myth in deciding who is acceptable and who is not, with whom one should mix and whom one should exclude. Of course, a major reason for this selectivity is that so many in the former GDR are suffering the economic and social pains of transition. Germany has, like Europe generally, experienced significant economic problems in the 1990s—although these are more directly related to and exacerbated by its attempts to develop what was once its communist neighbour than is the case for West European countries generally. Germany, too, has in the 1990s been fundamentally re-assessing its conception of citizenship, to no small extent because of the influx of foreigners and the related issue of increased racism. And now that Germany is one, the old West German 'Basic Law' (*Grundgesetz*) should in principle be replaced by a new pan-German constitution (*Verfassung*). But above all, what is common to both Germany and Europe as a whole is that strong centripetal and centrifugal forces currently co-exist and are causing tensions, even instability; the increased salience of identity politics is a reflection of this.

On Identity, Citizenship and Rights

The changing conception of citizenship in the context of the changing nature of the state is not the only major issue of citizenship and identity currently being hotly debated. Another relates more to society than to the state. In many parts of the world, traditional communities—often reflected in particular political organisations, the nation-state proper—have been changing more rapidly than ever before. The decline of empires, the need for relatively unskilled workers, the ramifications of wars, capitalism's push for ever more fluid boundaries and fewer constraints—these and other factors have led to an increase in population movements in Europe and elsewhere.[42] As ever more refugees, asylum-seekers, employment-seekers and others arrive and attempt to settle in what had previously been perceived to be relatively homogeneous societies, so theorists have been devoting increasing attention to the concept of multiculturalism. One of the most controversial aspects of this is the debate on group rights.

As writers such as Nicola Girasoli have pointed out,[43] most aspects of international law that might be invoked to protect group rights in fact focus on the rights of *individuals*, which can then be aggregated to promote or defend the rights of, for instance, an ethnic minority within a particular country and society. In order to address and overcome this putative gap in liberal democratic theory, writers such as Will Kymlicka have developed sophisticated and, at least in Kymlicka's case, initially persuasive arguments in favour of collective (group) rights.[44]

Kymlicka justifiably and sensibly highlights the differences between minority groups in contemporary multicultural societies. For example, he distinguishes immigrant groups from 'non-immigrant' national minorities, such as indigenous (aboriginal) peoples and groups whose traditional homelands have been incorporated into larger states as the result of colonisation, the redrawing of state boundaries following wars, etc. In the European context, the Turks in Germany would constitute an example of the first group, the Hungarians in Transylvania/Romania an example of the second. Having drawn such distinctions, he argues for differentiated approaches in various areas, such as language and land rights. His argument is nuanced, sensitive and, as indicated above, at first sight convincing to many. It also appears to be sensible, since it recognises a fact of modern life in so many countries, including his own Canada, that conflict exists between groups within the same country, and that measures must be taken to address such conflicts and avoid further ones.

Unfortunately, there is a potentially serious flaw in the very notion of recognising group rights. This is that recognition can become legitimation of difference, exclusion and inequality. It can encourage individuals to think of themselves as members of a particular group, and therefore as different from 'others', whether this be individuals of another gender, sexuality, ethnicity, class, or some other label. Moreover, if the concept of group rights becomes dominant in society at the expense of individual rights, members of very small groups may become even more marginalised than they already are, as politics becomes focused on the relations between the dominant group and the more significant (numerically) minorities or disadvantaged groups. Hence, in the commendable and, given the tensions in the contemporary world, understandable attempt to deal with exclusion and notions of 'otherness', arguments in favour of group rights might unintentionally exacerbate the very problems they are attempting to overcome or lessen.

It might be objected that to argue against the development of group rights is to avoid confronting a real and serious problem in the contemporary world. This is not necessarily the case. Some who believe that the advocacy and development of group rights is a method for dealing with present conflicts have to accept that some conflict will always exist wherever there are human beings. Once there is a fuller appreciation of the potential costs (negative implications) of recognising group rights, we might be able to move beyond predominantly legalistic approaches to dealing with conflict and towards more adequate analyses of the underlying causes of conflict and exclusion, including various kinds of inequality and inadequate recognition of individuals.

Before concluding this section on identity, citizenship and group rights, it is important to make two further observations. The first harks back to Meehan's point about dual or multiple citizenship, but focuses more explicitly on the implications for identity. Many who argue against further integration in Europe do so on the basis that any attempt to foster a European identity among citizens of member-states will have negative implications for national identities. But there is no obvious reason why the question of identification should be conceived as a zero-sum game. As has often been noted, most Bavarians appear to be quite capable of considering themselves simultaneously as Bavarian, German, European and Western; they are comfortable with multi-layered spatial (territorial) identities, and typically see no need to make a choice between these.

Leading on from this point, the recognition of multiple identities—not merely spatial—in any one individual should be encouraged. Other things being equal, the more identities we have, the less likelihood there is that one of these will become extreme and exclusive of others. Furthermore, the more identities each of us has—in terms of ethnicity, territory, gender, sexuality, age, employment, parenthood, etc.—the more obvious each individual's uniqueness becomes. Far from discouraging such an individualism-oriented approach to identity, it should be acknowledged that such a focus on uniqueness can help to overcome the identity crisis many people appear to be suffering; precisely the recognition of the uniqueness of a particular identity permutation could help to overcome the *thymos* problem referred to above.[45] If such crises are overcome or reduced, so the tendency towards exclusive *group* identities should also be reduced, which in turn would render the world a more civilised and less aggressive place. Tolerance should increase the more individuals can recognise their own uniqueness and worth; it is when these qualities are either not recognised or else insufficiently acknowledged that people band together to exclude 'others', since at least single identity groups can demand recognition.

Layout of This Book

It was with an interest in exploring many of these topics that CESAA (the Contemporary European Studies Association of Australia) adopted 'Citizenship and National Identity in Europe' as the title of its 1994 annual symposium. The one-day conference was held in Melbourne in August; the current volume is the outcome of our deliberations.[46] Each of the papers was reworked and updated in late-1997.[47]

In the next two chapters, Martin Vranken and Stephen Hall respectively examine the EU citizenship that was introduced in November 1993 with the implementation of the Maastricht Treaty. The concept of a citizenship that is not linked to a 'nation-state' is so novel and radical that it was felt appropriate to include two analyses of it. In the first, Martin Vranken focuses on legal aspects of an EU citizenship. He maintains that citizenship and national identity both evoke a sense of belonging, but also that the *legal* concept of citizenship is difficult to unravel. Having briefly listed the citizenship rights entailed in the Maastricht Treaty, he argues that the concept of a European citizenship must be approached from a dynamic perspective, and that a legal framework actually facilitates the evolution of a European citizenship and identity. Much of his chapter focuses on two key dimensions of EU citizenship—the enforcement of EU rights by individuals, and the relevant non-economic aspects of EU law. While concentrating on legal aspects of citizenship, Vranken also emphasises that the political will to act is at least as important as the legal framework if the concept of an EU citizenship is to make headway.

In chapter three, Stephen Hall justifiably identifies EU citizenship as a symbolic move of major significance, at the same time as he highlights its unique nature. Citizenship normally attaches to and is granted by a state; yet the EU is not a state. Citizenship also typically confers political rights; yet there are a number of limitations on the political rights conferred by EU citizenship. Most notably, while EU citizenship grants its holders the right to vote and stand in both local and EU-level elections, they must be nationals of a given state to be able to vote and run in national elections. Since it is national politicians who ultimately exercise greatest power—certainly in a negative (veto) sense—within the EU, there is clearly a democratic deficit inherent in the present conception of EU citizenship. For EU citizenship to be seen as true citizenship by most Western criteria, it must guarantee full political rights. Since it does not, Hall has appropriately sub-titled his chapter 'Unfinished Business'.

In chapter four, Stephen Castles argues that rapid political changes have rendered it necessary to reconsider models of democracy and citizenship. A major reason is the large number of immigrants or members of new ethnic minorities who are excluded from full participation in society in various ways. The chapter identifies three dilemmas—formal inclusion of immigrants as citizens, which can threaten a 'nation' if this is perceived primarily in terms of ethnic belonging and cultural homogeneity; substantial citizenship or the problem of overcoming marginalisation; the need for cultural openness and structural change in a national political community—and examines how different countries are addressing these. There is a particular focus on the different approaches to citizenship adopted by Germany and France; according to Castles, neither has resolved these dilemmas.

In the fifth chapter, Gisela Kaplan addresses the issue of gender in European politics. She begins by providing a brief overview of the role of women in resistance movements, as one way of demonstrating the significant role women have played in European history in the last half century. Kaplan then cites Helen D'Ancona's 1988 statement that the EU was the legislatively most progressive political community for women in the world, before comparing and contrasting the abstract and formal situation of women within Western Europe with present realities. After highlighting their gross under-representation in parts of the workforce and the political system, she criticises the structural inequalities within the European administrative apparatus, and argues for change within this. Only if such changes are introduced, she maintains, will women in general become full citizens of the new Europe.

Linda Hancock also considers the *de facto* citizenship inequality between men and women in chapter six, but concentrates on the ramifications of divorce laws. She points out that, until recently, integrative measures within the EU have been taken mostly in the economic sphere. But the social and political implications of integration are now firmly on the agenda. One of the most important social issues to be addressed is divorce, in particular the marginalised position of divorced women. Hancock locates her argument in a broader one to the effect that the rights of women, immigrants and refugees must be fully respected if a satisfactory 'supranational citizenship' of Europe is to be achieved. Like a number of contributors to the current debate on citizenship rights, Hancock argues that the EU's laws and legal rulings will have to move beyond the consideration of *individual* rights and directly address the issue of *group* rights if both justice and substantive equality are to be advanced.

In chapter seven, Leslie Holmes considers the issues of inclusion and exclusion in the post-communist states of CEE. While this is related primarily to problems of nationalism, racism and citizenship, there are also references to the issue of gender inequality. It is argued that many of the examples of exclusion in contemporary CEE can be explained largely in terms of the very nature of post-communism. One of the most obvious factors is the legacy of communist rule that acts as the backdrop to everything the post-communist states are attempting. Another is the international context in which post-communism arose at the end of the 1980s and beginning of the 1990s. It is further argued that it is easy to exaggerate the extent of intolerance of 'otherness' in many European post-communist countries so far in the 1990s. But the West needs to be more inclusive itself if it is not indirectly to encourage more exclusionary politics (for instance, in terms of policies on citizenship, or racism between ethnic groups) in the future. One major reason for this is that extremist exclusionary politics in CEE could have significant negative spillover effects on other parts of Europe, on an even bigger scale than occurred as a result of the wars in former Yugoslavia during the first half of the 1990s.

The focus of Aleksandar Pavkovic's chapter (eight) is on one of the most troubled parts of post-communist Europe during the 1990s, former Yugoslavia. According to Pavkovic, from its inception in nineteenth century Croatia, the Yugoslav idea was one of both political unification of Southern Slavs and the creation of a single national identity for the disparate Southern Slav 'tribes'. Enthusiasm for the latter idea appears to have reached its peak among young Serb and Croat intellectuals just before the outbreak of the First World War. But its appeal declined after 1929, as the concept was associated with King Aleksandar's unsuccessful attempts to impose political unity on Yugoslavia by political *diktat*. By the time the country was divided up by the Axis Powers in 1941, the Yugoslav idea had lost most of its supporters, according to Pavkovic. The concept was resurrected by Tito's communists after 1945 as a supranational identity which, being socialist, was supposed to transcend traditional national identities. But the communist leadership's aspirations were frustrated. By the mid-1960s, various national—albeit formally communist—elites in the different republics of Yugoslavia were discrediting the idea, arguing that it was an ideological deviation that masked Great Serbian unitary nationalism. Yet, as Pavkovic points out, some 1.2 million Yugoslav citizens described themselves as ethnically 'Yugoslav' in the 1981 census. Having no clear national allegiance—for instance, because their parents were of different nationalities—they opted for this 'non-national' identity. Pavkovic considers what this identity had to offer those who chose it, many of whom had a completed higher education. He also asks what such an identity could offer now, in the absence of a common Yugoslav homeland. His answer is that it could offer little more than it did when it was first mooted in the nineteenth century.

Taken as a whole, the various chapters of this book raise and address many of the most contested and important issues in contemporary political and social theory, even if most of these are considered here specifically in their European contexts. One is the very meaning of citizenship. Whereas the concept of nationality focuses on the relationship between the individual and the state in terms of their mutual rights and duties of serving and protecting, the concept of citizenship connotes a more positive political role for the individual; and whereas nationality relates primarily to the international sphere, conceptions of citizenship typically focus more on the domestic.[48] While there would probably be relatively little disagreement about this conception of citizenship, there are serious differences over what citizens can legitimately expect, and what can legitimately be expected of them.

It will be clear from the synopsis of the chapters that contributors sometimes adopt radically different perspectives from each other on a number of key issues, including the notion of group rights. On one level, these differences reflect those that currently exist more generally, both in and on Europe and its future. Far from attempting to hide these differences or encouraging compromise and conformity, we considered it appropriate to display them openly, since the topics analysed in this volume are not and should not be seen as finished projects. Europe is dynamic, and is experiencing many problems that cannot readily be solved at either the theoretical or the practical level; to imply they could be by imposing cosy interpretations would be insulting to those directly suffering the ramifications of these problems, to those attempting to find solutions, and to the readers of this book. But we hope that the interpretation and sometimes clarification of the sources of such problems will constitute a modest contribution to their reduction and—who knows?—perhaps their eventual solution. Unfortunately, that still appears to be a long way off.

Notes

1. The literature on both topics is very extensive, and no attempt at comprehensive listings will be attempted here. But readers interested in citizenship could start their search with some of the following: Turner, B., *Citizenship and Capitalism* (London: Allen and Unwin, 1986); Barbalet, J., *Citizenship: Rights, Struggle and Class Inequality* (Milton Keynes: Open University Press, 1988); Vogel, U. and Moran, M. (eds.), *The Frontiers of Citizenship* (Basingstoke: Macmillan, 1991); Meehan, E., *Citizenship and the European Community* (London: Sage, 1993); Turner, B. (ed.), *Citizenship and Social Theory* (London: Sage, 1993); Clarke, P., *Citizenship* (London: Pluto, 1994); van Steenbergen, B. (ed.), *The Condition of Citizenship* (London: Sage, 1994); Turner, B. and Hamilton, P. (eds.), *Citizenship* (London: Routledge, 1994); Cesarani, D. and Fulbrook, M. (eds.), *Citizenship, Nationality and Migration in Europe* (London: Routledge, 1996). On various aspects of identity from different perspectives see, to start, Smith, A., *National Identity* (London: Penguin, 1991); Garcia, S. (ed.), *European Identity and the Search for Legitimacy* (London: Pinter, 1993); Laclau, E. (ed.), *The Making of Political Identities* (London: Verso, 1994).
2. See Taylor, C., 'Examining the Politics of Recognition', in Gutmann, A. (ed.), *Multiculturalism* (Princeton: Princeton University Press, 1994), 25–74.
3. Fukuyama, F., *The End of History and the Last Man* (New York: Avon, 1993), 163. Fukuyama's preferred term for this 'desire for recognition' is *thymos*, which is a classical Greek term usually translated as 'spiritedness'—see *ibid.*, esp. 162–91.

4. See e.g. *Der Spiegel*, No.49, 1992, 15. Unfortunately, after a period of declining numbers of racist attacks in Germany, their numbers have been increasing again recently, particularly in the eastern parts of the country. More generally on racism in Europe see Read, M. and Simpson, A., *Against a Rising Tide: Racism, Europe and 1992* (Nottingham: Spokesman for Nottingham Racial Equality Council and European Labour Forum, 1991); European Parliament (rapporteur G. Ford), *Report of the Committee of Inquiry into Racism and Xenophobia* (Luxembourg: OOPEC, 1991); Feteke, L. and Webber, F., *Inside Racist Europe* (London: Institute of Race Relations, 1991); Bunyan, T. (ed.), *Statewatching the new Europe: a handbook on the European state* (Nottingham: Statewatch, 1993); Castles, S. and Miller, M. J., *The Age of Migration* (London: Macmillan, 1993); Harris, G., *The Dark Side of Europe* (Edinburgh: Edinburgh University Press, 1994).
5. Buzan has pointed out that, on both sides of the former East–West divide in Europe, and in the interplay between them, Europe is undergoing a sociopolitical revolution involving migration of peoples, the formation of new societal identities, and the forging of a new political forms and frameworks. See Buzan, B., 'Introduction: The changing security agenda in Europe' in Waever, O., Buzan, B., Kelstrup, M., Lemaitre, P. (eds.), *Identity, Migration and the New Security Agenda in Europe* (London: Pinter, 1993), 5.
6. The European Community (EC) became known as the European Union (EU) in 1993 and will hereafter be called the EU even when referring to the pre-1993 situation.
7. Waever and Kelstrup point out that in the Danish debate on the EU, the future of the Danish nation is an issue, with the cultural community being the first to approach these new themes—'almost exclusively in terms of cultural security policy'; see Waever, O. and Kelstrup, M., 'Europe and its nations: political and cultural identities' in Waever *et al., op. cit.*, 70.
8. The term 'nation-state' is an unfortunate one, since it implies the common identification of a political unit with a nation. In fact, not only has the term long been quite inappropriate for historically multi-ethnic countries such as Switzerland, but it is ever more obvious in today's multi-cultural societies of the West that it implies a unity that no longer exists (to the extent it ever did). Unfortunately, the fact that federal countries such as Australia and the USA have opted to call their component units states—rather than provinces as in Canada, for instance—means that the problematic term nation-state is likely to be used for some time to come, primarily to avoid confusion both with federal units and with the abstract concept of the state.
9. The results of the referenda on the Maastricht Treaty were as follows: in Denmark, June 1992, 50.7% voted against and 49.3% in favour; in the second Danish referendum, May 1993, 56.8% voted in favour and 43.2% against; in the French referendum of September 1992, 51.05% voted in favour, 48.95% against; in the Irish referendum of June 1992, 69.1% voted in favour of the Treaty and 39.9% against. The results of the referenda on the Amsterdam Treaty were as follows: in Ireland, May 1998, 61.7% in favour, 38.3% against; in Denmark, May 1998, 55.1% in favour, 44.9% against.
10. Franklin, Marsh and McLaren have argued that the notion of the permissive consensus, which had allowed integration in the past and had until the present decade been expected to continue into the future, had appeared to be an unduly optimistic concept already by the end of 1992. See Franklin, M., Marsh, M., and McLaren, L., 'Uncorking the bottle: popular opposition to European unification in the wake of Maastricht', *Journal of Common Market Studies*, 32 (4) 1994, 455–72, esp. 468–71.
11. For a recent comparative analysis see Dogan, M., 'Classe, Religion, Parti: Triple Déclin dans les Clivages Electoraux en Europe', *Revue Internationale de Politique Comparée*, 3 (3) 1996, 515–40, esp. 524–31. See also Gallagher, M., Laver, M., and Mair, P., *Representative Government in Western Europe* (New York: McGraw Hill, 1992), 89–117.

12. For a recent radical perspective on the decline of class and of the utility of class analysis see Pakulski, J. and Waters, M. *The Death of Class* (London: Sage, 1996). See also Flanagan, S.C. and Dalton, R.J., 'Parties Under Stress: Realignment and Dealignment in Advanced Industrial Societies', *West European Politics*, 7 (1) 1984, 8–23; Van Deth, J. and Geurts, P., 'Value orientation, left-right placement and voting', *European Journal of Political Research*, 17 (1) 1989, 17–34.

13. This said, the decline in trade union membership in Europe has often been exaggerated— see Fuchs, D. and Klingemann, H-D., 'Citizens and the State: A Relationship Transformed' in Klingemann, H-D. and Fuchs, D. (eds.), *Citizens and the State* (Oxford: Oxford University Press, 1995), 424; and Aarts, K., 'Intermediate Organizations and Interest Representation' in *ibid.*, 239–40. Unfortunately, many of the data in this large-scale empirical analysis of various forms of participation only go as far as 1990, and can therefore neither confirm nor deny further perceived declines this decade.

14. The process of globalisation is described here as a quasi-ideology because there is much mythology embedded in it, which can nevertheless be a powerful tool for exercising control over sections of the population. As some Asian car manufacturers have discovered, it can be to their advantage to establish plants in the UK (e.g. Nissan) or elsewhere in Europe or North America, and the notion that developing countries will invariably constitute a more attractive investment proposition to transnational corporations is not true. Brand loyalty among British buyers can be higher if a 'Japanese' car is produced in the UK, for instance. The workforce can be better skilled and more experienced in a developed than in a developing country. Indeed, it can even be cheaper and less strike-prone, as could be proving to be the case in a comparison of South Korean and British workers in the late-1990s.

15. See, e.g. Buzan, B., 'Societal security, state security and internationalisation', in Waever *et al.*, *op. cit.*, esp. 41–6.

16. Sassen has argued that economic globalisation has led to the denationalising of key economic institutions within the nation state, so that there is a growing consensus in the community of states to lift border controls on the flow of capital, services, information and other factors of globalisation. Yet, on the other hand, the nation state is reasserting its right to control its borders with regard to immigration policy. See Sassen, S., 'The De-Facto Transnationalizing of Immigration Policy', *Jean Monnet Chair Papers*, No. 35 (Florence: European University Institute, 1996), 7.

17. See e.g. Buckley, M. and Anderson, M., *Women, Equality and Europe* (London: Macmillan, 1988); Lovenduski, J., 'Feminism and West European Politics: An Overview' in Urwin, D. and Paterson, W. (eds.), *Politics in Western Europe* (London: Longman, 1990), 137–161; Ellis, E., *European Community Sex Equality Law* (Oxford: Clarendon, 1991); Zmroczek, C. and Duchen, C., 'What are these Women up to? Women's Studies and Feminist Research in the European Community' in Aaron, J. and Walby, S. (eds.), *Out of the Margins: Women's Studies in the Nineties* (London: Falmer, 1991); Glaesner, A., 'Gender and Europe: Cultural and Structural Impediments to Change' in Bailey, J. (ed.), *Social Europe* (London: Longman, 1992), 70–105; Hoskyns, C., 'The European Community's Policy on Women in the Context of 1992', *Women's Studies International Forum*, 15 (1) 1992, 21–8; Kofman, E. and Sales, R., 'Towards Fortress Europe?', *Women's Studies International Forum*, 15 (1) 1992, 29–39; Mushaben, J.M., 'The Other Democratic Deficit: Women in the European Community Before and After Maastricht' in Lutzeler, P. (ed.), *Europe After Maastricht* (Providence, RI and Oxford: Berghahn, 1994), 251–75; Elman, R.A. (ed.), *Sexual Politics and the European Union* (Providence, RI: Berghahn, 1996).

18. For the best-known elaboration and examination of the backlash phenomenon in relation to feminism (albeit particularly in the USA) see Faludi, S., *Backlash* (New York: Crown, 1991).

19. For various perspectives on this see e.g. Seidler, V., *Rediscovering Masculinity* (London: Routledge, 1989); Morgan, D., *Discovering Men* (London: Routledge, 1992).
20. The term regionalism is often used loosely, and hence confusingly. It can refer both to the growing role of sub-state units (component parts of existing states), and to the development of supra-state bodies such as the EU. To avoid ambiguity, the former is here described as micro-regionalism, the latter as macro-regionalism.
21. On all this see Amin, A. and Tomaney, J., 'The Regional dilemma in a neo-liberal Europe', *European Urban and Regional Studies*, 2 (2) 1995, 170–87; Anderson J. and Goodman J., 'Regions, states and the European Union: Modernist reaction or postmodernist adaptation?', *Review of International Political Economy,* 2 (4) 1995, 600–32; Jones B. and Keating M., *The European Union and the Regions* (Clarendon: Oxford, 1995); Rhodes, M. (ed.), *The Regions and the New Europe* (Manchester: Manchester University Press, 1995); Ritchie, M. 'Growing pains of the fledgling body', *European Voice*, 23–9 November 1995; Jeffery, C., 'Towards a 'Third Level' in Europe? The German Länder in the European Union', *Political Studies*, 44 (2) 1996, 253–66; Special Issue: The Regional Dimension of the European Union, *Regional and Federal Studies,* 6 (2) 1996.
22. Allardt has considered the mobilisation of new or revived ethnic groups since the 1960s and 1970s in terms of the positive aspects of this development. He points to four general characteristics in the new ethnicity. First, the ethnic characterisations were not performed by the majority populations, but by the minorities themselves. Second, a coincidence of the timing of the revival indicates a pattern of a rapid diffusion of political ideas. Third, there was a marked professionalisation of the ethnic activists. Finally, governments showed an increased willingness and ability to manage conflict. See Allardt, E., 'Political Sociology and Comparative Politics' in Daalder, H. (ed.), *Comparative European Politics* (London: Pinter, 1997), 276.
23. This is despite the fact that there has been increased cooperation between police and security forces in the EU member states, particularly in the context of the pillar of the Maastricht Treaty dealing with cooperation on Justice and Home Affairs (JHA). This cooperation has resulted in more coordinated action in the fight against organised crime, terrorism, fraud and drugs.
24. See e.g. Statistisches Bundesamt, *Statistisches Jahrbuch 1997 für die Bundesrepublik Deutschland* (Stuttgart: Metzler-Poeschel, 1997), 371–5, tables 15.6, 15.7 and 15.9.
25. For details see Albrecht, H. J., 'Minorities, Crime, and Criminal Justice in the Federal Republic of Germany' in Marshall, I. H. (ed.), *Minorities, Migrants, and Crime* (Thousand Oaks CA: Sage, 1997), 86–109, esp. 92–8. A similar picture can be found in France; for an analysis of this, and an equally sensitive approach to and interpretation of the data to Albrecht's, see Jackson, P., 'Minorities, Crime, and Criminal Justice in France' in *ibid.*, 130–50. For data on rising crime rates in CEE see Holmes, L., 'Crime, Corruption and Politics: International and Transnational Factors', a chapter to be published in a forthcoming (as yet untitled) volume edited by Alex Pravda and Jan Zielonka, esp. Table 1.
26. See, for example, Mazey, S. and Richardson, J., 'The logic of organisation: Interest groups', and Keating, M. and Hooghe, L., 'By-passing the nation state? Regions and the EU policy process' in Richardson, J. (ed.), *European Union: Power and Policymaking* (London: Routledge, 1996), 200–15 and 216–29 respectively.
27. On this, see for example Heller, A. and Feher, F., *The Postmodern Political Condition* (Cambridge: Polity, 1988).
28. For a particularly depressing argument to the effect that the recent 'Balkan Wars' in former Yugoslavia undermine claims that a post-modern tolerance is spreading in Europe see Meštrovic, S., *The Balkanization of the West* (London: Routledge, 1994).
29. See, for example, Perduca, A. and Pinto, F. (eds.), *L'Europa degli Stranieri: Stranieri extracomunitari tra accoglienza e rifiuto alla soglia del 1993* (Milan: Franco Angeli,

1991), esp. the chapters by Guichard, F. 'France: Immigration, nationalité, citoyenneté', 83–8 and Gelli, R. 'France: Le statut des étrangers', 89–97; Helms, L. 'Right-wing Populist Parties in Austria and Switzerland: A Comparative Analysis of Electoral Support and Conditions of Success', *West European Politics*, 20 (2) 1997, 37–52; Chapin, W., 'Explaining the Electoral Success of the New Right: The German Case', *West European Politics*, 20 (2) 1997, 53–72; Halfmann, J., 'Immigration and Citizenship in Germany: Contemporary Dilemmas', *Political Studies*, 45 (2) 1997, 260–74.

30. Marshall, T.H., *Class, Citizenship and Social Development* (New York: Doubleday Anchor, 1965), 78.

31. Newman points out, moreover, that Marshall's work has been criticised as being complacent, based on an inaccurate one-dimensional, evolutional view of history that is gender biased, ethnocentric, paternalistic and too narrow. See Newman, M., *Democracy, Sovereignty and the European Union* (New York: St Martin's Press, 1996), 143.

32. Marshall, *op. cit.*, esp. 71–134.

33. For a particularly accessible listing of the broad rights and responsibilities that citizenship might confer and entail see Guild, E., 'The Legal Framework of Citizenship of the European Union' in Cesarani and Fulbrook, *op. cit.*, 30–54. Guild directly compares what she calls the general 'hallmarks of citizenship' with what is offered and expected under EU citizenship.

34. Michael Newman has argued this persuasively with reference to Britain under the Tories— see Newman, *op. cit.*, esp. 138–41.

35. Newman, M. , *op. cit.*, 140. See also Melucci, A., *Nomads of the Present: Social Movements and Individual Needs in Contemporary Society* (London: Century Hutchinson, 1989).

36. By this we mean that the notion that the post-communist countries have 'only' had radically to transform their economic and political systems is simplistic, and obfuscates attempts to understand why these states have in general been so troubled. Other transformations they have been attempting in the 1990s include of their boundaries, social class structures, underlying ideologies, and international trade and military allegiances.

37. See Brewin, C., 'Society as a kind of community: communitarian voting with equal rights for individuals in the European Union' in Mohood, T. and Werbner, P., *The politics of multi-culturalism in the new Europe* (London: Zed books, 1997), 224.

38. Heater, D., *Citizenship: The Civic Ideal in World History, Politics and Education* (London: Longman, 1990), 314–47.

39. Meehan, E., 'The debate on citizenship and European Union' in Murray, P. and Rich, P. (eds.), *Visions of European Unity* (Boulder, CO: Westview, 1996).

40. *Ibid.*, 202.

41. See Preuss, U., 'Prospects of a Constitution for Europe', *Constellations*, 3 (2) 1996, 209–24. Juergen Habermas suggests that a European Constitution would help to foster a common multicultural European identity, assuming it were based on shared political principles rather than traditional cultural bonds—see Dieter Grimm's article 'Does Europe need a Constitution?' and Habermas' response 'Reply to Grimm' in Gowan, P. and Anderson, P. (eds.), *The Question of Europe* (London: Verso, 1997), 239–58 and 259–64 respectively.

42. See Castles, S. and Miller, M., *The Age of Migration* (London: Macmillan, 1993); Collinson, S., *Beyond Borders: West European Migration Policy Towards the 21st Century* (London: Royal Institute of International Affairs and Wyndham Place Trust, 1993).

43. See Girasoli, N., *National Minorities* (Budapest: Akadémiai Kiadó, 1995); Girasoli, N., *Compromise and Minority Rights* (Budapest: Akadémiai Kiadó, 1996).

44. Kymlicka, W., *Multicultural Citizenship* (New York: Oxford University Press, 1995)

45. See note 3.

46. The paper by Stephen Hall was added later, after Dr. Hall kindly agreed to submit a

chapter based on his book on the same topic.
47. The reasons for this delay are explained in the Preface to this book.
48. This point is based on Elster, J., Offe, C., Preuss, U. *et al.*, *Institutional Design in Post-communist Societies* (Cambridge: Cambridge University Press, 1998), 88.

2 Citizenship and the Law of the European Union

MARTIN VRANKEN

Introduction

The purpose of this chapter is to discuss legal aspects of a European citizenship. The comments that follow are limited to developments within the European Union (EU); the ever expanding membership of the Union notwithstanding, they therefore do not extend to Europe as a whole.

When used in a general sense, the concept of citizenship has much in common with the notion of national identity, since each evokes a sense of belonging. The legal concept of citizenship is somewhat more difficult to explain. Admittedly the 1992 Maastricht Treaty on European Union (MTEU) has added a new Part Two to the European Community Treaty, entitled 'Citizenship of the Union'. Thus a citizenship of the EU has formally been created. Specifically, anyone holding the nationality of one of the Member States (MS) becomes a citizen of the Union. This Union citizenship triggers certain rights. The Maastricht Treaty lists five such legal entitlements as follows:

1. A right of free movement on Union territory;
2. A right to participate in municipal and European Parliament (EP) elections (both actively and passively);
3. A right to diplomatic protection;
4. A right to petition the EP;
5. A right to apply to the Ombudsman.

Some legal commentators have been very critical of these provisions for a European citizenship. Hartley, in particular, has argued that the establishment of a Union citizenship is largely of symbolic importance, for the simple reason that there is very little by way of hard law here.[1] To be clear, most of the above-listed rights indeed require further implementation action, either by way of measures to be adopted by the Council (acting unanimously!) or by means of agreement between the various Member States.

Be this as it may, a discussion of a European citizenship need not end here. European integration—it is trite to observe—is a gradual, dynamic process. Similarly, the concept of a European citizenship is most usefully approached as a dynamic rather than as a static concept. In this essay it will be argued that the law—both in substantive and in procedural terms—facilitates this evolving notion of a European citizenship. This thesis will be demonstrated by discussing legal developments not only as regards certain non-economic aspects of the European Community (EC) but also as regards the enforcement of Community law by private individuals. As a practical matter it seems convenient to commence with this second, procedural dimension of EC law.

European Citizenship: Procedural Aspects

A Article 177 EC

The original design of the European Court of Justice (ECJ) dates from 1952 and is reminiscent of French administrative law. As has been noted elsewhere,[2] this French 'reflex' was both deliberate and accidental. It was deliberate in that the Court in its legal technique was conceived of as an administrative tribunal in essence. This approach is reflected in the text itself of the Treaty establishing the European Coal and Steel Community (ECSC).[3] Accidental was that the dominance of French administrative law in the national legal scene of several West European nations predates the formation of the ECSC.[4] Interestingly, as pointed out by Brown and Garner, all six founding members of the EC at one time formed part of the Napoleonic empire.[5]

Of more direct relevance to this discussion of European citizenship is that the ECJ was not intended to be a people's court. Even though Article 173 EC allows private parties to bring proceedings into the European Court for the review of Community acts that are 'of direct and individual concern' to them, that Treaty provision has traditionally been interpreted in a restrictive fashion. Rather, access to the Court by private parties was to occur—first and foremost—through a 'filter' of national courts and tribunals. The main mechanism to this effect remains the so-called technique of requests for preliminary rulings, as embodied in Article 177 of the EC Treaty.

Whenever a question as to the interpretation or the validity of Community law is raised before any court or tribunal of a Member State, the domestic court or tribunal may or—in some instances—must request the ECJ to give an interpretative ruling. It is expected that the domestic institution will call for the assistance of the European Court whenever the former considers that a decision on a question of EC law is necessary in order to enable it to pass judgement. It must be stressed, though, that the procedure for preliminary rulings applies to cases that are (and remain!) national court cases. Requests for preliminary rulings therefore originate as well as end in the domestic court. Pending the interpretive ruling from Luxembourg, the national proceedings are temporarily suspended, i.e. they are put on hold or 'frozen' for the duration of the Article 177 proceedings.

B The Doctrine of Direct Effect

Even though the rule is for private parties not to have direct access to the ECJ, significant in-roads have been made as regards the protection of Community rights by the Court of Justice. Especially noteworthy in this regard has been the judicial development of the so-called doctrine of direct effect. This doctrine, created with the active albeit not unqualified support of the legal scholarly community,[6] has proved to be a most useful weapon in ensuring that private parties do not suffer unduly in instances of non-compliance with Community obligations by the Member States. A case in point is the decision in *Francovich*.[7]

Mr. Andrea Francovich claimed he was owed six million lire by his insolvent employer. The legal basis for this claim was Council Directive 80/987/EEC concerning the protection of employee rights in the event of employer insolvency.[8] The Directive created an obligation for the Member States to ensure that the payment of any worker claims is guaranteed. Specifically, so-called 'guarantee institutions' had to be set up, the assets of which were to be kept separate from the employer's operating capital.

The Member States had three years within which to implement the Directive, but Italy failed to do so. In proceedings before the Italian courts, Mr Francovich claimed that the Italian government should pay him the money due under the non-implemented Directive (or compensation *in lieu*). The Italian court referred the matter to the European Court in Luxembourg for a preliminary ruling.

The Court of Justice confirmed that the Directive was intended to create individual rights. Yet, it found that the Directive was not sufficiently specific and unambiguous to have direct effect, i.e. to create enforceable rights without the need for further implementation action by the State. The main problem seemed to be a determination as to who was the debtor. Was it the guarantee institution or the state itself? In the event, the Court ruled that the Italian state could not be sued as the debtor. However, the Court did not stop there. It went on to consider the issue of the State's liability in damages for failure to implement the Directive. And here, Italy did not get off the hook. Technically, while the State did not incur any liability as debtor, Italy could be sued as a tort-feasor. As a practical matter, this means that private parties are no longer allowed to suffer at the hands of a Member State that fails to live up to its EC obligations!

The European Court of Justice's reasoning in *Francovich* drew immediate attention from the legal scholarly community.[9] Clearly, *Francovich* was significant, in that the case established that State liability for damage to individuals, caused by a breach of EC law for which it is responsible, constitutes an inherent principle of EC law. But the case also raised a number of important questions. Does State liability exist only in relation to those provisions of Community law which do not have direct effect, or can it be treated as a more general principle?[10] What should happen in case of a partial failure to implement Directives?[11] Subsequent judicial decisions in *Brasserie du Pêcheur, Factortame*[12] and, even more recently, *Dillenkofer*[13] confirm that the emerging principles governing State liability operate at two levels. On the one hand, the case law of the ECJ acts as a powerful incentive for Member States to fully comply with both the letter and the spirit of their Community obligations. On the other hand, these cases actively assist in the building of a meaningful notion of European citizenship as they 'improve and extend the possibilities open to individuals to secure effective remedies'.[14]

European Citizenship: A Substantive (Labour) Law Approach

A   The 1957 version of the Treaty of Rome

The EC may have started as an exercise in economic integration but, of course, it is no longer just that. To be clear, economic integration continues to be important to date. However, over the years the 'reach' of Brussels (and Luxembourg!) has widened to include non-economic aspects in this integration process. The domain of social policy best allows us to illustrate this proposition, as it is manifest that the Community has come a fair way, notwithstanding the rather unspectacular Title 3 of the 1957 Treaty, especially the provisions in Articles 117-128 EC.

Article 119 EC on equal pay (together perhaps with Article 120 EC on paid holiday leave) is one of the few 'hands-on' provisions on social integration in the pre-Single European Act (SEA) version of the Treaty of Rome. It must be appreciated, though, that even that provision lay largely dormant or unused for some two decades before the Court of Justice took the opportunity to 'activate' it in the *Defrenne* case.[15]

Defrenne was decided in the mid-1970s. From a social policy perspective, the second half of that decade has been referred to as the 'golden period of harmonisation'.[16] The official trigger was provided in the form of a Solemn Declaration in October 1972, issued by the Heads of State and Government in Paris. This Solemn Declaration is important for two reasons. First, it signalled the end of the neo-liberal phase in the EC and its associated beliefs that social policy issues in general and labour law concerns in particular did not need any special attention. Throughout the 1960s the prevailing idea had indeed been that social harmonisation would be the inevitable by-product of economic integration. The 1972 Declaration was an opportunity to state openly that progress as regards social policy is just as important as the achievement of an economic union. Secondly, and with the benefit of hindsight, the 1972 Declaration also proved important because it actually resulted in specific action. A so-called Social Action Program was put together in 1974. Subsequently, no fewer than five significant labour law directives were adopted in rapid succession. They are sufficiently important to warrant being listed here, because they can be seen as emanations of a functional approach to a social citizenship in the EU.

Two Directives were adopted in 1975. Council Directive 75/117/EEC of 10 February 1975 seeks to 'approximate' the laws of the Member States relating to the application of the principle of equal pay for men and women.[17] In particular, this Directive clarified the meaning of the principle of equal pay as contained in Article 119 EC by stipulating that the principle covers both the same work and work to which equal value is attributed. The second Directive adopted in 1975 was Directive 75/129/EEC,[18] as amended in 1992 by Directive 92/56/EEC.[19] It introduced a duty for employers to inform and consult with the employees' representatives on the social implications of collective redundancies. Community action in this field had been triggered by the AKZO case. In 1973 a Dutch-German multinational company by that name decided upon a program of restructuring which involved job losses for some 5,000 of its workers. AKZO had a number of subsidiaries in different European countries. Its strategy was to compare the cost of dismissal in the various countries and to carry out the dismissals in that country where the cost was the lowest. The 1975 Directive on collective redundancies is the direct result of the outrage in some European quarters about the perceived lack of 'fair play' by AKZO.[20]

In 1976 a further Directive was adopted on the implementation of the principle of equal treatment for men and women as regards access to employment, vocational training and promotion, and working conditions.[21] A fourth Directive on the safeguarding of employees' rights in the event of a 'transfer of undertakings, businesses or parts of businesses' aims at enabling workers to remain in employment with the new employer on the same wages and employment conditions that used to apply with the transferor.[22] A fifth and final labour law Directive was adopted in 1980. Directive 80/987/EEC concerns the protection of workers' rights in case of employer insolvency. Generally, the purpose of this last Directive is the same as that of the 1977 Directive on transfer of undertakings or even that of the 1975 Directive on collective redundancies: to ensure that the inevitable restructuring of companies within a progressively unified economic market does not adversely affect the Community's citizens.

It is interesting to note that, with the exception of the 1976 Directive on equal treatment, the legal basis for all of the above Directives is Article 100 EC. This Treaty provision requires unanimity in the Council of Ministers. The fact that so many social laws nonetheless could be adopted illustrates the unwritten rule in the Community that the political will to act can be just as important as, if not more important than, the legal framework within which to place that action. As will be discussed below, that same unwritten rule arguably helps explain the difficulties experienced in achieving social progress in the post-1970s era, the availability of a somewhat more facilitating legal framework under the SEA notwithstanding.

B The Single European Act

To be fair, the SEA did not do much in the way of promoting social integration—not directly anyway. The Act introduced qualified majority voting in matters of occupational health and safety only. Legislative proposals concerning any other 'rights and interests of employed persons' continued to require unanimity in the Council of Ministers. Frustration with this very limited advance in promoting social integration helped pave the way for the adoption of the Charter of Fundamental Social Rights of Workers in 1989. The Charter, adopted by the Heads of State and Government of the Member States minus the United Kingdom, is not legally enforceable as such. Even so, its significance in political and symbolic terms is beyond doubt. Blanpain and Engels refer to Title I of the Charter as 'the twelve Commandments' because it lists certain basic social rights under twelve headings ranging from the general right to freedom of movement to the more specific legal entitlement to a safe and healthy workplace.[23]

It has been suggested that most of the social rights contained in the 1989 Charter are already provided for by other instruments at international law, and that consequently they 'do not contain much added social value'.[24] However, some of the Charter's headings do comprise new elements. A case in point is the assurance of an equitable wage, i.e. a wage sufficient to enable workers to maintain a decent standard of living. This entitlement expressly extends to workers in employment relationships that are atypical because of their engagement by the employer under fixed-term, part-time, temporary or seasonal contracts. The Charter also pays attention to the unemployed. These people must be able to access public placement services free of charge, and they are entitled to an 'adequate' level of social security benefits. In particular, persons who have been unable either to enter or re-enter the labour market and who have no means of subsistence must be able to receive 'sufficient' resources and social assistance 'in keeping with their particular situation'.[25]

C Maastricht

The MTEU set out to build upon the momentum created by the 1989 Charter of Fundamental Social Rights of Workers. It sought to do this by turning a politically significant text into a legally enforceable one. However, it must be remembered that a Conservative government in the United Kingdom opposed the re-writing of the original provisions on social policy in the Treaty of Rome. Thus a compromise had to be worked out which involved, initially at least, putting any changes on social policy in a separate text from the (to be amended) Rome Treaty. But not even that compromise proved acceptable to the British. In the final analysis, a special Protocol had to be annexed to the Maastricht Treaty in which the (then) twelve Member States authorised eleven of the Member States to enter into an Agreement on Social Policy.

This is neither the time nor the place for a detailed discussion of the contents of the Agreement. Ample authoritative analysis is available elsewhere.[26] What may need to be stressed, though, is that qualified majority voting (currently 62 out of a total of 87 votes) in the Council of Ministers is now possible on a much larger scale than ever before as it is no longer restricted to matters of occupational health and safety. In particular, qualified majority voting is henceforth available on the equally broad as vague subject matter of 'working conditions'.[27] Even though important exceptions to the qualified majority rule remain in place for the time being—the main exceptions being social security, dismissal protection and employee participation other than information sharing and consultation[28]—the Community treatment of labour law is visibly coming of age.

A psychologically significant milestone in the post-Maastricht era undoubtedly proved to be the adoption, on 22 September 1994, of a Council Directive on the establishment of European works councils.[29] Various proposals to this effect had been on the table for more than a decade without much progress until the idea of a European law on employee involvement in the management of companies was relaunched in October 1993 under the Social Policy Protocol procedure. The Directive aims at improving the information and consultation rights of employees in 'Community-scale undertakings'. Targeted are companies with a minimum of 1,000 employees within the Community and 150 employees in each of at least two Member States. Responsibility for the establishment of a European works council (or an alternative procedure for informing and consulting employees) rests with the central management of the relevant companies. Negotiations towards a European works council must be initiated by the central management, either on its own motion or at the (written) request of the workers or their representative. The Directive stipulates that the negotiations must occur 'in a spirit of co-operation with a view to reaching an agreement'.[30] Failure to agree within the time frame set by the Directive triggers the application of so-called subsidiary requirements as listed in an Annex to the Directive.[31]

The European works council Directive represents the first successful attempt in the history of EC social policy to create a transnational scheme for employee participation.[32] It is also the first Directive not to legally bind all Member States. The legal basis for the Directive is the social policy Agreement annexed to the TEU and from which the UK obtained an 'opt out'. That country therefore need not implement the Directive on European works councils. Interestingly, it has been estimated that, when the number of multinational companies likely to be affected by the Directive in each country is compared with the number of companies that have established European works councils voluntarily, the highest penetration rate is among companies with their headquarters in the UK![33] This would seem to suggest a sound degree of business pragmatism which contrasts rather unfavourably with the ideological stance of the pre-Blair government administration in Britain.

A second Directive to be adopted under the social policy Agreement 'route'—and therefore not binding upon the UK—was a Council Directive of 3 June 1996 on parental leave. In essence, men and women workers are given a non-transferable individual right to take time off at the occasion of the birth or adoption of a child so as to enable them to look after that child.[34] But the real significance of this particular Directive lies in that it is the first to 'rubber stamp' an earlier agreement between European-level trade unions and employers' organisations as envisaged in the Agreement on social policy.[35]

D Amsterdam

(1) The Chapter on Employment

At the time of writing the text of the Treaty of Amsterdam was available in draft form only.[36] The Treaty—the result of some 15 months of negotiations culminating in an intergovernmental summit at Amsterdam on 16-17 June 1997—comprises separate Chapters on Employment and on Social Policy. As regards the former, in essence, a high level of employment henceforth constitutes an official goal of the EU. The precise manner in which actual job creation is to be encouraged remains a matter for the Member States to decide, though. Apparently, this approach reflects the views of a number of conference delegations that specific job-creation measures should not be decided at the level of the Union.[37]

Article 1 of a new Title on Employment, to be inserted after Title VI of the EC Treaty, states that the Member States and the Community shall work towards developing a co-ordinated strategy for employment and, in particular, for the promotion of a skilled, trained and adaptable work force that is responsive to economic change. According to Article 2 of this new Title, the Member States must regard the promotion of employment as a matter of common concern, which means that they are expected to coordinate their action in this respect with the Council of Ministers. Pursuant to Article 4, the European Council will each year consider the employment situation in the Community and adopt conclusions on the basis of a joint annual report to be submitted by the Council of Ministers and the EC Commission. These conclusions must in turn form the basis for the EC Commission to devise proposals and for the Council of Ministers to formulate guidelines which the Member States 'shall take into account in their employment policies'. Article 5 confers discretionary powers upon the Council of Ministers to adopt incentive measures designed to encourage inter-state cooperation where to do so is deemed appropriate.

In an attempt to avoid accusations as to an unwarranted usurpation of power by the Community at the expense of national sovereignty, the adoption of measures for the harmonisation of national laws or regulations has expressly been excluded from the incentives referred to in Article 5 above. Furthermore, any such incentive measures must specify the grounds for taking them 'based on an objective assessment of their need and the existence of an added value at Community level'. They must state the maximum amount for their financing, which should reflect the incentive nature of such measures. And finally, the duration of these incentive measures has been limited to a maximum of five years.[38]

(2) The Chapter on Social Policy

Great symbolic significance attaches to the willingness of the new Blair administration in Britain to bring the Agreement on Social Policy, previously annexed to the EC Treaty at Maastricht, within the main body of the EC Treaty. The Treaty of Amsterdam amends Articles 117 to 120 EC so as to incorporate the text of Articles 1 to 7 of the Maastricht Agreement on Social Policy. The practical importance of this move remains to be seen. A possible wild card in this regard could prove to be the applicability of the notion of subsidiarity.[39] Some commentators have never been particularly optimistic in this regard.[40] A Commission report to the European Council on the application of the subsidiarity principle suggests that the Community is serious in limiting the number of new legislative proposals by, for example, making greater use of alternatives to legislation, encouraging prior consultation and improving the interplay between national and supranational law makers.[41]

(3) The Union and the Citizen

All of the above changes on employment and social policy are contained in Section II of the draft text of the Treaty of Amsterdam. It carries the title of 'The Union and the Citizen'. Other Chapters within Section II deal with, *inter alia*, the Environment, Public Health and Consumer Protection. Although these are all topics that elaborate upon the non-economic aspects of the European citizenship image, their discussion is beyond the scope of this paper. One further aspect of European citizenship needs to be addressed, though. Because of its crucial nature, the drafters of the Amsterdam Treaty devoted a separate Chapter to the issue of fundamental rights, including the principle of non-discrimination. Somewhat surprisingly, perhaps, the relevant Chapter does not feature within the Section on 'The Union and the Citizen'. Instead, no doubt for reasons of exposure maximisation, it constitutes the first Chapter of Section I of the Amsterdam Treaty on 'Freedom, Security and Justice'. The main purpose of this Chapter I is to amend Article F of the MTEU by formally stating that the Union is founded on the principles of liberty, democracy, respect for human rights and fundamental freedoms, and the rule of law. These principles are said to be common to all Member States. Specifically, the fundamental rights guaranteed by the European Convention for the Protection of Human Rights and Fundamental Freedoms—negotiated under the auspices of the Council of Europe and signed in Rome on 4 November 1950, i.e. several years before the official establishment of the (then) European Economic Community (EEC)—as well as any other fundamental rights that may result from the constitutional traditions common to the Member States, are formally acknowledged as forming general principles of Community law. Thus the ground-breaking work of the ECJ in this area has now received the official seal of approval from the supreme EU legislature. The express formulation of the general principles underlying the Union is also of direct relevance to any (Central or East) European nation that seeks to obtain membership of the Union.[42]

The drafters of the Treaty of Amsterdam singled out the principle of non-discrimination for special attention. Under a new Article 6a of the EC Treaty, the Council of Ministers has been given powers to take 'appropriate action' to combat discrimination based on sex, racial or ethnic origin, religion or belief, disability, age or sexual orientation. Any such action requires unanimity in the Council of Ministers, though. Provision is also made for the protection of individuals with regard to the processing and the free movement of personal data. Pursuant to a new Article 213b of the EC treaty an independent supervisory body is to be established for the internal monitoring of the conduct of the various Community institutions and bodies. From 1 January 1999, any applicable EC laws on the protection of individuals with regard to the processing of personal data and the free movement of such data will apply to these Community institutions and bodies.

Conclusion

European citizenship is a dynamic, not a static concept. It is a concept that is intertwined with the progress of European integration itself. It will therefore inevitably acquire fuller meaning over time. Even though the formal creation of a European citizenship only occurred in the 1992 TEU, its origins clearly pre-date Maastricht. And Maastricht, or for that matter Amsterdam, is unlikely to be the last word on the subject either.

Nor is the concept of a European citizenship unitary. Rather, it is a multi-dimensional notion with procedural as well as substantive (legal) connotations. It has been argued in this chapter that, an apparent reluctance by the drafters of the 1957 version of the Treaty of Rome to create a fully-fledged people's court notwithstanding, a pro-active use of its powers has enabled the ECJ to enhance the practical relevance of the Community's legal order for all those who live and work in the EU.

The legal notion of European citizenship is evolving in substantive as well as in procedural terms. As for the substantive law of the Community, the focus of this chapter has been on the social dimension of a European citizenship. The Community's achievements in harmonising the labour laws of the Member States take pride of place in this regard. But, ultimately, labour law must be seen in the wider context of a social Europe that also encompasses other aspects of the integration effort, such as education, culture, public health and even consumer protection, to list but a few. Together they form the composite parts of a more global citizenship ideal.

Notes

1. Hartley, T.C., 'Constitutional and Institutional Aspects of the Maastricht Agreement', *International and Comparative Law Quarterly*, 42, 1993, 213–37.
2. Vranken M., 'Role of the Advocate General in the Law-making Process of the European

Community', *Anglo–American Law Review*, 25, 1996, 41.

3.   Lagrange, M., 'Le Rôle de la Cour de Justice des Communautés européennes' in *Les Problèmes juridiques et économiques du Marché Commun* (Librairies Techniques, 1960), 41–2; Rasmussen, H., *On Law and Policy in the European Court of Justice* (Dordrecht, Boston: Martinus Nijhoff, 1986), 201.

4.   Brown, L.N., and Garner, J.F., *French Administrative Law*, 3rd ed. (London: Butterworths, 1983), 162–71.

5.   *Ibid.*, 166.

6.   The origins of the doctrine of direct effect can be traced back to the writings of Winter, J.A., 'Direct Applicability and Direct Effect: Two Distinct and Different Concepts in Community Law', *Common Market Law Review*, 9, 1972, 425–38.

7.   Joined Cases C-6/90 and C-9/90, *Francovich v Italian Republic* and *Bonifaci v Italian Republic*, (1991) *European Law Reports* I-5357 and *Common Market Law Reports* 66, 2, 1993.

8.   *Official Journal* L283, as amended by Directive 87/164/EEC, 1980; *Official Journal* L66, 1987.

9.   See the short but illuminating discussions in Barav, A., 'Damages against the State for Failure to implement EC Directives', *New Law Journal*, 1991, 1584–1604; Szyszczak, E., 'New Remedies, New Directions? Joined Cases Francovich and Bonifaci', *The Modern Law Review*, 55, 1992, 690–7; and Ross, M., 'Beyond Francovich', *The Modern Law Review*, 56, 1993, 55–73.

10. Craig, P.P., 'Once More unto the Breach: The Community, The State and Damages Liability', *The Law Quarterly Review*, 113, 1997, 67–8.

11. Irmer, W., and Wooldridge, F., 'The return of Francovich', *European Business Law Review*, 8, 1997, 67–8.

12. Cases C-46 & 48/93, *Brasserie du Pêcheur S.A. v Germany, R. v Secretary of State for Transport, ex parte Factortame Ltd*, 1 *European Law Reports* 1996, 1029; 1 *Common Market Law Reports*, 1996, 889.

13. *Dillenkofer and Others v Germany*, joined cases C-178,179,189 and 190/94, decision of 8 October 1996, [1996] *All ER (EC)*, 917.

14. Jarvis, M., 'The Liability of Member States for Legislative Omissions: A Summary of Conference Proceedings', *European Business Law Review*, 7, 1996, 230.

15. Case 43/75, *Defrenne v Sabena (No. 2)*, *European Court Reports*, 1976, 455; 2 *Common Market Law Reports*, 1976, 98.

16. Blanpain, R., and Engels, C., *European Labour Law*, 3rd and Revised ed. (Deventer/ Boston: Kluwer, 1995), 118.

17. *Official Journal* L45/19, 1975.

18. *Official Journal* L48, 1975.

19. *Official Journal* L245/3, 1992.

20. See Vranken, M., *Fundamentals of European Civil Law and Impact of the European Community* (Sydney: The Federation Press, 1997), 164–7.

21. Directive 76/ 207/EEC of 9 February 1976.

22. Directive 77/187/EEC, *Official Journal* L61, 1977.

23. Blanpain and Engels, *op.cit.*, 122.

24. *Ibid.*

25. Point 10 of the Charter.

26. See, in particular, the discussion by Weiss, M., 'The Significance of Maastricht for European Community Social Policy', *International Journal of Comparative Labour Law and Industrial Relations*, 8, 1992, 3–14. See also the chapter on European labour law by Hepple, B. A., in Blanpain, R, and Engels, C., *Comparative Labour Law and Industrial Relations in Industrialised Market Economies*, 6th ed. (Deventer/Boston: Kluwer, 1997).

27. Article 2 of the Agreement on Social Policy.
28. Article 3 of the Agreement on Social Policy.
29. Directive 94/95/EEC on the establishment of a European Works Council or a procedure in Community-scale undertakings and Community-scale groups of undertakings for the purposes of informing and consulting employees, *Official Journal* L254/65, 1994.
30. Article 6,1 of the Directive.
31. Vranken, M., 'Update on European Social Policy: the European Works Council Directive', *Contemporary European Studies Association of Australia Newsletter*, 12, 1995, 12–13.
32. 'European Works Councils—The Action Begins', *European Industrial Relations Review*, 250, 1994, 14.
33. 'EWCs Directive comes into Force', *European Industrial Relations Review*, 273, 1996, 11.
34. For a fuller discussion see 'Into the Unknown: Implementing the Parental Leave Agreement', *European Industrial Relations Review*, 267, 1996, 19–23.
35. 'Community social policy continues, despite the UK', *European Industrial Relations Review*, 270, 1996, 1.
36. Conference of the Representatives of the Governments of the Member States, Brussels, 19 June 1997, CONF/4001/97.
37. 'New Treaty of Amsterdam is Agreed', *European Industrial Relations Review*, 282, 1997, 1.
38. Declaration to the Final Act on incentive measures referred to in Article 5 of the new Title on Employment, CONF/4001/97 CAB, EN, 57.
39. Article 3b EC was introduced at Maastricht. It comprises a new general principle of EC law to the effect that, in areas that do not fall within its exclusive competence (e.g. social policy), the Community shall take action in accordance with the principle of subsidiarity. This means that the Community can take action 'only if and in so far as the objectives of the proposed action cannot be *sufficiently* achieved by the Member States and can therefore, by reason of the scale or effects of the proposed action, be *better* achieved by the Community'(emphasis added).
40. See Weiss, *op.cit.*
41. Commission of the European Communities, *'Better Lawmaking' 1996*, Brussels, 27 November 1996, CSE (96) 7 final.
42. Article O of the Maastricht Treaty on European Union as amended by the Treaty of Amsterdam.

3 European Citizenship —Unfinished Business

STEPHEN HALL

Introduction

On 1 November 1993, the *Treaty on European Union* (TEU) instituted a 'Citizenship of the Union' on a formal legal basis and attached certain rights to that status. It did this by inserting a new Part Two into the *Treaty establishing the European Community* (EC Treaty).[1] This new citizenship status is established by Article 8 EC which provides as follows:

> 8. (1) Citizenship of the Union is hereby established.
> Every person holding the nationality of a member state shall be a citizen of the Union.
>
> (2) Citizens of the Union shall enjoy the rights conferred by this Treaty and shall be subject to the duties imposed thereby.

The insertion of the Union citizenship provisions into the EC Treaty has been described by the European Commission as '[o]ne of the most significant steps on the road to European integration taken by the authors of the Treaty on European Union'.[2]

Union Citizenship and National Citizenship

Nothing in the TEU abolishes nationality or citizenship of the individual member states. Indeed, the second sentence of Article 8(1) EC links citizenship of the Union with tenure of member state nationality.[3] A person cannot be a Union citizen without holding the nationality of at least one member state, unless perhaps s/he has been deprived of his/her member state nationality in breach of the fundamental rights protected by the Court of Justice.[4] Thus, nationals of the EU's fifteen member states enjoy both the citizenship of their own country and citizenship of the EU.

39

Citizenship and Equality

The idea of citizenship strongly suggests that people who possess a common citizenship status are entitled to be treated on a basis of (at least formal) equality with each other. This is especially so in relation to those matters which typically affect citizens uniquely; i.e. participation in the political process and the right to enter and reside within the territory of the entity conferring the citizenship status. Indeed this notion of the legal equality of citizens is enshrined as a constitutional principle in most of the Union's member states, and is observed as a matter of practice in all of them.

European Union citizenship does not, however, meet the expectation of equality inherent in the general idea of citizenship. A Union citizen who is not a national of the member state in which s/he seeks to move or reside (hereafter 'inter-state Union citizen') does not enjoy the equal protection of Community law with his/her fellow Union citizens who are nationals of the host member state. This inequality subsists, moreover, precisely in the core citizenship rights to entry, residence and democratic participation.

Entry and Residence Rights

The Union citizen's rights of entry and residence are set out in Article 8a EC:

8a. (1) Every citizen of the Union shall have the right to move and reside freely within the territory of the member states, subject to the limitations and conditions laid down in this Treaty and by the measures adopted to give it effect.

(2) The Council may adopt provisions with a view to facilitating the exercise of the rights referred to in paragraph 1; save as otherwise provided in this Treaty, the Council shall act unanimously on a proposal from the Commission and after obtaining the assent of the European Parliament.[5]

Article 8a confers certain movement and residence rights within the 'territory of the member states' on 'every' citizen of the Union. The provision does not, however, provide a complete statement of movement and residence rights for every Union citizen wherever they might be within the Union. If it did, it would take away more rights than it confers. In particular, citizens of the Union residing in a member state of which they are a national would find that their hitherto unconditional right of residence was suddenly hedged about with a variety of 'limitations and conditions' previously applicable only to nationals from other member states. This could not have been the intention of the contracting member states or the drafters of the treaty.[6]

Consequently Article 8a applies only to Union citizens who are entering, moving within or residing in a member state whose nationality they do not possess. These inter-state Union citizens must be treated on a basis of equality with the host member state's own citizens, subject to the 'limitations and conditions' applicable to inter-state Union citizens. It is this feature of Article 8a which makes possible an inferior class of citizenship in the field of movement and residence rights. Inter-state Union citizens are given a right to move and reside 'freely' within the territory of a host member state. But, unlike Union citizens possessing the nationality of the host member state, their right is made subject to 'the limitations and conditions laid down in this Treaty and by the measures adopted to give it effect'. It is therefore plain that Article 8a does not fully extend to inter-state Union citizens the same entry and residence rights that are available to Union citizens possessing the nationality of the host member state.

Thus in any given member state there are different classes of Union citizens; those with the full array of citizenship rights of entry and residence, and those without. How great in practice is the difference between these classes of Union citizen?

The answer to this question turns on just what Article 8a means when it says that the Union citizen's entry and residence rights are 'subject to the limitations and conditions laid down in this Treaty and by the measures adopted to give it effect'. This phrase is, on its face, somewhat enigmatic. The first point worth noting is that the EC Treaty nowhere lays down 'limitations and conditions' expressly applying to the Union citizen's Article 8a mobility rights, just as the Treaty nowhere spells out the 'duties' of Union citizenship to which there is a reference in Article 8(2).

One might be tempted to conclude that the inter-state Union citizen's right to move and reside freely within the territory of host member states cannot be encumbered by limitations or conditions. This is so, it might be said, because there are no limitations or conditions in the EC Treaty expressly applicable to Union citizens exercising their rights under Article 8a, and because Article 8a is clearly intended as an important new constitutional provision in the EC Treaty. In other words, it is an absolute right which permits of no restrictions by the Community institutions or member states. Further Treaty amendment would be required in order to insert the 'limitations and conditions' which Article 8a envisages.

Such an approach, however, flies in the face of the clear language of the Treaty, which strongly suggests that somewhere in the Treaty, and in measures adopted giving effect to the Treaty, there are some limitations and conditions to which the inter-state Union citizen's mobility rights are subject. Furthermore, such an expansive reading of Article 8a raises an absurd spectre. While inter-state Union citizens *as* Union citizens would have unrestricted mobility rights, the same Union citizens *as* workers, service providers, service receivers or established self-employed would continue to be subject to the limitations and conditions which are left in place by the TEU. These economic actors, all of whom must be member state nationals[7] and thus Union citizens, are subject to limitations on their mobility rights on grounds justified by public policy, public security and public health.[8]

Thus an inter-state Union citizen seeking to enter a host member state as a worker could be excluded by State authorities on public health grounds if s/he suffered from certain infectious diseases,[9] whereas the same person seeking to enter simply in his/her capacity as a Union citizen could not, on the expansive reading of Article 8a, be refused entry. Clearly, Article 8a is not open to this expansive reading. What then are we to make of Article 8a's express restrictions on the entry and residence rights of inter-state Union citizens?

The reference to limitations and conditions 'laid down in this Treaty' points to the existing limitations on mobility rights already applicable to inter-state Union citizens who are workers, service providers, service receivers or established self-employed. Nothing in Article 8a, therefore, can be construed as relieving these economically active inter-state Union citizens from the limitations and conditions justified on grounds of public policy, public security and public health which are authorised by the EC Treaty provisions applying specifically to them.[10] The Article 8a mobility rights are subject, however, not only to the limitations and conditions 'laid down in this Treaty' but also to the 'measures adopted to give it effect'. Article 8a therefore permits its mobility rights to be subject to measures adopted 'giving effect' to the EC Treaty.

The TEU was signed against the background of a suite of three directives designed to extend Community mobility rights to new classes of people: EEC Directives 90/364 (residence rights for persons of independent means),[11] 90/365 (residence rights for pensioners),[12] and 90/366 (residence rights for students engaged in vocational training).[13] All three directives were required to be implemented by not later than 30 June 1992.[14] Directive 90/366 was annulled by the European Court of Justice (ECJ) in 1992 on the ground that it had been adopted by the Council on an incorrect legal base.[15] The Court, however, ruled that the effects of the annulled measure should be maintained until the entry into force of a replacement directive adopted on the correct legal base.[16]

The annulled students' residence directive was eventually replaced by Directive 93/96[17] adopted on the legal base required by the Court, but in substantially identical terms to the annulled directive. The Court of Justice has held, however, that Article 7 EEC[18] (the provision proscribing nationality discrimination generally provided it falls 'within the scope and application of this Treaty') was directly effective so as to confer on nationals of member states who have been admitted to a course of vocational training in a host member state a right of residence in the host member state.[19] Directive 90/366 merely aimed 'to give effect to and organise the right of residence'[20] conferred by the Treaty itself. The same will be true of Directive 93/96. Thus only Directives 90/364 and 90/365 provided substantially new mobility rights for member state nationals. The movement and residence rights contained in the Directives 90/364, 90/365 and 93/96 are subject to certain restrictions.

In the case of member state nationals who have 'pursued an activity as an employed or self-employed person', covered by Directive 90/365, they must be in receipt of 'an invalidity or early retirement pension, or old age benefits, or of a pension in respect of an industrial accident or disease'.[21] There is no requirement that they have pursued their employment in the territory of the host member state.[22] This directive would therefore appear to be outside the scope of Article 48 EC, which confers on persons who have been employed in a host member state a qualified right to remain in that State.[23] In the case of students covered by Directive 93/96, they must be 'enrolled in a recognised educational establishment for the principal purpose of following a vocational training course' in the host member state.[24]

The right of residence[25] is also granted, by Directive 90/364, 'to nationals of member states who do not enjoy this right under other provisions of Community law'.[26] This directive might therefore appear to be a highly significant act extending mobility rights to every member state national who cannot make out a case under some more specific provision. Such a view would be mistaken. The beneficiaries of the movement and residence rights contained in Directive 90/364 must show that 'they themselves and the members of their families are covered by sickness insurance in respect of all risks in the host member state and have sufficient resources to avoid becoming a burden on the social assistance system of the host member state during their period of residence'.[27] Consequently, Directive 90/394 is only of practical use to those who might be described as the 'independently wealthy'. Similar conditions as to financial independence are imposed in respect of pensioners and students.[28] The rights enjoyed by all three categories of persons (sometimes referred to as the 'Three P's'—pensioners, pupils and playboys) are additionally enjoyed by certain members of their families,[29] subject to the conditions already adverted to.

Finally all three EEC non-economic residence directives permit member states to derogate from their provisions on grounds of public policy, public security and public health. In that event the three directives apply the provisions of Directive 64/221[30] which details the application of the Treaty's public policy, public security and public health exceptions to the mobility rights of economically active member state nationals.

The result of this array of provisions is that, for movement and residence purposes, Community law divides EU citizens into three categories. Firstly, and by far the most numerous, are Union citizens who are nationals of the member state in which they reside. These Union citizens enjoy the full array of movement and residence rights within the member state, determined by the member state's own laws, and are not subject to the limitations and conditions on mobility rights authorised under the EC Treaty.

The next category are economically active inter-state Union citizens. These are Union citizens in a member state of which they are not a national and who are, or who seek to be, workers, service providers, service receivers or established self-employed. For movement and residence purposes, these Union citizens are entitled to be treated on a basis of equality with the host member state's own citizens, subject to limitations justified on grounds of public policy, public security and public health. These people are second class citizens of the Union.

The last category consists of inter-state Union citizens who are not economically active. Into this category fall Union citizens in a member state of which they are not a national and who draw a pension, who are vocational training students, or who do not have a right of residence 'under other provisions of Community law' (i.e. all other inter-state Union citizens). In the enjoyment of Community mobility rights these Union citizens are, like their economically active cousins, entitled to be treated on a basis of equality with the host member state's own citizens, subject to limitations justified on grounds of public policy, public security and public health.

Economically inactive inter-state Union citizens are, however, subject to an additional raft of limitations on their Community mobility rights. They must also show that they are 'covered by sickness insurance in respect of all risks in the host member state and have sufficient resources to avoid becoming a burden on the social assistance system of the host member state during their period of residence'.[31]

Inter-state Union citizens wishing to exercise their constitutionalised citizenship mobility rights must not be too poor. Community law, in respect of a fundamental right of modern citizenship, treats its own citizens differently according to the size of their bank balances. Union citizens thus stigmatised on account of their financial status do not enjoy the equal protection of the law.

Democratic Participation

The inter-state Union citizen's rights to participate in the electoral life of his/ her host member state are set out in Article 8b EC:

8b. (1) Every citizen of the Union residing in a member state of which he is not a national shall have the right to vote and to stand as a candidate at municipal elections in the member state in which he resides, under the same conditions as nationals of that State. This right shall be exercised subject to detailed arrangements adopted before 31 December 1994 by the Council, acting unanimously on a proposal from the Commission and after consulting the European Parliament; these arrangements may provide for derogations where warranted by problems specific to a member state.

(2) Without prejudice to Article 138(3) and to provisions adopted for its implementation, every citizen of the Union residing in a member state of which he is not a national shall have the right to vote and to stand as a candidate in elections to the European Parliament in the member state in which he resides, under the same conditions as nationals of that State. This right shall be exercised subject to detailed arrangements adopted before 31 December 1993 by the Council, acting unanimously on a proposal from the Commission and after consulting the European Parliament; these arrangements may provide for derogations where warranted by problems specific to a member state.

Inter-state Union citizens are thus given two specific democratic rights by the EC Treaty. They may vote and stand for election to (i) municipal authorities and (ii) the European Parliament (EP), under the same conditions as the nationals of the host member state.

The detailed arrangements for the exercise of municipal electoral rights are set out in Directive 94/80[32] while the corresponding arrangements for elections to the EP are contained in Directive 93/109.[33] In each case, the preamble to the implementing directive describes the electoral right as 'an instance of the application of the principle of equality and non-discrimination between nationals and non-nationals and a corollary of the right to move and reside freely enshrined in Article 8a' EC.

The rights conferred by the two electoral directives are largely faithful to Article 8b's promise to extend equal treatment to inter-state Union citizens in municipal elections and elections to the EP. For example, where national laws require that the member state's own citizens must have been resident in the member state's territory for a certain minimum period before being eligible to vote or stand as a candidate, inter-state Union citizens 'shall be deemed to have fulfilled that condition where they have resided for an equivalent period in other member states'.[34]

The electoral directives also contain several provisions designed to ensure that inter-state Union citizens do not receive more favourable treatment than a member state's own nationals. Inter-state Union citizens, for example, are not entitled to stand as candidates for election in a host member state if they have been disqualified from doing so in their own member state as a result of an 'individual decision' under the civil or criminal law of those member states.[35] Both directives also permit special limited derogations in respect of any member state (in fact only Luxembourg) 'where the proportion of citizens of voting age who reside in it but are not nationals of it exceeds 20% of the total number of citizens of the Union residing there who are of voting age'.[36]

Inter-state Union citizens are thus, as a matter of Community law, given important political rights which foreign Community nationals did not possess prior to the TEU. They may now participate, both as voters and as candidates, in the supranational and much of the sub-national electoral life of host member states under conditions of substantial equality with Union citizens who are nationals of the host member state. Some anomalies have also no doubt been removed, such as the ability of Commonwealth citizens to vote in European Parliamentary elections in the United Kingdom (UK) when Community nationals from other member states were ineligible.[37]

But inter-state Union citizens are, as a matter of Community law, still shut out from the national-level electoral life of their host member states. At the current stage of European integration, with the continuing dominance of the Council in the Community's legislative processes, it is the national level which is the real locus of political power in the Union.

The TEU effectively gave the EP a new power to veto the appointment of a new Commission nominated by the Council[38] in addition to its existing power to censure and remove the Commission *en bloc*.[39] These powers are symbolically significant, but when the really important political deals are cut in Brussels they are mostly done by and among national politicians answerable to national constituencies via national political processes. The organs of the member states, furthermore, play a vital role in the performance of the Union's executive functions.

It is probable that the specifically supranational European political institutions (especially the EP and the Commission), even after almost four decades, still lack the popular recognition, affection, loyalty and trust necessary to enjoy much political legitimacy. Why this is so, and who if anyone is mainly responsible, is well beyond the scope of this paper. But it seems clear at present that the member states 'remain, for their peoples, the principal focus of collective loyalty and the principal forum of democratic political activity'.[40]

The continuing predominance of the member state polity in the life of the EU calls into question the exclusion of inter-state Union citizens from the national electoral life of their host member states. These Union citizens are, as a matter of Community law, not entitled to participate as voters or candidates in national elections. This of course remains true even where issues of European concern are prominent in national electoral politics. The boundary between issues which are national and those which fall within the Union's domain is often difficult to determine, and is frequently non-existent. Consequently, these Union citizens are, in most member states, excluded from direct participation in electoral politics even where Union policies, or the future directions of European integration itself, are an issue.

The exclusion of the national level from Community law electoral rights was no doubt motivated by a concern to preserve the member states' national identities. Article F(1) TEU commits the Union to respect these identities,[41] and it is possible to point to Articles 48(4) and 55 EC[42] as provisions authorising exceptions to important Community freedoms on the same basis of concern. Indeed the inter-state Union citizen's rights to participate fully in municipal elections is also affected by this concern. Member states are authorised to provide that only their own nationals may hold the office of elected head, deputy or member of the governing college of a municipal authority.[43] Furthermore, inter-state Union citizens elected to representative councils may not participate in certain functions associated with the selection of delegates to, or members of, national parliamentary assemblies.[44]

Nevertheless, the European Union has among its basic objectives 'to strengthen the protection of the rights and interests of the nationals of its member states through the introduction of a citizenship of the Union'.[45] It is to achieve this objective 'while respecting the principle of subsidiarity as defined in Article 3b' EC. The second paragraph of Article 3b EC provides as follows: 'In areas which do not fall within its exclusive competence, the Community shall take action, in accordance with the principle of subsidiarity, only if and in so far as the objectives of the proposed action cannot be sufficiently achieved by the member states and can therefore, by reason of the scale or effects of the proposed action, be better achieved by the Community'. The preamble to the TEU also declares the member states' resolve 'to continue the process of creating an ever closer union among the peoples of Europe, in which decisions are taken as closely as possible to the citizen in accordance with the principle of subsidiarity.' The precise significance of the subsidiarity principle in Article 3b is not yet settled.[46] At the very least, however, it means that the Community should, as a guiding political principle, leave action to the member states unless the desired objectives can be better achieved by action at the Community level.

The subsidiarity principle does not apply to areas which fall within the small area constituting the Community's exclusive competence,[47] but it does apply to all other areas of Community competence. Hence the vast majority of action which clearly falls within the Community's competence should, wherever possible in accordance with the subsidiarity principle, be performed by the member states. It is, furthermore, a prominent feature of the Community's constitutional arrangements that the member states have practical responsibility for the execution of almost all Community law. And yet inter-state Union citizens resident in host member states are not entitled, as a matter of Community law, to participate in the democratic supervision of these actions by voting and being candidates in national elections.

Inter-State Union citizens may thus be subject to discrimination on the sole basis of their nationality, and deprived of a political right of considerable importance in the Union's democratic life by no less an authority than the Community's constitutional charter itself.

Although there can be no doubting the legality of this situation, it sits very uneasily with Community law's general principle of equality and with the TEU's express commitment to 'the principles of liberty, democracy and respect for human rights and fundamental freedoms'.[48] Citizens of the Union residing in a member state of which they are not a national are, electorally speaking, Union citizens of an inferior class as a matter of Community law.

Conclusion

The establishment of a common European citizenship on a constitutional basis is a development of the most significant symbolic importance. The conferral of citizenship is a step ordinarily undertaken by States, and is a sign that the person possessing it enjoys a special legal relationship with that State and with the other persons upon whom citizenship has also been bestowed.

A person possessing citizenship in a modern democracy is entitled to assume that s/he is a full member of the political community and that s/he enjoys the equal protection of the law in relation, at the very least, to the core citizenship rights of entry, residence and democratic participation.

According to Germany's Federal Constitutional Court, the EU is not, at its current stage of development, a *Bundesstaat* but a *Staatenverbund*. Thus it is not a federal State, but a confederation of States from which Germany could withdraw.[49] It is certainly the case that the Union does not possess all the attributes of Statehood in international law, but its establishment of a Union citizenship powerfully reinforces the proposition that it is very much more than an international organisation or a league of sovereign States.

Whatever its status in international law, in its internal arrangements the Union is now much more State-like than ever before as a result of creating a common Union citizenship. The Commission has noted that 'the Treaty has created a direct *political* link between citizens of the member states and the European Union such as never existed within the Community'.[50]

Some member states were more enthusiastic than others about the inclusion of Union citizenship provisions in the TEU. Those that were less inclined to support it were no doubt concerned to confine it within limits. Several of those limits have been explored in this article. But citizenship is such a potent element in modern democratic theory, and in modern democratic practice, that once it is established among free peoples its tendency is always to grow towards full maturity. European citizenship has already outgrown its infancy in the guise of the various enthusiasms of the 1980s collectively referred to, mainly by the Commission, as 'People's Europe'.

With the TEU, European citizenship attains its adolescence and stands independently but uncertainly on its own constitutional base. It is not yet at a stage where it has attained its full vigour, but adolescence is an unsteady stage of life. It is frequently besieged by unsettling conflicts and contradictions which play their role in the passage to adulthood.

The contradiction at the heart of Union citizenship is its failure to ensure that its subjects enjoy the equality which citizens can ordinarily expect to take for granted. In relation to those very matters where citizenship should be the best legal safeguard of formal equality, the present arrangements create privileged and non-privileged categories of fellow citizens. This is a state of affairs which should be anathema to any self-respecting democracy. Equal treatment for EU citizens is necessary in a democracy not only in respect of electoral rights, though here the case is at its most obvious. It is also necessary that a democratic Union afford all its *de jure* citizens equal treatment in respect of mobility rights.

The connection between political democracy, a common citizenship status and the right of interstate movement was addressed by the Supreme Court of the United States shortly after the American civil war:

> He [the Union citizen] has the right to come to the seat of government to assert any claim he may have upon that government, or to transact any business he may have with it. To seek its protection, to share its offices, to engage in administering its functions, he has a right to free access to its seaports, through which all the operations of foreign trade and commerce are conducted, to the sub-treasuries, the land offices, the revenue offices, and the courts of justice in the several States, and this right is in its nature independent of the will of any State over whose soil he must pass in exercise of it.[51]

The same court, some seventy years later, also condemned as incompatible with possession of common citizenship in a democratic Union restrictions on interstate migration which discriminated against the economically marginalised:

It would ... introduce a caste system utterly incompatible with the spirit of our system of government. It would permit those who were stigmatised by a State as indigents, paupers, or vagabonds to be relegated to an inferior class of citizenship. It would prevent a citizen, because he was poor, from seeking new horizons in other States. It might thus withhold from large segments of our people that mobility which is basic to any guarantee of freedom of opportunity. The result would be a substantial dilution of the rights of national citizenship, a serious impairment of the principles of equality.[52]

None of this was as seriously problematic before Maastricht. Community nationals from other member states were, as a matter of law and fact, simply privileged foreigners. But the existence of a shared constitutionally-based formal citizenship status in circumstances where its holders do not enjoy the equal protection of Community law, in those very matters central to citizenship, is a challenge to the European Union's democratic credentials. Even more importantly, by denying its own citizens the limited protection of formal legal equality the Union also denies them 'the negative condition of the good life'.[53]

There is a gap between the expectations reasonably created by instituting a formal citizenship of the Union and the reality which is delivered under the current state of Community law. It is in the bridging of this gap that much unfinished business lies.

Notes

1.   Articles 8, 8a, 8b, 8c, 8d and 8e.
2.   Commission of the European Communities, *Report from the Commission on the Citizenship of the Union* COM(93) 702 final, 1.
3.   The Treaty of Amsterdam will add the following sentence to Article 8(1): 'Citizenship of the Union shall complement and not replace national citizenship'.
4.   Hall, S., 'Loss of Union Citizenship in Breach of Fundamental Rights', *European Law Review,* 21, 1996, 129.
5.   The Treaty of Amsterdam will replace the present text of Article 8a (2) with the following: 'The Council may adopt provisions with a view to facilitating the exercise of the rights referred to in paragraph 1; save as otherwise provided in this Treaty, the Council shall act in accordance with the procedure referred to in Article 189b. The Council shall act unanimously throughout this procedure'.
6.   The ECJ has recently expressly left open the question as to whether Article 8a EC confers a right on Union citizens to take up residence in a member state whose nationality they do not possess (Case C-85/96 *Martinez Sala v Freistaat Bayern*, 12 May 1998, paragraph 60 of the Court's judgement). At the very least, according to the ECJ, Article 8 renders all Union citizens already lawfully resident in a host member state within the scope *ratione personae* of the EC Treaty even if the lawfulness of their residence stems from national law alone on grounds outside the scope of Community law. Such Union citizens are thereby protected by, *inter alia*, the non-discrimination entitlements enshrined in Article

6 EC (at paragraph 62 of the Court's judgement).

7. See for example: Joined Cases 50-58/82 *Administrateur des Affaires Maritimes, Bayonne v Dorca Marina* [1982] E.C.R. 3949, 3958-9, paragraphs 10-11 of the Court's judgment; Case 238/83 *Caisse d'Allocations Familiales de la Région Parisienne v Meade* [1984] E.C.R. 2631, 2638, paragraph 7 of the Court's judgment; Case C-105/89 *Buhari v Institut national d'assurances sociales pour travailleurs indépendants* [1990] E.C.R. I-4211, I-4239, paragraph 26 of the Court's judgment.

8. See especially Articles 48(3) (workers), 56(1) (established self-employed) and 66 (suppliers and receivers of services) of the EC Treaty.

9. Article 4(1) of Directive 64/221 and Annex A point 3: O.J. Sp Ed, 1963–4, 117.

10. See note 7.

11. O.J. L180/26, 1990.

12. O.J. L180/28, 1990.

13. O.J. L180/30, 1990.

14. Article 5 of each directive.

15. Case C-295/90 *European Parliament v Council ('Re Students' Rights')* [1992] E.C.R. I-4193; [1992] 3 C.M.L.R. 281. The Court ruled that Directive 90/366 should have been adopted on the procedure set out in Article 7(2) EEC (now Article 6(2) EC), which requires a qualified majority on the Council and the legislative cooperation of the European Parliament (EP). The Council had instead adopted Directive 90/366 under the procedure allowed under Article 235 EEC, which requires Council unanimity and merely consultation with the EP.

16. The Court adopted this approach without express legislative authority in the EEC Treaty, but relied principally on the Community law general principle of legal certainty.

17. O.J. L317/59, 1993.

18. Article 7 EEC became Article 6 EC after the TEU came into force.

19. Case C-357/89 *Raulin v Minister van Onderwijs en Wetenschappen* [1992] E.C.R. I-1027.

20. Case C-295/90 *European Parliament v Council ('Re Students' Rights')* [1992] E.C.R. I-4193; [1992] 3 C.M.L.R. 281, 300, paragraph 14 of the Court's judgment.

21. Article 1(1) of Directive 90/365.

22. In the case of workers, the right to remain in a host member state after having been employed in the same member state is covered by Article 48(3)(d) EC and Regulation 1251/70 (O.J. Special Ed. 1970, L142/24, 402). The corresponding right for self-employed persons is covered by Directive 75/34 ([1975] O.J. L14/10).

23. Article 48(3)(d). Although the Commission's proposal for Directive 90/365 was based on Articles 49 and 54 EEC, the Council refused to adopt it on this basis.

24. Article 1(1) of Directive 93/96. As to the meaning of 'vocational training' see Wyatt, D. and Dashwood, A., *European Community Law*, 3rd edition (London: Sweet and Maxwell, 1993), 640–50.

25. The right of residence is granted by Article 1 of each directive. The right of movement is granted by the first paragraph of Article 2(2) of Directives 90/364 and 90/365, which apply Articles 2, 3, 6(1)(a), 6(2) and 9 of Directive 68/360 (abolition of restrictions on movement and residence for workers and their families) *mutatis mutandis* to the beneficiaries of those Directives. Article 2(2) of Directive 93/96 does not extend Articles 6(1)(a) and 6(2) of Directive 68/360 to the students covered by the former directive, thereby implying that such beneficiaries do not enjoy a freedom to reside anywhere within the territory of the host member state and that short breaks in residence and absence on military service may affect the continuing validity of a residence permit.

26. Article 1(1) of Directive 90/364.

27. The first paragraph of Article 1(1).

28. The first paragraph of Article 1(1) of Directive 90/365 and Article 1 of Directive 93/96. Curiously, these directives do not expressly require the beneficiaries' accompanying families to be covered by sickness insurance. Furthermore in the case of pensioners, the pensions which they are required to be receiving must themselves be of a sufficient amount to prevent the pensioner from becoming a burden on the host member state's social security system. Consequently a pensioner who is not in receipt of a sufficiently lucrative pension, but who has sufficient income from his or her pension combined with income from other sources as would prevent him or her from becoming a burden on the host member state's social security system, would need to rely on Directive 90/364 should s/he desire to reside in a member state of which s/he is not a national.

29. Article 1 of each directive. The family provision is rather less liberal in the case of Directive 93/96 than in the case of Directives 90/364 and 90/365. Whereas only a student's spouse and dependent children may accompany him, the beneficiaries under the other two directives may be accompanied by their spouses and dependent 'descendants', as well as dependant relatives in the ascending line of the beneficiary (but not, it seems, of the beneficiary's spouse).

30. The third paragraph of Article 2(2) of each directive. In the case of students, only Articles 2 to 9 of Directive 64/221 apply.

31. Article 1 of Directives 90/364, 90/365 and 93/96.

32. O.J. L368/38, 1994. The inter-state Union citizen has electoral rights in respect of each 'basic local government unit' as defined in the directive. What this term means in respect of the diverse local government systems in each of the member states is set out in an Annex to the directive. In England, for example, the electoral rights extend to counties, districts, London boroughs, parishes and the City of London in relation to ward elections and common council men. In Germany the federal *Länder* are not included and the inter-state Union citizen's electoral rights are confined to certain sub-*Land* governmental units.

33. O.J. L329/34, 1993.

34. Article 4(1) of Directive 94/80 and Article 5 of Directive 93/109.

35. Article 5(1) of Directive 94/80 and Article 6 of Directive 93/109.

36. Article 12(1) of Directive 94/80 and Article 14(1) of Directive 93/109.

37. Commonwealth citizens do not lose their right to vote in the United Kingdom as a result of anything in the TEU, the EC Treaty or the two electoral directives.

38. The new Article 158 EC, inserted by Article G(48) TEU.

39. Article 144 EC.

40. Dashwood, A., 'The Limits of European Community Powers', *European Law Review*, 21, 1996, 113.

41. The preamble to the TEU also records the member states' desire 'to deepen the solidarity between their peoples while respecting their history, their culture and their traditions'.

42. Article 48(4) provides that freedom of movement for workers 'shall not apply to employment in the public service'. Article 55 provides that the right of establishment 'shall not apply ... to activities which ... are connected, even occasionally, with the exercise of official authority'. Article 66 extends the exemption in Article 55 to the freedom to supply services.

43. Article 5(3) of Directive 93/80.

44. Article 5(4) of Directive 93/80.

45. Article B TEU.

46. See for example Cass, D.Z., 'The Word that Saves Maastricht? The Principle of Subsidiarity and the Division of Powers within the European Community', *Common Market Law Review*, 29, 1992, 1107; Emiliou, N., 'Subsidiarity: An Effective Barrier Against the 'Enterprises of Ambition'?', *European Law Review*, 17, 1992, 383, and 'Subsidiarity: Panacea or Fig Leaf?' in O'Keeffe, D. and Twomey, P.M. (eds.), *Legal Issues of the Maastricht Treaty* (London: Chancery, 1994); Lord Mackenzie Stuart, 'Subsidiarity: A

Busted Flush?' in Curtin, D. and O'Keeffe, D. (eds.), *Constitutional Adjudication in European Community and National Law* (Dublin: Butterworths, 1992); Steiner, J., 'Subsidiarity under the Maastricht Treaty' in *Legal Issues of the Maastricht Treaty, op.cit.*; Toth, A., 'A Legal Analysis of Subsidiarity' in *Legal Issues of the Maastricht Treaty, op.cit.*; *The Principle of Subsidiarity*, Fide Congress Vol. 1, 1994; Pope Pius XI, *Quadrigesimo Anno* (papal encyclical, 1931), para 79.

47. According to John Temple Lang ('What Powers Should the European Community Have?', *European Public Law*, 1, 1995, 98 and materials there noted), the Community has exclusive power over only four areas: Commercial Policy, conservation of marine biological resources, treaties on supply of nuclear materials, and certain mergers. Implementation of the TEU's provisions on monetary union will extend the Community's exclusive competence to the common currency. See also Dashwood, *loc.cit.*, 113, for an even more restrictive view of the Community's exclusive competence.

48. Third paragraph in the preamble. Also see Article F(2) TEU, which commits the Union to respect fundamental rights.

49. Decision of 12 October 1993, 2 BvR 2134 & 2159/93. English translation, *Brunner v European Union Treaty* [1994] 1 C.M.L.R. 57.

50. *Report from the Commission on the Citizenship of the Union*, COM(93), 702 final, 2. Emphasis in original.

51. *Crandall v Nevada*, 6 Wall 35, 18 L Ed. 745 (1868) at 747, per Miller, J., delivering the opinion of the court.

52. *Edwards v California*, 314 US 160 (1941) at 181, per Douglas, J., concurring with the opinion of the court.

53. Lewis, C.S., 'Equality' in Hooper, W. (ed.), *Present Concerns: Ethical Essays, essays by C.S. Lewis* (Fount, 1986), 18.

4 Democracy and Multiculturalism in Western Europe

STEPHEN CASTLES

Introduction

The 1990s have been a period of turmoil and re-orientation in West European politics. At least five major factors have made it necessary to rethink models of democracy and citizenship. First, the end of the Cold War and the collapse of socialist regimes in Eastern Europe have caused major changes in political and economic relationships throughout Europe. Second, the economic changes brought about by globalisation and the rise of new industrial countries have resulted in economic restructuring and rapid social change in Europe. De-industrialisation has been closely linked to the erosion of Keynesian and social-democratic models for achieving 'social citizenship'—not only in Thatcherite Britain but even in social democratic Sweden. This has led to a critique of the evolutionary and perhaps ethnocentric assumptions of Marshallian ideas of citizenship.[1]

Third, the crisis of the West European Left is partly a result of the two previous factors. One sign of the crisis is the decline in strength of trade unions and working class parties. In the face of globalisation, the left is struggling to find new economic and social models, which are not premised on the notion of relatively autonomous nation-states. At the same time, the absence of any economic alternative to capitalism, or any political alternative to parliamentary democracy, have made it essential to re-examine the emancipative potential of liberal-democratic principles.[2] Fourth, the expansion of the European Community (EC) from a central group of originally six countries to 15 now, and its development into a European Union (EU) with much further-going political, economic and social functions is a significant factor. This raises many questions about citizenship, national identity and cultural interaction. On the institutional level, the growing significance of the European Parliament (EP), Commission and judicial system questions national sovereignty. At the same time, tendencies towards regionalism can perhaps be better accommodated in a supranational system than in nation-states. Discussions on long-term

55

policies to incorporate Central and Eastern European states have brought new uncertainties into already difficult processes of integration.

Finally, there is the presence of large numbers of immigrants of many different origins in Western Europe. The foreign (ie. non-citizen) resident population of European Organisation for Economic Co-operation and Development (OECD) countries was about 20 million in 1993.[3] Of these, over half were non-EU citizens and about a quarter were non-Europeans. At least five million people have citizenship of their country of residence but belong to ethnic minorities—such as Afro-Caribbeans and South Asians in the United Kingdom (UK) or North Africans in France. This makes around 25 million people who are excluded from formal citizenship rights or who do not enjoy full economic and social participation. The share of immigrants and ethnic minorities in total population is around 7–10% in Belgium, France, Germany, the UK, Sweden and Austria, with the highest level in Switzerland: 18%. Southern European immigration countries have lower immigrant populations—for instance 1.7% in Italy (if official figures can be believed)—but entries are growing fast.[4]

The challenge posed by the presence of immigrant minorities for democracy and citizenship in Western Europe is the central theme of this chapter. But it is important to be aware of the close and complex links between all the topics just mentioned. Here is an example: the rise of the extreme right and the escalation of racist violence are obviously related to immigration, for anti-immigrant campaigns have been at the centre of right-wing mobilisation. But these phenomena are also closely linked to economic restructuring and the decline of the welfare state, which lead to declining living standards and socio-economic insecurity for many people. The decline of the labour movement has been another factor which has created the 'social space' for the rise of the extreme right.[5] European integration has been ambivalent in this context: on the one hand it has been seen as an attack on national identity, of which extreme-right parties have become the self-appointed defenders. On the other hand, some far-right groups have seen themselves as the bearers of 'European values and culture' against the 'invading hordes'—especially those from Islamic countries. Finally, the end of the Cold War—which had after all provided a sense of political purpose and unity in both West and East—is a further factor of uncertainty clearly linked to extreme-right mobilisation, particularly in Germany.

Immigration and Citizenship

Immigration presents three main dilemmas for citizenship and democracy. The first concerns *access to citizenship*—that is the rules governing the extent to which immigrants and their children can formally become members of the national political community. The dilemma is that failure to make immigrants into citizens undermines a basic principle of parliamentary democracy: that all members of civil society should have rights of political participation. But making them into citizens questions concepts of the nation based on ethnic belonging or cultural homogeneity. Such ideas have been central to historical processes of nation-building and are still important, despite attempts to develop purely political models of citizenship. This dilemma of formal inclusion is the main issue in many European countries which deny naturalisation to immigrants and do not readily confer citizenship on children born to immigrants in the country.

The second dilemma concerns *substantial citizenship*—that is the rights and obligations connected with being a member of a national political community. Granting immigrants formal access to citizenship is an important first step, but it does not ensure that they actually obtain all the rights regarded as part of modern citizenship. Where immigrants have become socio-economically marginalised and are targets for racist violence, access to citizenship does not guarantee equal civil, political and social rights. Achieving full participation requires a whole range of policies and institutions concerned with combating discrimination, and improving labour market status, education and housing. This dilemma of overcoming marginalisation has led to very different responses in various countries.

But even this is not enough. The third dilemma is that immigrants often cannot simply be incorporated into society as individuals. A large proportion of immigrants and their immediate descendants cluster together, share a common socio-economic position, develop their own community structures, and seek to maintain their languages and cultures. This is partly an issue of cultural affinity, but it is above all a reaction to experiences of racism and marginalisation. Culture and ethnicity are vital resources in the settlement process. This means that immigrants cannot become full citizens unless the state and the national community are willing to accept—to some extent at least—the right to cultural difference. In the long run, this may make it necessary not only to change concepts of national culture and identity, but also to overhaul institutional structures which claim to be universalistic, but which are in fact based on specific cultural values and traditions. The third dilemma then is that of the need for cultural openness and structural change in a multicultural society.

I will now examine current debates on immigration and citizenship in Germany and France—two countries with very different models—and then look more briefly at a few other countries. It is important to realise that being a citizen is not always a clear-cut issue of whether one has a certain passport or not. As already mentioned, members of ethnic minorities may be formal citizens and yet be excluded from many rights. Conversely, non-citizens may be granted certain rights, such as long-term residence, the right to work, or social security entitlements. Millions of immigrants in European countries have a special status, known for instance as the *Aufenthaltsberechtigung* (residence entitlement) in Germany, or the *Niederlassungsbewilligung* (settlement permit) in Switzerland. They may be regarded as 'quasi-citizens', who have some but not all of the rights of citizenship.[6] This in-between status is problematic. Partial integration into citizenship creates expectations and conflicts—it cannot be a stable condition: sooner or later, either the immigrants must leave, or they must be allowed to become full citizens.[7]

Germany

The first example is Germany, which is in the paradoxical situation of being officially regarded as not being a country of immigration, and yet having had some of the largest inflows of any country since 1945: nearly 20 million people in all, including no less than 1.5 million per year in 1991 and 1992—as many as the USA!

The largest groups were *Aussiedler* (ethnic Germans) from the East immediately after 1945 (some 8 million) and then again since 1989 (about 2.5 million). The *Aussiedler* have an immediate right to citizenship, even though their ancestors may have left Germany to settle in the Volga valley or in Romanian Siebenbürgen centuries ago. Indeed, many of the recent arrivals speak archaic dialects, and their culture and values are often worlds apart from contemporary Germany. Why are the *Aussiedler* seen as Germans who have an immediate right to all the privileges of being a citizen of one of Europe's richest countries? It is because of the principle of *jus sanguinis* (the law of the blood). You are German if you are of German blood. Since German blood is chemically no different from any other, the proof is a social one: a person must be able to show cultural belonging through use of the German language and belonging to a German community—as demonstrated for instance through parish birth and marriage records. In other words, Germany is a *Kulturnation*—a nation defined through cultural rather than political belonging—which is a linked to its turbulent history and late emergence as a nation state in 1871.[8]

However, in the last few years the principle of *jus sanguinis* has come into conflict with a more rational principle—that of limiting strains on the welfare state. A *de facto* quota system was introduced in the early 1990s, through which the number of *Aussiedler* was limited to about 220,000 per year through complex bureaucratic rules.[9]

The situation of Germany's other immigrants is quite different. Most of the foreign residents are there because of mass labour recruitment between 1955 and 1973. The Government brought in 'guest workers', mainly from Southern Europe and Turkey, who were meant to work in Germany for a few years and then go home. The Government stopped recruitment in 1973, hoping that surplus foreign workers would leave. In fact, many stayed on, and family reunion continued. By the late 1970s it was clear that permanent settlement was taking place.[10] Since the mid–1980s, increasing numbers of temporary workers from Poland and other East European countries have been employed in building, domestic work and other informal sector jobs—a resumption of historical patterns dating back to the nineteenth century. In addition, there have been substantial inflows of asylum seekers, with an upward curve from 100,000 in 1986 to 438,000 in 1992.[11] Many came from Africa and Asia, but the main growth since 1989 has been in East-West movements.

There are over seven million foreign residents in Germany today. The main groups in 1993 were Turks (1.9 million), former Yugoslavs (929,600), Italians (563,000), Greeks (352,000) and Poles (260,500).[12] The myth of temporary sojourn still shapes the legal status of foreigners, except those from EU countries, who enjoy social and economic parity with German citizens. Non-EU residents are denied many rights, particularly concerning political participation. It is hard for foreigners to become citizens. Apart from a ten year waiting period, there are high fees and restrictive rules concerning employment situation, financial security and police records. In 1992, there were just 37,042 naturalisations (0.5% of the foreign population).[13] On that basis it would take 200 years for all foreign residents to become citizens! The *jus sanguinis* principle also means that children born to immigrant parents in Germany have no automatic right to citizenship. Young people who have been born in Germany and know no other country can, under certain circumstances, be deported. This hardly leads to clear future perspectives or political integration!

The political exclusion of foreign residents is linked to socio-economic marginalisation. Most were recruited as manual workers and have had few chances of upward mobility. Many are concentrated in poor housing areas with few amenities. Inadequate educational opportunities and discrimination in training and employment have carried this disadvantaged position over to much of the second generation. Such marginality and exclusion has fed into the stereotypes of difference and inferiority fostered by extreme-right racist groups, especially since 1989. One result is growing racist violence against both long-standing foreign residents and new asylum-seekers. Another consequence has been growing mobilisation of immigrant youth—especially Turks—to fight racism and discrimination. Since mainstream political expression is blocked, mobilisation is largely around cultural and religious symbols—further strengthening fears of 'otherness' and fundamentalism.

Citizenship for immigrants has become a major political issue. The growth of violent neo-Nazi groups has made many people aware of the dangers of excluding a large group from full participation in society. After four Turkish girls and women were burned to death in a neo-Nazi attack in the small industrial town of Solingen in May 1993, there were large anti-racist demonstrations all over Germany. One of the main slogans was the demand for dual citizenship. This is an important issue especially for Turks, who cannot easily give up their previous citizenship. Current German law requires renunciation of any other citizenship as a precondition for naturalisation, although exceptions are made. The 'asylum compromise' of 1993—a change in Germany's Basic Law (or constitution) to restrict the right of asylum—did at last create a legal right for third generation immigrants (children of foreigners themselves born in Germany) to choose German citizenship, although again the new rules stopped short of allowing dual citizenship. In fact, in Germany—as in all other immigration countries—there are growing numbers of people with dual or multiple citizenship, which is the natural result of bi-cultural marriages. The official estimate for Germany is 1.2 million such people.[14]

The situation in Germany is in flux. On the one hand, there are widespread fears of further immigration, for Germany has indeed borne the brunt of the mass movements since 1989. The constitutional change of 1993 was the culmination of a long series of measures designed to increase border control and reduce entries. An important element of this was international cooperation such as the Schengen agreement of 1985, the Dublin Convention of 1990 and agreements with Hungary, the Czech Republic and Poland to stop people using their countries for transit to the West. Germany has thus been influential in erecting the walls of 'Fortress Europe'.

But, on the other hand, views on integration of long-standing immigrants within Germany are changing fast. The myth of not being 'a country of immigration' has become unsustainable.[15] That has been clear on the social policy level for many years: whatever the political doctrine, welfare agencies and education authorities have had to set up special services and adopt effective multicultural policies to deal with problems in neighbourhoods and cities with immigrant concentrations. Such policies are beginning to be institutionalised by offices of multicultural affairs, or commissioners for foreign citizens, at the municipal, state and federal levels.

In the political arena, the left—the Green Party, some sections of the Social Democratic Party (SPD) and the unions—has advocated stronger rights for immigrants and anti-discrimination measures for many years. A key demand was for local voting rights for resident non-citizens—a measure introduced in Schleswig Holstein but subsequently ruled invalid by the Constitutional Court in 1990. This idea has now been replaced with the further-reaching demand for dual citizenship. However, the left has an ambivalent attitude towards multiculturalism. It has often been seen as a model for cementing the identity of ethnic groups, and for maintaining cultures which are seen by some as anti-modern and repressive—especially towards women. Some immigrants fear that it would commit them to a group identity which they do not want. Other people on the left, however, see multiculturalism in terms of creative cultural interaction, and welcome the changes it brings for social and cultural life.[16]

The extreme right of course remains opposed to immigration and to the extension of rights to immigrants. Until recently, the parliamentary right— the CDU-CSU—was strongly opposed to recognition of permanent settlement. Now the CDU is rethinking its position, influenced by municipal politicians like Mayor Rommel of Stuttgart, who know the situation in the big cities at first hand. From the mid-1980s, a group around then CDU General Secretary Heiner Geißler called for recognition of permanent settlement, and significant improvements in immigrant rights. The initiative was unpopular, and contributed to Geißler's dismissal from his influential post.

More recently, some theorists of the right have called for radical changes. A significant expression of this is a book entitled *Der Wahn des Nationalen* (roughly: 'the madness of the national idea') by Dieter Oberndörfer, a prominent political scientist and adviser to the CDU. Oberndörfer calls for the replacement of the nation-state by an 'open European republic', based on liberal-democratic principles. Such a republic would be based not on ethnic belonging, but on liberal-democratic principles. The key principle would be *'Verfassungspatriotismus'* [constitutional patriotism], the active identification of the citizens with the political order and values of the republic.[17]

In this model (which, as we shall see, is very like the French 'Republican model'), granting citizenship to immigrants is no problem, because the idea of the nation as ethnic or cultural belonging is replaced by the idea of a purely political community. However, citizenship is conceptualised in terms of individual political participation, and there is no room for ideas of social citizenship, nor for multiculturalism based on the collective integration of groups with diverse cultures. In other words, Oberndörfer's model addresses only the issue of access to citizenship. It does nothing to resolve the other dilemmas mentioned earlier: of overcoming marginalisation and of the need for cultural openness and structural change in a multicultural society.

Oberndörfer's approach has some similarities with Jürgen Habermas' writing on the subject. Indeed the concept of *Verfassungspatriotismus* seems to have been coined by Habermas. However, there is an important difference. In an article published in 1993 in the weekly magazine *Die Zeit,* Habermas argued that, in the long run, a democratic society has no alternative but to incorporate immigrants, even if this means fundamental changes in culture and politics. He described 'two stages of assimilation':

> The first requires acquiescence to the principles of the constitution—that is assimilation to the way in which the autonomy of the citizen is conceived, and to the way in which the 'public use of reason' (Rawls) is practised in the receiving society. The second stage requires preparedness for a considerable degree of acculturation, that is adaptation to the life-style, practices and customs of the indigenous majority culture. That means an assimilation which takes place on the level of ethical and cultural integration...[18]

According to Habermas, a democratic state should demand the first type of assimilation: political acculturation and acceptance of basic constitutional principles. But it has no right to demand the second type, which would mean interference in the rights of citizens (both indigenous and immigrant) to their own forms of cultural identity. Habermas goes on to present a perspective for future development in multicultural societies:

> This principle, however, does not guarantee that the initially asserted identity of the community will be protected from changes *in the long run.* Since the immigrants must not be forced to give up their own traditions, the consequence of waves of immigrants with newly-established forms of life is a widening of the horizon within which the citizens interpret their common constitutional principles. Then a mechanism becomes active, through which a changed composition of the active citizenry also changes the context within which the citizens' fundamental ethical and political discourses take place.[19]

Thus Habermas argues that incorporation of immigrants as citizens will, in the long run, lead to institutional change in major sub-systems of society, such as political and economic structures—an answer to the third dilemma mentioned above. Resolving the second dilemma—that of combating marginalisation—would no doubt be a pre-condition for the type of political assimilation that Habermas has in mind.

France

It is far easier for newcomers to become citizens in France than in Germany, yet citizenship for immigrants remains an important political issue. France has been a country of immigration ever since the mid-19th century, when the *grève des ventres* ('belly strike') led to an early fall in birth rates. Polish and Italian workers were vital to industrialisation, and their descendants have become largely assimilated.[20] France's large current immigrant population is a result of four main factors: (1) France's colonial past, which has led to large inflows from North and West Africa and the Caribbean; (2) foreign labour recruitment, mainly in Southern Europe, from 1945 to 1974; (3) mobility of people within the European Community; and (4) inflows of refugees and asylum-seekers.

The 1990 Census showed a foreign population of 3.6 million (6.4% of the total population). The main groups were Portuguese (650,000), Algerians (614,000), Moroccans (573,000), Italians (253,000), Spaniards (216,000), Tunisians (206,000) and Turks (198,000).[21] In addition, there are over 1 million immigrants who have become French citizens, about half a million French citizens of non-European origin from 'Overseas Departments and Territories', and an unknown number of Algerians who entered as French citizens before Algerian independence in 1961. French-born children of Algerians who were born before 1961 have a special status: they are considered French by the French Government (because born in France of French-born parents), but Algerian by the Algerian Government (because their parents are Algerian citizens).

Foreign immigrants can obtain naturalisation fairly easily after five years residence. About 60,000 foreigners were naturalised in 1993.[22] Until 1993, children born in France to foreign parents automatically became French at the age of 18, unless they renounced this right—which few did. Children whose parents became naturalised also received French citizenship. About 35,000 people received French citizenship in these ways in 1993, making a total of 95,000 acquisitions. The *Loi Pasqua* of 1993 ended this situation: now the young person of immigrant origin has to make a specific declaration of the desire to become French between the age of 16 and 21. French citizenship can be refused in the case of a previous criminal conviction. Acquisition of French citizenship often means dual citizenship, which is accepted by the authorities. According to Jacqueline Costa-Lascoux, 'French law is a subtle combination of *jus sanguinis, jus soli* and the will of the applicant'.[23] (*Jus soli* is the law of the soil: the principle that someone born on the territory of a nation is a citizen by virtue of that fact).

The official policy is to classify the population as citizens or non-citizens, with no shades of grey in between. Once immigrants become citizens, they enjoy full equality of rights. Special policies for ethnic groups and recognition of their leaderships are seen as barriers to integration.[24] Citizens are meant to display civic virtues (*civisme*), and fulfill their obligations to the secular, unitary state. The principles of this 'Republican model' go back to the Revolution of 1789 and the Declaration of the Rights of Man, according to which any resident of France could be a citizen (irrespective of origins), if he or she is loyal to the nation as a political community. The contradiction of this model is that it appears to be purely political and as such to guarantee individual equality to all citizens, yet it requires acceptance of French culture and language, as necessary attributes of *civisme*. There is no room for cultural diversity or for formation of ethnic communities.

The tradition of political and cultural centralisation, imposed by French monarchs in building one of the first nation-states and continued in a revolutionary guise by the Jacobins, plays a large part here. The belief is widespread that immigrants who are offered the benefits of liberty and the rights of man should be willing to assimilate in return. As Dominique Schnapper writes: 'French people doubted neither the superiority of their genius and happiness, nor the fact that those who were going to become French and participate in a glorious national destiny would recognise the same'[25]. The instruments for this assimilation were to be the school, the church, the army, and work—the great institutions of the Republic—which would socialise immigrants and above all their children into French culture.

Two factors negate this ideal 'republican model': socio-economic marginalisation and racism. Many immigrants have become highly disadvantaged on the labour market and in social life. Their living standards and housing are below the national average, and they have become concentrated in inner-city areas, or in the huge public housing areas on the periphery of Paris, Marseilles, Lyons and other cities. These have becomes 'quarters of exile'[26]—marked by isolation, disadvantage and conflict. Such marginalisation is linked to ethnicity: it affects non-Europeans most, followed by Europeans of non-European Union origin. Thus the idea of citizenship as conferring equality applies only in a formal political sense, not in social reality.

Racism has increased sharply in France since the 1970s. Statistics of the Ministry of the Interior show a five-fold increase in acts of anti-immigrant violence from 1978 to 1985.[27] The 1980s were a period of increasing political mobilisation by the extreme-right *Front National* (FN), which by 1984 was commanding around 10% of votes, through campaigns against immigrants.[28] The FN emphasised law and order, and claimed that North Africans were bringing in drugs and criminality. Anti-immigrant violence became frequent, and the growth of the anti-racist group *SOS-Racisme* was fuelled particularly by experience of police aggression against young *beurs* (second-generation descendants of North African parents). Racism made nonsense of the idea that becoming a citizen meant equality, for the violence was directed against people of non-European appearance—whether citizens or not.

The neat distinction between foreigner and citizen became overlaid by a graduation based on ethnicity. EU nationals enjoy all basic rights, except the right to vote. Immigrants from non-EU European countries lack such privileges, and many have an irregular legal situation. People of non-European birth or parentage, whether French citizens or not, constitute the ethnic minorities. These include Algerians, Tunisians and Moroccans, young Franco-Algerians, black Africans, Turks and settlers from the Overseas Departments and Territories. The importance of ethnicity rather than citizenship has been tacitly recognised in housing and social policies. From the 1970s, local councils introduced the concept of the *seuil de tolérance* (threshold of tolerance), according to which ethnic minority members (i.e. those of non-European origin) should not constitute more than 10-15% of tenants in public housing or students in schools.[29] This focus on ethnicity can also be found in many of the programs designed to deal with urban issues of housing, education, training and youth.[30]

Thanks to anti-immigrant campaigns by the Communist Party in the 1970s and by the FN since, the position of ethnic minorities is a central issue in party and electoral politics. In 1986, the Chirac Government attempted to amend the *Code de Nationalité* to make it harder for second-generation immigrants (especially those of North African origin) to become citizens. Faced by a storm of protest against this attack on the French tradition of citizenship, the Government withdrew its Bill, and set up a Commission on Nationality. After lengthy deliberations, no major changes were made in the Code.[31] Yet by 1993, the climate had changed sufficiently to allow such restrictions through the *Loi Pasqua*.

The then centre-right government introduced immigration restrictions in the wake of terrorist attacks by Algerian Islamic fundamentalists in 1995. The issue of further tightening the conditions for acquisition of citizenship has also been raised. Since the 1970s, immigrants have become politically active, taking an important role in major strikes, and demanding civil, political and cultural rights. Youth discontent with unemployment and police practices led to riots in Lyon, Paris and other cities in the 1980s. The growing political role of Muslim organisations has become a controversial issue,[32] while young people of North African origin (the *beurs*) have established anti-racist movements such as the afore-mentioned *SOS-Racisme* and *France Plus*. Locally-based movements have had some success in achieving improvements in housing, education and vocational training. At the national level, *beurs*-led movements helped prevent changes to the Nationality Code in 1986, but were unable to do so in 1993. Such activities have done much to construct a political identity for the *beurs*.[33]

France is at a cross-roads. The assimilationist model of turning immigrants into citizens at the price of cultural conformity no longer works adequately.

On the one hand, the institutions of integration (school, church, army, labour market, trade unions, etc.) are no longer fully effective, due to cleavages based on xenophobia, corporatism and unemployment.[34] The abolition of conscription announced in 1996 further erodes the Republican model. On the other hand, many immigrants are no longer willing to accept full assimilation when it brings neither social equality nor protection from racism. Organisations based on cultural identity are increasingly seen as the only way of combating racism and achieving a political voice. The traditionalists still argue that multiculturalism in the sense known in Australia is unthinkable in France. For instance, Dominique Schnapper writes: 'In France, true multiculturalism is the power to elect [as] a President of the Republic a Jew, Muslim, Asian who has been a former student of the Ecole Polytechnique and the Ecole Nationale d' Administration'.[35] This hardly seems a realistic model for the *beurs* of the satellite cities, who demand both citizenship and cultural rights.[36]

Other Countries

These brief accounts of the situation in Germany and France indicate the complexity of issues of immigration, citizenship and participation in society. How do other countries compare? Each has its own traditions of nation-building and incorporation of minorities, and has had distinct experiences of post-1945 immigration. Yet there are also common features: the large volume of immigration, the unexpected emergence of new ethnic minorities, the upsurge of racism and extreme-right mobilisation since the 1980s, and growing public debates on the meaning of ethnic diversity for politics, culture and national identity.[37] It is possible to roughly divide Western European countries into two categories.[38]

Countries which have based nation-building on ethnic belonging and the principle of *jus sanguinis* have generally had immigration models based on temporary labour recruitment and rejection of family reunion. This includes supposedly mono-ethnic countries like Germany and Austria, as well as countries with more than one 'founding people': Belgium and Switzerland. In all these cases, naturalisation is hard to obtain for the first generation, and there is no automatic right to citizenship for the second generation. However, the realisation is growing that immigrants are going to stay permanently, and that a situation of legal exclusion is problematic.

The main solution has been to introduce forms of limited quasi-citizenship: more secure rights of residence and various forums for political consultation, especially at the local level. Such countries have strong anti-immigrant movements, concerned not only with stopping further entries, but also with restricting rights for those already present. Denied a voice in mainstream politics, immigrant organisation often focuses around homeland politics or religious and cultural symbols. The choice in such countries is between sustaining national myths of culture and identity at the price of a divided society with a permanent marginalised minority, or alternatively incorporating immigrants at the price of rethinking national identity.

A second group of countries are those, like France, which have models of assimilation for some sections of their immigrant populations. Britain and the Netherlands resemble France in that they made the peoples of their colonial empires into citizens (or, in the case of Britain, subjects of the Crown) as a form of ideological control. This paved the way for migration of colonial workers and their families to the metropoles after 1945. These migrants had all the rights of citizenship upon arrival. In the meantime, such rights have been rescinded, so that new immigrants from former colonies have the same status as foreigners. But the majority of Afro-Caribbeans and Asians in Britain, and of Surinamers and other colonial immigrants in the Netherlands, are citizens. These countries have also generally based their citizenship on mixtures of *jus soli* and *jus sanguinis*, and have granted citizenship to foreign immigrants and their children.

The problem in these countries is the contradiction between formal citizenship, and socio-economic exclusion and vulnerability to racism. The 2.7 million ethnic minority members in Britain have low average occupational status and high unemployment, and are heavily concentrated in run-down areas of the inner cities. Organised racist groups and racist violence are major problems, while black youth discontent exploded into inner-city riots in the 1980s. The response of government has been to embrace a limited form of multiculturalism, which makes use of ethnic cultures in education and social work. There have also been measures to combat youth unemployment, make education more accessible to minorities, improve the conditions in urban areas, and to change police practices.[39] Ethnic minority organisations argue that such measures are designed to re-define issues of racism and discrimination as problems of cultural difference. In any case, de-industrialisation and the attack on the welfare state by Conservative Governments after 1979 undermined integration policies.

In 1983, the Netherlands introduced a Minorities Policy, based on the need for specific social policies to integrate minorities, while at the same time preserving cultural identity. This was combined with strong anti-racism laws, and local voting rights for resident foreigners. However, in recent years, this quasi-multicultural approach has been much criticised, on the grounds that it has done little to prevent socio-economic exclusion, as shown by high unemployment and residential concentration. The 1991 government Action

Program on Minorities Policy has largely dropped the former goal of minority group emancipation and participation, instead emphasising the need for socio-economic and legal integration.

Sweden, however, appears as an anomaly, for it does not fit into either the exclusionary or the assimilationist category. It was a society with a high degree of ethnic and cultural homogeneity until recently. Its national traditions seem closer to those of Germany than those of the 'classical immigration countries'. Yet it has had large-scale settlement, and adopted multicultural policies very close to those of Australia and Canada. The Swedish model includes easy naturalisation, anti-discrimination laws, a wide range of social policies to achieve integration, finance for ethnic associations and support for linguistic and cultural maintenance. The roots of the model lie in the tradition of state interventionism of Swedish social democracy, which has used the same approaches to integrating immigrants into civil society and the state as were used earlier to integrate the working class and reduce class conflict.[40] However, the model is currently under serious strain: there is a strong popular backlash against further immigration; rising unemployment makes it hard to finance the social policy measures; and many immigrants have begun to criticise the multicultural policies as manipulative and paternalistic.[41]

Democracy and Multiculturalism

Debates on citizenship and multiculturalism arising from recent mass immigration are having important effects on West European notions of democracy. There is no doubt of the importance of the issue in every West European country. Recognising the permanent effects of immigration and ethnic diversity is a test-case for political realism and flexibility. Failure to resolve the pressing issues would endanger democracy in two ways: firstly, it would cement a 'two-thirds society' in which certain groups would be permanently excluded from socio-economic and political participation; secondly, it would open the door to the extreme-right, which feeds on myths of national homogeneity and the threat from outside.

Both the traditional European models of nation-building are finding it difficult to respond to these new challenges. The exclusionary *jus sanguinis* approach in Germany and similar countries clearly cannot facilitate the incorporation of immigrants. Major changes in citizenship law and naturalisation practices need to be introduced, if Germany's 7 million foreign residents are to become part of society. At the moment, there is confusion about how to bring this about: the tentative move towards formal inclusion through individual access to citizenship will not be sufficient in itself, for it takes no account of the social and cultural rights that are necessary to guarantee real participation for ethnic minorities.

The assimilationist approach, which was discussed for France, seems preferable to the German approach, for it does allow immigrants to gain formal access to citizenship. Yet the insistence of the 'Republican model' on incorporation as individuals, and the rejection of any notion of cultural pluralism, seem problematic. The existing high levels of socio-economic marginalisation, anti-immigrant racism, and second-generation political mobilisation all contradict the French model of citizenship. Here too, some rethinking of basic political notions and institutions seems vital.

In his *Critique de la Modernité*, Alain Touraine mentions the debate on citizenship in 1986–7 as an important example of the process of constituting the subject in a democracy. He argues that the Commission on Nationality rejected the traditional dichotomy between *jus sanguinis* and *jus soli,* and arrived at a consensus that nationality should be the result of a choice by the newcomer. The state should facilitate this choice through 'a policy of integration, rather than rejection or marginalisation'. Touraine writes that the French definition of nationality should be based on 'the will to live together', but this should not mean giving up other attachments.[42] As a statement of principle this sounds excellent, and reminds us of the quotation from Habermas above. However, the problem is that this statement of the Commission on Nationality seems to be mere rhetoric. Little seems to have changed in actual French practices concerning acceptance of cultural difference.

This raises the question of how multiculturalism can fit in with different models of citizenship and democracy. In both the German and French models, multiculturalism appears unacceptable: in Germany because it contradicts the principle of ethnic homogeneity, in France because it contradicts the link between political integration and acceptance of French culture. In both countries, current debates are complex. Even on the left, multiculturalism is often rejected on the grounds that it would lead to a nation of separate cultural groups. For the German left, this means cementing cultures which are seen as anti-modern and repressive. For the French left, it means undermining the equality and secularity of the 'Republican model'. Such views are not universal: some groups in both countries argue that cultural diversity is an integral part of globalisation and mobility, which must lead to multicultural approaches.

For an Australian observer, the conceptual problem in European debates lies in the frequent equating of multiculturalism with an ethnic group model. In what I have referred to elsewhere as a 'citizenship model' of multiculturalism,[43] cultural rights (both for individuals and groups) should be seen as a vital part of citizenship and democracy. By accepting and supporting cultural rights, within a universal system of law and political institutions, we can encourage socio-economic and political participation, rather than forcing people to withdraw into closed-off—and possibly conservative—cultural enclaves. But this requires a high degree of cultural openness and the willingness to change both institutional structures and notions of national identity.

Notes

1. See Turner, B., 'Outline of a theory of democracy' in Mouffe, C. (ed.), *Dimensions of Radical Democracy* (London: Verso, 1992).
2. The following recent works are indicative of this trend: Habermas, J., *Theorie des kommunikativen Handelns*, 2 vols. (Frankfurt: Suhrkamp, 1988); Touraine, A., *Critique de la Modernité* (Paris: Fayard, 1992); Mouffe, *op. cit.*; and Held, D. (ed.), *Prospects for Democracy* (Cambridge: Cambridge University Press, 1993).
3. OECD, *Trends in International Migration: Annual Report 1994* (Paris: OECD, 1995), 27.
4. Castles, S. and Miller, M.J., *The Age of Migration: International Population Movements in the Modern World* (New York: Guilford Press, 1993).
5. Wieviorka, M., *L'Espace du Racisme* (Paris: Seuil, 1991); Wieviorka, M., 'Tendencies to racism in Europe: does France represent a unique case, or is it representative of a trend?' in Wrench, J. and Solomos, J. (eds.), *Racism and Migration in Western Europe* (Oxford: Berg, 1993).
6. Compare Hammar, T., *Democracy and the Nation-State: Aliens, Denizens and Citizens in a World of International Migration* (Aldershot: Avebury, 1990).
7. For Australia, incidentally, one could argue that the real citizenship decision is the granting of a permit for permanent immigration. This confers nearly all citizenship rights, and more or less automatically gives an entitlement to formal citizenship after two years.
8. Hoffmann, L., *Das deutsche Volk und seine Feinde* (Cologne: Pappyrossa Verlag, 1994).
9. Thränhardt, D., 'European migration from East to West: present patterns and future directions', *New Community*, 22 (2), 227–42.
10. Castles, S., Booth, H. and Wallace, T., *Here for Good: Western Europe's New Ethnic Minorities* (London: Pluto Press, 1984).
11. OECD, *Trends in International Migration: Annual Report 1993* (Paris: OECD, 1994), 78.
12. OECD, *Trends in International Migration: Annual Report 1994* (Paris: OECD, 1995), Table B1.
13. *Ibid.*, 225
14. Beauftragte der Bundesregierung für die Belange der Ausländer, *Das Einbürgerungs- und Staatsangehörigkeitsrecht der Bundesrepublik Deutschland* (Bonn: Beauftragte der Bundesregierung für die Belange der Ausländer, 1993), 9.
15. See Bade, K.J. (ed.), *Das Manifest der 60: Deutschland und die Einwanderung* (Munich: Beck, 1994).
16. See Leggewie, C., *Multi Kulti: Spielregeln für die Vielvölkerrepublik* (Berlin: Rotbuch, 1990); Cohn-Bendit, D. and Schmid, T., *Heimat Babylon: Das Wagnis der multikulturellen Demokratie* (Hamburg: Hoffmann und Campe, 1993).
17. Oberndörfer, D., *Der Wahn des Nationalen* (Freiburg: Herder, 1993), 14.
18. The English version is my translation. The original reads: '...zwei Stufen der Assimilation... Die erste verlangt Zustimmung zu den Prinzipien der Verfassung—eine Assimilation also an die Art und Weise, wie in der aufnehmenden Gesellschaft die Autonomie der

Bürger verstanden und wie der 'öffentliche Gebrauch der Vernunft' (Rawls) praktiziert wird. Die zweite Stufe erfordert Bereitschaft zu einer weitgehenden Akkulturation, und zwar zur Einübung in der Lebensweise, in die Praktiken und Gewohnheiten der einheimischen Mehrheitskultur. Das bedeutet eine Assimilation, die auf die Ebene ethisch-kulturelle Integration durchschlägt...'
See also a very similar but more detailed discussion in Habermas, J., 'Struggles for recognition in the democratic constitutional state' in Gutmann, A. (ed.), *Multiculturalism: Examining the Politics of Recognition* (Princeton NJ: Princeton University Press, 1994), 107–48.

19. 'Dieser Grundsatz garantiert wiederum nicht, daß die anfangs behauptete Identität des Gemeinwesens auch *auf Dauer* vor Veränderungen bewährt wird. Weil die Einwanderer nicht zur Preisgabe ihrer eigenen Traditionen genötigt werden dürfen, erweitert sich in der Folge von Immigrationswellen mit neu etablierten Lebensformen auch der Horizont, in dem die Bürger alsdann ihre gemeinsamen Verfassungsgrundsätze interpretieren. Dann greift nämlich jener Mechanismus ein, wonach sich mit einer veränderten Zusammensetzung der aktiven Staatsbürgerschaft auch der Kontext ändert, innerhalb dessen sich die ethisch-politischen Selbstverständigungsdiskurse der Staatsbürger bewegen.' Habermas, J., 'Die festung Europa und das neue Deutschland', *Die Zeit,* Hamburg, 28 May 1993 (emphasis in original).
20. Noiriel, G., *Le Creuset Français: Histoire de l'Immigration XIXe-XXe siècles* (Paris: Seuil, 1988), 297–312.
21. OECD, *Trends in International Migration: Annual Report 1993* (Paris: OECD, 1994), Table B1.
22. OECD, *Trends in International Migration: Annual Report 1994* (Paris: OECD, 1995), Table B5.
23. Costa-Lascoux, J., *De l'Immigré au Citoyen* (Paris: La Documentation Française, 1989), 121.
24. Weil, P., *La France et ses Étrangers* (Paris: Calmann-Levy, 1991).
25. Schnapper, D., 'A host country of immigrants that does not know itself', *Diaspora,* 1 (3) 1991, 354.
26. Dubet, F. and Lapeyronnie, D., *Les Quartiers d'Exil* (Paris: Seuil, 1992).
27. However, these figures are of limited value, for they clearly under-report the absolute number of acts of violence.
28. Lapeyronnie, D., Frybes, M., Couper, K. and Joly, D., *L'Intégration des Minorités Immigrées, Étude Comparative: France–Grande-Bretagne* (Paris: Agence pour le Développement des Relations Interculturelles, 1990).
29. Verbunt, G., 'France' in Hammar, T. (ed.), *European Immigration Policy: a Comparative Study* (Cambridge: Cambridge University Press, 1985).
30. Weil, P., *La France et ses Étrangers* (Paris: Calmann-Levy, 1991).
31. See Costa-Lascoux, *op. cit.*
32. de Wenden, C., *Citoyenneté, Nationalité et Immigration* (Paris: Arcantère Editions, 1987).
33. *Ibid.*
34. Compare Costa-Lascoux, *op.cit.,* 115–6; Schnapper, *loc.cit.,* 360.
35. *Ibid.,* 361–2.
36. Bouamama, S., Cordeiro, A. and Roux, M., *La Citoyenneté dans tous ses États* (Paris: CIEMI L'Harmattan, 1992).
37. See Castles and Miller, *op.cit,* Chapters 8 and 9.
38. Castles, S., 'How nation-states respond to immigration and ethnic diversity', *New Community,* 21 (3) 1995, 293–308.
39. Layton-Henry, Z. and Rich, P.B. (eds.), *Race, Government and Politics in Britain* (London: Macmillan, 1986); Solomos, J., *Race and Racism in Contemporary Britain,* Second ed. (London: Macmillan, 1993).

40. Hammar, T., 'Sweden' in Hammar, *op.cit.* 1985.
41. Ålund, A. and Schierup, C.-U., *Paradoxes of Multiculturalism* (Aldershot: Avebury, 1991); Ålund, A. and Schierup, C.-U., 'The thorny road to Europe: Swedish immigrant policy in transition' in Wrench and Solomos, *op. cit.*
42. Touraine, *op. cit.*, 391.
43. Castles, S., 'Democracy and multicultural citizenship: Australian debates and their relevance for Western Europe' in Bauböck, R. (ed.), *From Aliens to Citizens* (Aldershot: Avebury, 1994).

5 Pluralism and Citizenship: The Case of Gender in European Politics

GISELA KAPLAN

In 1988, Helen D'Ancona declared that the European Community (EC) was, legislatively, the most progressive political community for women in the world.[1] From the point of view of legislation this may well be true, but what does this mean in practice? Where is 'gender' located in European level politics today? My reading of current opinions and literature would suggest only qualified support for the achievements of the EC/European Union (EU)[2] in terms of the 1979 UN declaration for the elimination of all forms of discrimination against women. European countries signed this UN declaration, sometimes referred to as the 'Magna Carta for Women'. But how serious were they and how well have they managed the processes of change? This chapter will raise questions concerning the present and future success of the stated aims of the EU, confining itself to observations of the EU decision making levels.

The Heritage

Part of the present difficulty for women in Western Europe stems from the political and philosophical division of the private from the public realm. In the history of European jurisprudence the boundaries of the private and public realms were very clearly defined. The private realm was denoted as one of 'desire, affectivity and the body' (love, sex and woman). By contrast, the public realm was reserved exclusively for men as a space determined by rational and impartial thought. The separation of the two spheres over centuries was anything but arbitrary.[3] In practice it achieved two things, on the one hand relegating woman to the private sphere and therefore barring her from public life, on the other privatising pluralism, dissent and diversity, thereby ensuring that anything she might have to say could be viewed as *private* opinion and privatised dissent.

Both of these elements of European jurisprudence have worked heavily against women's interests. Laws penetrated deeply into the private sphere and decreed in detail how women had to behave even within the marital home. At the same time, entry into public life was hampered or prohibited by law. Up to the twentieth century, many European governments were opposed to active citizenship and would react against *any* expressions of discontent, whether staged by men or women. Some European countries saw a decline in public space and public self-expression in the 20th century occurring as a consequence of dictatorial regimes, be these fascist (Spain, Portugal, Italy), National-socialist (Germany, Austria), totalitarian regimes such as Stalinist Russia and the GDR, or military dictatorships such as Greece.

The new wave feminists had a formidable task against the weight of these traditions, both in the history of ideas and in everyday life. As mentioned elsewhere,[4] Italian writer Rossana Rossanda has pointed out that feminists faced exactly the problems which Georg Lukács had raised in his book *History and Class-Consciousness* (1923): How can a class which is not perceived as a separate group think of itself, and how must that class think in order to change the world?[5] Western European feminism has asked the same question and started to 'perceive itself', not as a class in the socio-economic sense of the old working class, but as a loose, horizontal, democratic association with a strong collective identity.[6] Feminism may seem historically condemned to suffer a 'permanent state of incompletion',[7] but there is no doubt that there has barely been a set of movements so influential on everyday public life as the feminist dissent of the 1970s and 1980s.

The women's movements, whilst now subsided, have left a legacy and more than just a foot-print on the European landscape. It is true that the more radical proponents of the West European movements, such as communist, anarchist, utopian, socialist, and communitarian groups, have had few inheritors, not so much of their ideas as in the practice of their ideas. Bourgeois, liberal feminist reform movements have fared better because their methods and goals were more manageable within existing structures. They were also less threatening and demanding.[8] Second wave feminists were fully cognisant of the fact that 'one exists only to the extent as one is thought of by others'.[9] In the current European climate of change and transition, the extent to which one is thought of by others is first and foremost a race for retaining visibility. For women, the evolution of the EU has brought into sharp relief once again the issue of gender, and of their own role in public life.

There is one recent proposal that may have some explanatory power for women's legitimate claims to a changed role in European politics. This explanation for one possible source of inspiration for the modern idea of a united Europe is worth elaborating here because of the connection that can be made to women. Tassin has argued that the idea of modern Europe stems largely from the political experience of resistance to Nazism.[10] Many of those countries dragged into the wars, especially outside Europe, may not have forgotten that their fellow-countrymen and -women died for wars not of their own making but for the sake of alliances and against the evil emanating from Europe.

It is instructive that the *Centre d'action pour la fédération européenne* published a collection of documents in 1945 relating to the Declaration of European Resistance Movements. To this group of statements belongs the following:

> Resistance Europe—that is where France's place is. There is its mission. Not in the theoretical Europe that 'great power' diplomats are carving up on a green cloth, but in that Europe of suffering which is anxiously rising at daybreak, in that underground Europe of masks and false papers, in that Europe of blood which is struck and gives blow for blow. There is our fraternity. There is our future... The European Resistance will remake Europe. A free Europe of free citizens, because we have all known slavery. A Europe united both politically and economically, because we have paid the price of division.[11]

Most of these statements, too lofty and probably too full of pathos for today's pragmatists and sceptics, make no mention of women, of their courage, their deaths, their sacrifices. Elsewhere, I have traced the importance of women for resistance movements in World War II.[12] I have argued that the presence of women in underground organisations was one of the roots of the modern feminist movements. Women joined political underground resistance movements, not just risking their lives but acquiring political literacy, political thinking, skills and strategies in political dissent. French women were granted the vote (rather belatedly in 1944) as a gesture of gratitude by the French government for women's work in the resistance which helped to liberate France. In Italy, too, there existed a well-organised resistance movement. For instance, in Italy just as in Bulgaria, Luxembourg and France, the majority of Jews survived. Altogether 80% of Italian Jews were saved by well organised underground activities.[13]

It is estimated that of the 200,000 partisans throughout Italy over 70,000 were women.[14] Women were partly organised within such special war groups as the *Gruppi di difesa* (defence groups), *Gruppi femminili di assistence ai combattenti della liberazione* (women's groups for aid to resistance fighters) and *Gruppi femminili antifascisti* (antifascist women's groups). By 1943, the protests of men and women alike became visible, especially in centres like Milan and Turin, demanding an end to deportations to Nazi concentration camps and the end of fascist and Nazi massacres. Women's defence groups such as *Gruppi di difesa della donna* formed in 1943, providing strike support to partisans. This anti-fascist unity gave the feminist movement its strength in those last war years. In fact, Camilla Ravera, the grand leader of women's resistance against fascism, rejoined the resistance once her prison term was over. She said of the time:

> The participation of women in the movement to liberate Italy from fascism and build a more just society actually signified their place under the new conditions. Not for nothing was one of the first depositions among the laws established after Liberation the granting of the vote to women. And in the first Parliament of the Republic there were more than fifty women representatives. At that point in time women gave such a convincing, clear display of the fact that they did know how to think politically, how to choose, take decisions, get together even in struggle.... And during the reconstruction, when there was still a sense of anti-fascist unity, women worked miracles.[15]

The importance of the organised resistance lay less in its political clout during the war than in the assessment of its role after the war. As in other European countries, there was much that Italians wanted to forget after 1945, such as the accusations that the Italian soldiers were cowardly, Italy's alliance and collaboration with Hitler, and the excesses of fascism within Italy. The discovery of the existence of a strong resistance movement provided just the right ingredients to rid many Italians of their feelings of shame.

The resistance movement in Italy and elsewhere certainly lent a new respectability and legitimacy to those who had been participants in the resistance movement, and this helped to reconstitute communist, socialist and other parties after the war. The PCI (Italian communist party) and the PSI (Italian socialist party) were instrumental in the drafting of a new republican constitution. It gave women the right to vote and it enshrined the concept of equality between men and women. Like the French, the Italians took measures to recognise the crucial role of women in the resistance movement. But unlike the French, they were willing to concede that in peace times women should retain an important political role in order to create and defend democracy. Therefore the Italian Women's Union, *Unione Donne Italiane* (UDI) was created; this initially consisted of women from all political parties, but it was financed and run by the PCI. This Women's Union developed directly out of several resistance groups, among them the partisan *Gruppi di difesa della donna*.[16] Hence the core membership of the UDI initially consisted largely of women who had been anti-fascist political activists during the war and Mussolini era, and who were experienced enough to take on an important leadership role.

Portugal provides another example of the strength of resistance. In 1933, the Portuguese dictator Antonio Salazar decreed a new constitution, which established the equality of citizens before the law; but it did not include women, 'in view of the differences deriving from her nature and interests of her family'.[17] When Salazar resigned in 1968, women and men who had stood close to the Communist Party secretly formed the *Movimiento Democrático das Mulheres* (Women's Democratic Movement). Once Salazar was dead and the last vestiges of his support were overturned, it was this long-standing underground resistance of over thirty years which initially took the lead in the reshaping of Portugal. In 1976, a new, progressive constitution was written and proclaimed.

Equally noteworthy was the resistance in Spain. Spain had developed a strong leftist political culture in the 1920s. In the 1920s and 1930s, the role of women was an explicit agenda item within the context of republican and democratic ideas. The Spanish Second Republic, like the Portuguese Republic earlier, gave women the vote, the status of equality before the law, and permitted divorce. In a whole range of ways, its constitution and legislation attempted to remove the gender bias and the oppression of women. One of the Republic's remarkable offshoots was the foundation, in 1936, of *Mujeres Libres* (Free/ or freethinking women), an explicitly proletarian feminists' organisation in Barcelona and the first autonomous feminist organisation in Spain.[18] Many of the women in this movement were also members of an international antifascist organisation, called *Solidaridad Internacional Antifascista* (SIA). Once the Spanish Civil War (1936-9) ended in defeat for the leftist forces in favour of the fascist Falange, women's organisations and other leftist political bodies were brutally suppressed.[19] Yet they never ceased to exist in the underground. Illegal women's organisations, largely linked with equally illegal communist and socialist parties, had also extended into a vast net of clandestine activity. In 1963, the *Movimiento Democrático de Mujeres* (Women's Democratic Movement) was founded in Madrid, and many other organisations sprung to life. After Franco's death, the first task of the new *Cortes* (Parliament) was the drafting of a new constitution, which was adopted in a national referendum in December 1978. The new constitution in many ways reconfirmed over 40 years later the constitution of the Second Republic.

Significantly, apart from the UK, the only west European countries which made *full* allowance for women's rights and women's equality in all areas of life (employment, and family/marriage) were Portugal, Spain and Italy, all countries in which socialist forces came to dominate at the time the constitutions were drafted. In other words, there is evidence in these and in some other countries, such as Denmark, France and the Netherlands, that resistance was relatively widespread even though it was unable to change the direction of power politics throughout Europe.

From the perspective of resistance, the political left of Europe has legitimate reasons for seeing itself as a chief defender of a united Europe of the future.

However, sceptics would not be entirely wrong in regarding these claims with some reservation, because the left scarcely had any political clout either before or in the first decades after World War Two. Yet a very special place in the history of resistance is occupied by women. In most current debates, these historical circumstances and conditions are often forgotten, much to the detriment of a Europe that wishes to move forward into the future.

European Citizenship and Women

Since World War Two, the signposts of citizenship have shifted, and it is not clear at this moment whether the shift is to the detriment or advantage of women. Without a doubt, the role of women is a litmus test for the meaning and extent of citizenship practice. Individual countries have now all extended citizenship rights to women, both in political and legal public arenas. These provisions applied formally at a national level, but have often fallen short in practice. Women's groups in individual countries have fought the discrepancies between formal rights and social practice for over twenty years. Now the stage has changed to the larger European theatre. Here, it was hoped, would be a supranational forum which could wipe away national and regional idiosyncrasies and vested traditions. The EU is, after all, pluralist in composition and has to be pluralist in outlook. Pluralism here refers to federative balances of national institutions and even to cultural differences.

Whether such pluralism includes 'gender' as a perception of equal rights, powers and participation in public life is ultimately questionable. On the one hand, policy developments at the EU level suggest strongly that gender balance is a high priority within the European Commission's programs. At all levels of management in the Commission, the recent positive action programs have recorded an increase in women's participation, although usually not to the expected targets.[20] On the other hand, there are also major forces that continue to militate against women, be this in the sphere of economics, or in the ideological underpinning of public life itself. In addition, women, including political theorists, are divided amongst themselves as to how best to achieve certain goals, and even what the focus for women in public life should be. The divisions drawn historically between the private and public, and between the political and the social, have so far not really been broken down. Citizenship is first and foremost a political concept (rather than a social one), but the extent to which it bestows rights on the bearer is another matter. In his typology of citizenship, Bryan Turner has reminded us that the concept of citizenship can exist in a multitude of political settings. It seems unnecessary to emphasise here that citizenship traditions in individual European countries vary widely and, historically, are often not compatible. For our purposes here, Turner's characterisation of an active-passive dimension of citizenship across different traditions is useful, indicating that citizenship models either grow from above or below (or in a combination of these forces). The passive dimension of citizenship stems from the descending view of monarch/ruler as the all-powerful sovereign whose subjects were recipients of privileges. In the ascending view, citizenship developed from below. It signifies freedom and the bearing of active citizenship rights.[21] The French Revolution challenged the descending view of citizenship, and 20th century liberation movements, such as the women's movements, were largely based on the insistent claims for ascending citizenship.

Until now, questions of citizenship have been tied to specific nations. The possibility of a new supranational European citizenship raises new questions. I tend to disagree with the suggestion that current western social trends towards both regional autonomy and localism as well as towards globalism are contradictory.[22] Rather, the opposite may be the case, i.e., globalisation and regionalism are two divergent but complementary responses away from or even against the nation-state and a national identity forged from this model. As yet, the theoretical framework for a supranational, let alone global, citizenship is far from evident. But I concur with Turner that national identities might eventually become anachronistic and hence superfluous. In Europe, there are interesting trends in this direction.

As a consequence of integration processes in Europe, and of globalisation trends in general, it is possible to conceive of the development of a political or group identity away from or at least apart from a *national* identity. Women can take a major role in such conceptual changes. As an interest group with a self-proclaimed identity *as* women, women are theoretically well equipped to ponder such developments. The women's movements in Europe (and globally) learned decades ago to organise supranationally. European networks of women existed well before any explicit structural and political presence of a European Community. Indeed, current trends towards greater globalisation is well exemplified by the ever increasing number of international women's organisations and groups. However, women's strength lies in their vertical affiliations, arising from grassroots activism and the model of ascending citizenship that they propose.

Beyond the question of identity, European integration raises anew questions that were broached in the period of the second wave movements in the 1970s and 1980s. Arato and Cohen argued then that the new social movements began where existing large scale formal organisations left off; namely to expand, redefine, and democratise social spaces in which collective identities, new meanings, new solidarities and forms of democratic association can emerge.[23] Within the women's movements, but not only in that context, the concept of a collective identity[24] implies a commitment to collective action, as well as some notion of the possible effects of that action in causing change. It stands to reason that the question on 'how must that class think in order to change the world' is tied up with the formation of such an identity. Women have resorted to strategies to safeguard and promote a collective identity, as in self-management of services, of alternative business ventures, and new solidarity groups and structures.[25]

Democratic citizenship, so radical feminist groups have argued, is based on a number of moral claims, such as shared rights, social responsibility and solidarity. As movements outside the parliamentary system, they maintain it is the duty of democratic politics to make room for particularity and difference and the right to have these voices heard and dealt with within the political community as a whole. This concept of a 'political community' is much wider than the narrow liberal view of government. It includes action groups not as 'sub' groups but as an integral part of the political community. Communitarian thinkers, such as Sandel or MacIntyre, and writers like Walzer or Quentin Skinner have recently endorsed the view that individual liberty and political participation can be reconciled, or more, that individual liberty and social responsibility need to be reconciled.[26]

In political reality, Offe has argued, movements are *incapable* of negotiating because they do not have anything to offer in return for any concessions made to their demands,[27] bearing in mind that a substantial proportion of the west European women's movements were autonomous and in principle rejected partisan action with governments. In the present climate, negotiation is the one venue open in the absence of an active movement. This is one of the possible explanations why women felt they had to find a way into the maze of formal structures to find a position from which negotiation is at least possible and seen as necessary.

To say that it is the duty of democratic politics to make room for particularity and difference and to have these heard and dealt with within the political community as a whole opens yet another set of complex issues. These are not so much a matter of losses or gains for women, dictated in part by external circumstances, but represent theoretical problems which have remained unsolved amongst feminist political theorists. One problem concerns the contrast of pluralism with equality, often held up as being incompatible beyond superficial lip-service.[28] A second contrast, even more fundamental in terms of political applicability, is the contradiction of a politics of sameness (equality) and the politics of difference.[29]

Gatens, a strong defender of the French *écriture feminine* movement, has perhaps given one of the most pertinent objections to the pursuit of a politics of sameness or 'universal' political citizenship by doubting that a person can be split into a sexed body and an unsexed mind.[30] Indeed, the old mind/body distinction in philosophy has not entirely vanished from view in the sex/ gender distinction. Braidotti put it bluntly when she concluded that 'the paradox of feminist theory at the end of this century is that it is based on the very notions of 'gender' and 'sexual difference' which it is historically bound to criticise'.[31]

Participation and Representation

Eurostat information confirms that women continue to constitute 51% of the population.[32] Many formal publications by European women stress that true representation should require a presence of 51% of women in government. Some more radical proponents speak even more firmly of direct or participatory democracy. There are well-entrenched and also recent views that would dispute the soundness of these arguments. Representative government, as Rousseau argued two centuries ago, is a 'sham' and direct democracy is 'possible only in small states'.[33] More recent political theory, at least in some cases, argues that the political participation of individual citizens in large pluralistic societies is not just unrealistic but in many ways undesirable. Democratic governments, in order to function democratically, need a large base which is well served by a multitude of organisations and 'bodies' not directly linked to state institutions. Indeed, these should be independent of government and autonomous in their decision-making. These have been called 'sub-state' associations which relate only by way of *analogy* to political democracy[34] and relegate any influence and power of sub-state associations to a very indirect one, which cannot be guaranteed.

In the late 1980s, Giovanna Zincone from Italy once again drew a sharp distinction between social and political groups. In her definition, social groups (such as women) are groups with shared characteristics and markers of discrimination, and political groups are exclusively party groups concerned with decision-making processes. She argued that there was no direct link between the two forms and that, if there were, it would not be desirable. Nor did she support the view that women should have the right to 51% of posts in decision making arenas 'simply because they make up 51 percent of the population'. She did admit that today's democracies represent interests and are therefore partial rather than impartial governments.[35]

By contrast, some feminist literature still implies that numerically equal representation of women and men at government level alone is a sign of parity and of democracy at work. Therefore an increase from low representation to high representation is seen as a clear indication of progress, irrespective of the political view and value system of the women in question, and irrespective of the backwardness of the party any of them may represent. Usually, this is coupled with at least an oblique reference to the notion that women need to enter politics because they may be able to do something for women whilst in power. The dissatisfaction with low numbers, the celebration when the percentage of women's representation in the European Parliament (EP), or national governments, has increased by a few percent seems to suggest that the goals are narrowly defined as 'the more, the better—for women.'

Until 1994, the EP consisted of 518 delegate members. Since the first direct elections to the European Parliament in 1979, women have steadily increased their numbers in each parliamentary term. In 1979, 12% of delegates were women, in 1984 16%, in 1989 it rose to 18.9%, and in the 1994 election women gained again, assuming about 25% of the available seats, jumping from 100 to 140 members.[36] This increase for the new EP term (1994–9) was to some extent helped by the sudden increase of available seats by 49. Overall, women won 40 of the 49 new seats. Of course, there are substantial differences among countries (in Italy and Portugal the female contingent actually decreased), and not all countries have benefited from the changed member representation. Lobbyists for 'women into politics' are likely to attribute this major victory to an extensive and long pre-election campaign, guided by the European Women's Lobby and carried out within each nation separately. Indeed, at no time before have women lobbied so widely and effectively at European level.

The strength of the lobbying success was arguably based on three interrelated factors: formal, experiential, and numerical. At a formal level, the most noteworthy developments preceding the election success for women concerned several organisational events. One was the formation of the European Women's Lobby in 1990. Another was the summit meeting 'Women in Power' of the group 'women decision-makers' in November 1992 in Athens. From this meeting derived the platforms for action programs concerning women into politics and the now well-known 'Athens Declaration'.[37] A third was the meeting held by the Standing Committee on Women's Rights of the European Parliament in October 1993 in Thessaloniki. Here, the theme was once again 'Women in Decision-Making'.

The experiential domain, interlocked with the formal, concerns the level of public and political responsibility women have accepted. For the first time in European history, there is a pool of women, large enough for an assembly, who have experience in formal politics at the highest levels of parliamentary or governmental politics *and* who are willing to promote the cause of women. These experiences may have been made as government ministers (such as Melina Mercouri, Greece); chairs or heads of formal decision-making bodies, or of the upper or lower house (such as Rita Süssmuth, Germany); or even as heads of state (for instance, Mary Robinson). Some of these women have been active in political life for over a decade or even longer, and they are equipped with skills, insights and knowledge that can guide the way for other women to formulate public debates, policies and lobbies.

Even within the reticent and overall conservative EU, the numerical increase of women's organisations related to public life (chiefly concerned with the labour force, education and politics) appears remarkable to the onlooker from outside Europe. These increases are not just confined to local levels; their importance lies in having been conceived and organised at the *European* level. As has been shown recently in the case of the European Women's Lobby, such umbrella organisations are able to act transnationally, and do so effectively and quickly in the public arena. EP election results, one might add, are overall also higher than national participation rates of women in politics (see Figures 1 and 2 below).

Figure 1
Women in Parliamentary
Committees
by EU Member States

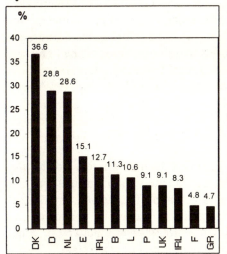

Source: Adapted from European Network
'Women in Decision-Making, 1992', p.21
Year of data: F 1988/89; NL 1989; DK, GR
1990; B,D,P 1991; remainder 1992

Figure 2
Percentage of Women in
Government
by EU Member States

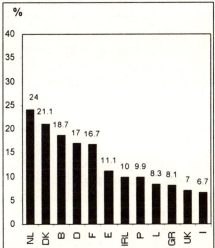

Source: European Network 'Women in Decision-
Making, 1992', p.65
Year of data: IRL and NL 1989; DK 1990;
E and P 1991; remainder 1992

Hence, it seems appropriate to regard both the formation of politically motivated organisations and their actions as positive steps towards a European citizenship. That these activities are regarded by European women as signalling only small steps *towards* such a citizenship can be gleaned from the Athens Declaration, as well as from the conclusions that the EP's Committee on Women's Rights drew at its Thessaloniki meeting in 1993, centred around the slogan: 'the democratic deficit in question'. The meeting's project was to expose, emphasise, question and challenge the deficits of the emerging European democracy. It concluded that:

> There can be no escaping the fact that women are markedly under-represented in political decision-making bodies. Although women account for 19.3% of members of the European Parliament (larger than the average member state of 11.3%), real equality between women and men is still very far off.[38]

The term 'equality' here also referred very specifically to a narrow political agenda of representation in government bodies and not to broader issues of equality in everyday life. There are problems in this conception, as I have elaborated elsewhere.[39] The assumption that there is a definable 'real' equality which happens to be achievable and, if not 'around the corner', is at least conceivable in the near or distant future, seems naïve. 'Real' equality, at least within schools of radical thought, has generally been held to be possible only after a total restructuring of society and after renegotiation of power hierarchies. The dominant economic system remains one of structured inequalities, and these are also reflected in systemic biases within institutions. The latter will be addressed in the following section, to exemplify that structural biases have disadvantaged women within the institutions of the EU.

Structural and Functional Biases in European Politics

This section addresses the questions of where women's issues are located and what definitional limits have been set for the various groups and task forces. Writers have recently questioned the potential effectiveness and efficacy of the European bureaucratic apparatus and have generally concurred that there are substantial disadvantages flowing directly from the way in which the various bodies have been set up to function and to interrelate.

First, the functions and powers bestowed upon the formal bodies of the EU from the start enshrined certain limitations and shortcomings, which have not disappeared in the various amendments and additional acts.

'The deficiency of the EECT and its amendments', Fabricius rightly argued, 'is that they do not contemplate any legal-normative basis on which social policies may be formulated'.[40] Hence, socio-political issues fall far short of the benefits that the European Union might have rendered to its members. Among the issues that need to be addressed are important social pre-conditions and/or consequences of work. Women especially are affected by consideration or lack thereof of the social context in which work is sought and maintained.

Interrelated with this issue is the absence of a specific 'right to work' clause in some individual member states, including Germany, the United Kingdom and Portugal. Portugal specifically abolished the right to work, once enshrined in its constitution, in the second constitutional amendment of 1989. The constitutions of Italy and the Netherlands make specific mention of the right to work, but these countries are in the minority.[41] In the late 1990s, of course, the radical concept of the right to work once espoused by leftist parties has long since disappeared from view. Hence, many of the proposals within the EU bodies create little pressure on individual countries and offer little incentive for individual nations to adopt them. In other words, this is one area in which the European Community had generally been reluctant to intervene, thereby maintaining national centres of decision making in favour of more easily attainable economic measures and goals at EU level.

The second major domain of democratic deficits within the basic framework of the EU concerns the structure of the various bodies of the EU particularly in relation to women. To elucidate this problem, it is necessary to briefly describe its structure. The major EU institutions are the Commission, the Council of Ministers, the European Council, the European Court of Justice (ECJ), and the European Parliament. Only the last of these is directly elected in European elections, and it is the only body to which European citizens have some access via voting. The most powerful body is the European Council which consists of the 15 prime-ministers of the member states and the French President.

The Council of Ministers is the major legislative power of the EU. It decides on proposals submitted by the Commission. It determines the speed of European integration and its particular character. It comprises the national ministers of all 15 member states according to the proposals under discussion. For this Council alone, the administration has over 2200 staff.[42]

The Commission is the most independent power broker in the EU. It consists of 17 members. The Commissioners are appointed by the Member States. The Commission is independent of directives from the Member States, and initiates and proposes as well as executes decisions by the Council. Its administration is composed of 26 Directorate Generals and nine additional specialised offices.

The European Parliament was first established in 1952 as an advisory body to the European Coal and Steel Community (ECSC). By 1970, its powers were increased to include participation in decision-making processes of the EC budget. When the first direct elections occurred in 1979, however, its main function was still largely to provide opinions. The Single European Act (SEA) and the Maastricht Treaty have further strengthened the EP's participation in decision making, especially in some co-decision procedures with the Council. In certain cases, the Council can take decisions only when the Parliament has given its assent to the decision. Parliament now, for the first time, has the power to reject or approve decisions of the Council.

This European administrative apparatus has been criticised for several reasons. First, Eurosceptics consider it large, unwieldy, and costly. Second, apart from the European Parliament, the entire EU institutional apparatus consists of non-elected members and personnel, a state of affairs that is broadly referred to as a 'democratic deficit'. Most positions are structurally fixed, e.g. by the portfolios of ministers, or by appointment, and are not accountable to a specific agency. However, while it can be argued that individual nations initially elect their own prime ministers and ministers, it cannot be assumed that the electorate would have voted for the same persons for the purpose of representation at European level. The Council has been able to make decisions without any noteworthy public accountability. Some feminist writers have referred to the Council as a cameralist secret diplomacy group.[43] Whatever these criticisms may be worth in the effective running of the EU, they at least reflect the aloofness of a remote bureaucracy and one that is fragmented for a variety of reasons. Page cites the absence of a focus of authority and its multinational character as reasons for the fragmentation.[44]

A third criticism comes exclusively from feminists. The presence of women, although seemingly large numerically, is generally found in marginalised spaces without direct powers. In recent years, the average percentage of women in senior positions in the EU machinery has been a meagre 6–8% and there is clearly a case to argue, as Page has recently, that women remain very under-represented.[45] It is worth pointing out that the average is distorted by the fact that the highest cluster of women has congregated in one service: the Translation Service of the Commission, not an area of great political impact. As a result of appointment procedures, women have continued to be largely absent from the most powerful bodies. There have been few women on the European Council, and only occasionally do one or two women appear in the specialised sessions of the Councils (depending on the portfolio). Even in the Commission, where there would appear to exist some freedom by individual governments to appoint a woman, there have rarely been any.[46] Concerning the most lucrative administrative positions in Brussels, women tend to be clustered at the bottom of the hierarchy and only a small percentage of women has achieved any notable seniority. In this regard, the EU record has so far not been impressive.

Amy Elman has argued that, in many crucial ways, it remains apparent that the idea of European unification was 'primarily an economically inspired plan', leaving whole complexes of issues and problems of social life untouched.[47] One can readily understand the cynicism and pessimism that many feminists have expressed when asked about the European bureaucracy. The very structural organisation and an inherent gender-bias continue to see women excluded from the main political fora of Europe.

The women's committees and task forces that *have* been established tend to function in the twilight of politics. These committees and units are usually destined to have low prestige value because, mostly, they also have little power and very circumscribed funding. As Schunter-Kleemann has argued, women's units are fragmented and at the same time 'walled-in'. Committees, be they advisory, standing, *ad hoc*, or otherwise, have suffered first and foremost from a lack of power to act.[48] They are there to recommend policies to committees for whom either the social agenda *ab ovo* may be of relatively little interest or for whom women's issues are of little importance beyond immediate economic wage equity concerns (remembering that the gender basis of the decision making bodies is exclusively or almost exclusively male).

Various EU bodies have appended to them small units and advisors, and these are strewn across the entire bureaucratic network. For instance, there is a standing Committee for Women's Rights in the EP. Further, women's issues are discussed within the Economic and Social Committee and Council. There are other informal and advisory bodies such as the Committee for Women's Questions (since 1982), expert circles for equal opportunity and observation of developments of national women's policy (1982-9), the European women's networks (since 1982) and the European Women's Lobby (since 1990). Clearly, from a structural perspective, such a dizzying array of organisations provides its own challenges and difficulties in communicating and networking. Without doubt, fragmentations of this kind are detrimental to overall consistent policy making and can significantly slow down implementation.

If few of these bodies and groups can put any of their proposals into practice, the question is to what avail all this very time-consuming networking might be? The Council has the right to amend or reject proposals under Treaty provisions. It is not regarded as acting with speed and, at least up to the point of signature of the Treaty of Amsterdam in 1997, it was at times not so enthusiastic to take social issues on board. For instance, issues such as sexual harassment have had a chequered and unimpressive career in the European Union. In the wage labour market, there has been formal recognition of sex discrimination; but when it is inherent to an industry (such as the pornography industry), or occurs outside waged labour, it has not been recognised.[49] The inability to effect change is also made clear in another context. The Committee for Women's

Rights, the standing committee of the EP, has undertaken important work, established important frameworks and important themes. Yet even if the EP has taken some of its proposals on board, there is an inadequate legal framework to enforce social legislation at the national level. Up to now its statements have remained mere declarations, and the game has been one of 'symbolic politics'.[50] The increased powers of the EP vis-à-vis the Council may result in some changes in future, but this alone is not sufficient. The legal-normative basis of the decision-making powers would have to become more inclusive, creating levers for legally enforcing change in areas of discrimination that so far fall outside the narrow definitional terms of the EU Treaties.

Probably the worst scenario is to be found in the Directorates General (DG) which support the tasks of the Commission. Here, the criticism that women's issues are being 'ghettoised'[51] finds some justification. The main location for women's issues is in DG V. Schunter-Kleemann rightly asks why gender issues are not represented in the other DGs and fall completely from view in DGs such as taxation, agriculture, development, and technology.[52] There is no cross-fertilisation or cross-referencing of programmes that might promise an overall strategy for gender, and ultimately for discrimination issues.

Finally, expectations of job specifications and briefs for areas concerned with women's issues are so manifold that it seems hardly possible to succeed in the tasks that have been set. For instance, The Equal Opportunities Unit in DG V of the Commission has a comprehensive list of tasks, including submitting draft proposals, organising seminars, fostering positive action, and liaison with international bodies.[53] Throughout the first half of the 1990s, those tasks were expected to be covered by a staff of 12 people.

A further point needs to be made with regard to prevailing ideological directions. The political climate of opinion within the committees has shifted from a social democratic preponderance in favour of conservative forces. This is reflected in attitude changes. Once these were pro-work and pro-independence for women, and hence pro-infrastructure development (such as kindergartens and other service provisions). During the first half of the 1990s, there was a trend towards more assertive conservative attitudes in favour of pro-privacy, pro-family and anti-infrastructure developments. Members of the various units concerned with women's issues, however, were largely recruited from around or within the field of experienced feminist lobbyists, administrators, academics and politicians. Once again, they found themselves fighting the same battles of opposition that had been fought twenty years ago, but this time from *within* a political context that was meant to specifically address women's issues. The frequency of the staff change-over in the Equal Opportunities Unit has been commented upon[54] and may well relate to the political, administrative and personal pressures associated with the everyday working realities in that task force.

An OECD study of 13 countries showed a strong correlation between centralised institutional controls of the labour market, such as central wage fixing systems, and a high component of public service employment.[55] In the study, it became clear that the bargaining system for wages is far more important and effective than specific policies targeting wage inequalities. The EU has policies for implementing wage equality, but these are applied in a context of deregulation and fragmentation of the bargaining systems, especially in the UK. In deregulated markets, the proportion of low wage earners, clustering in women's jobs, increases. Similar experiences have also been observed elsewhere in the western world.[56] The stronger a centralised wage fixing system, the higher the wages of women. Weiler draws the conclusion that the EU's orientation towards policies of changing gender structures will remain ineffectual. Unless the EU addresses general wage-fixing systems, no improvements will follow. Indeed, the situation may gradually worsen *despite* the existing policies.[57]

But even policies are no longer safe. One of the most dramatic examples of such a trend is the case of *Eckard Kalanke v Freie Hansestadt Bremen* (Case C-450/93) which sent shock waves through European feminist circles.[58] In October 1995, the ECJ delivered its judgement against a positive discrimination program legally enshrined in the state of Bremen. The Bremen law on equal opportunity in the public sector held that, as regards both recruitment and promotion, a female candidate must be given preference over a male candidate if women are under-represented in the sector in which she seeks employment or promotion (i.e. less than 50%). The Court ruled that this Bremen law was at variance with Directive 76/207/EEC (February 1976) because it went beyond the limits of the exception in Article 2(4) of the Directive.[59]

The legal uncertainty created by the decision seemed to allow ruling out positive discrimination actions in future, not just by degree but in principle.[60] The principle it established is that there cannot be an absolute and unconditional priority for appointment or promotion by gender. However, the Bremen law merely stipulated that provided both male and female applicants have the *same* qualifications, the female applicant should be given preference (and only up to the point of creating a gender balance). The law can also work in reverse order and favour males if they are under-represented. This is hardly the same as 'absolute' and 'unconditional' priority. The ruling was divisive because every attempt to redress the gender balance relies to some extent on positive measures—i.e. by attempting to overcome social practice based on vested interests and preconceived ideas at the local and everyday level. The *Kalanke* case has since been addressed (see below).

In 1995, the Commission drafted its fourth medium-term Community action program on equal opportunities for women and men for implementation in the years 1996-2000. This proposal includes as a distinct aim the promotion of gender-balance in 'a changing economy', in decision-making and the exercising of 'equality rights'.[61] The words are promising, but will the deeds and outcomes be? European politics displays the outward signs of pluralism and positive citizenship, but such posturing in an economic era which is more characteristic of a backlash against—rather than progress for— women means that the practice of 'equality rights' is awaited with some scepticism.

Conclusion

I began this chapter by pointing to the positive heritage of the resistance as a potential identity on which a European Union, inclusive of women, might build its future. However, there is another, negative way and different level of explaining the evolution of the current EU which is of considerable importance. Amongst the critics of the current direction of the EU were those[62] who saw the EU as an artificial construct of the Cold War. They have argued that its orientation is anti-democratic and extremely fragile. Entire political interest groups, not just women, are systematically excluded, and such organisations as unions, environmental or consumer protection authorities cannot even hope for a lever in public appeal.[63] Martens and Schumann argue that the absence of accountability and political responsibility is accompanied by a closed door policy on decision-making, poorly formulated laws, and chaotic committees which all only serve the purpose of 'pushing Europe more deeply into a paralysis against action'.[64] While I may not share this critique in full, it is at least worth bearing in mind that substantial parts of the European world feel plunged into inactivity by the developments of the EU, even if other countries are eager to join the EU for economic reasons. Whether one regards the current EU positively in the light of a stylised past of resistance or of a past determined by the secrecies of the Cold War is ultimately unproductive. Both options may well overdraw and overemphasise singular aspects of European history. However, if the current problems of the European Union are not seriously addressed in their socio-political breadth and beyond economic rationalism, one might well be as pessimistic as other critics have been[65] that a chance for a promising future is being missed here, if it has not failed already.

By labelling most issues identified as 'women's issues' as 'social', the political strength that women brought to the resistance has been watered down into the social domain, giving women, it seems, hardly more space than the tradition of political liberalism had once conceded: namely privatised dissent and the privacy of problems and difference. Even where gender issues have been raised successfully at EU levels, they have had little effect in preventing the gradual economic deterioration for women across the EU in the 1990s.[66]

Women in the past have devised a substantial number of declarations. The American *Declaration of Independence* was the basis for the feminist *Declaration of Sentiments*, presented by Elizabeth Cady Stone in the USA in 1848; so was the feminist *Declaration of Rights for Women* of 1876, which demanded justice and equality, and most notably 'that all the civil and political rights that belong to citizens of the United States be guaranteed to us and our daughters forever'. The *Athens Declaration* takes this a step further and argues for co-responsibility.[67] In a January 1994 session of the EP (Women in Decision-Making Bodies), the minutes record that *de jure*, women in Europe today face no barriers in the public domain as citizens, in political parties, by politicians or even in the private sector. *De facto*, however, women continue to be 'grossly and persistently under-represented'.[68]

Attempting to give reasons for this phenomenon, the document argues that fewer women than men tend to be in the pool of electable candidates because they lag behind in education, have less experience in the workforce, have family responsibilities which tie them down and, in addition, suffer from a political socialisation process that is gender biased and against their entry in the first place.[69] The negative slant of this report, and its implied tendency to evoke possible deficiencies in the current pool of women, is surprising. This is a view which cannot go unchallenged. The Scandinavian countries have made the transition to political representation (up to 40% in government) rather quickly and no one could reasonably argue that the political potential amongst women in Scandinavia is greater than in the rest of Europe. Structural inequalities are part of all nations and some are specific to western economic systems; yet the pool of appropriate women in *any* country is now large enough to fill just about all positions available in the public domain. It seems to me that it would have been more fruitful for European women to blame the structural inequalities within the EU apparatus, and have these changed, than for some to adopt a self-chastising attitude.

In 1996, the Committee of local and regional elected representatives of the Council of Municipalities and Regions (CEMR) created the European Network of Women Elected Representatives of Local and Regional Authorities. This was a sensible move supported by the European Commission. Data from 1995, made available in 1997, showed that the percentage of women in regional governments was considerably higher (about 26%) than in national governments (15.7%) across EU Member States and continued to show rising participation in 1997.[70] On 2 April 1997, the European Commission adopted its Third Action Program For Equal Opportunities, to be implemented between 1997 and the year 2000. Perhaps even more important, not just for the EU *in toto* but specifically for women, was the signing of the Treaty of Amsterdam on 2 October 1997 by the 15 Member States. Observers have argued that the Amsterdam summit not only propelled the EU along the road of a single currency and common foreign policy, but also strengthened 'social Europe'. For the first time (unlike the Maastricht Treaty), a European treaty contained a chapter on employment and a social chapter, raising hopes that the tensions and dissonances[71] between priorities and perceived areas of need, between policy at a formal level and economic and political realities of women's lives, will be eased.

Significantly, the Treaty of Amsterdam attempted to undo the damage created by the *Kalanke* case. The Treaty explicitly allows Member States to introduce positive action measures in favour of the 'under-represented sex' (either male or female), and has enshrined the principle of equality between women and men with regard to labour market opportunities and treatment at work.[72] These are positive signs, suggesting that doors may have opened concerning issues involving gender, ethnicity, environmentalism, even human rights and other pressing concerns, and that these can eventually be placed on the EU political agenda. But they are for the future.[73]

Notes

1.   D'Ancona, H., Statement bei dem EG-Seminar 'Die institutionellen Voraussetzungen für die Gleichberechtigung von Mann und Frau in den Mitgliedsstaaten der EG' Hannover, *IFG-Dokumentation*, 1988, 171–9.
2.   The European Community (EC) became known as the European Union (EU) in 1993 and will hereafter be called the EU even when referring to the pre-1993 situation.
3.   Young, I. M., 'Impartiality and the Civic Public: Some Implications of Feminist Critiques of Moral and Political Theory', *Praxis International* (Special Issue: *Feminism as Critique*, eds. Benhabib, S. and Cornell, D.), 5, 1986, 382 and 387–9; Pateman, C., 'The Fraternal Social Contract' in Keane, J. (ed.), *Civil Society and the State: New European Perspectives* (London: Verso, 1988), 115.
4.   Kaplan, G., *Contemporary Western European Feminism* (New York: New York University Press, 1992).
5.   Rossanda, R., 'Die Emanzipierte, die keine Buße tun will' trans. from Italian in Autonome Frauenredaktion (ed.), *Frauenbewegungen in der Welt: Vol.1—Westeuropa* (Hamburg: Argument, 1988), 162.
6.   Cohen, J. L., 'Strategy or Identity: New Theoretical Paradigms and Contemporary Social Movements', *Social Research* , 52 (4) 1985, 667.
7.   Riot-Sarcey, M. and Varikas, E., 'Feminist Consciousness in the Nineteenth Century: A Pariah Consciousness?', *Praxis International* (Special Issue, as detailed in fn.3), 443.
8.   Benhabib, S. and Cornell, D., *Feminism as Critique. Essays on the Politics of Gender in Late-Capitalist Societies* (Cambridge: Polity Press, 1987). Previously as Special Issue of *Praxis International*, as detailed in fn.3.
9.   Lukács, G., cited in Rossanda, *loc. cit.*, 162.

10. Tassin, E., 'Europe: A Political Community?' in Mouffe, C. (ed.), *Dimensions of Radical Democracy: Pluralism, Citizenship, Community*, (London: Verso, 1992), 178.
11. *Combat*, 53, 1954, cited in *ibid.*
12. Kaplan, G., *op. cit.*.
13. Birnbaum, L. C., *Liberazione della donna. Feminism in Italy* (Middletown: Wesleyan University Press, 1986), 34 and 43; Dawidowicz, L. S., *The War Against the Jews 1933–1945* (New York: Seth Press, 1986), 403; Zuccotti, S., *The Italians and the Holocaust. Persecution, Rescue and Survival* (London: Peter Halban, 1987).
14. Bassnett, S., *Feminist Experiences: the Women's Movement in Four Cultures* (London: Allen and Unwin, 1986), 104.
15. Scroppo, E., *Donna, privato e politico* (Milan: Mazzotta, 1979), 26—transl. in Bassnet, *op. cit.*, 104–5.
16. The latter had published its own newspaper, *Noi Donne*, founded in France in 1936 by exiled Italian women. By the end of 1943, this paper had appeared underground in Milano, Turin, Florence, Genoa and Reggio Emilia, and by 1944 officially as the new official paper of UDI. See Fiocchetto, R., 'Die Geschichte der italienischen Frauenbewegung' in Savier, M. and Fiocchetto, R. (eds.), *Italien der Frauen* (Munich: Frauenoffensive, 1988), 26.
17. Stocker de Sousa, M.M. and Dominguez, M.C.P., 'Women in Portugal', supplement. No. 11, *Women of Europe* (Brussels: Commission of the European Communities, n.d., though possibly 1986), 5.
18. Ackelsberg, M. A., 'Separate and Equal? *Mujeres Libres* and Anarchist Strategy for Women's Emancipation', *Feminist Studies*, 11 (1) 1985, 63.
19. Fishman, R. M., 'The Labor Movement in Spain: From Authoritarianism to Democracy', *Comparative Politics*, 14 (3) 1982, 281.
20. *Women of Europe Newsletter*, No. 61, 1996, 3.
21. Turner, B., 'Outline of a Theory of Citizenship', in Mouffe, *op. cit.*, 52.
22. *Ibid.*, 58.
23. Arato, A. and Cohen, J., 'Civil Society and Social Theory', *Thesis Eleven*, 21, 1988.
24. Pizzorno, A., 'Political Exchange and Collective Identity in Industrial Conflict' in Crouch, C. and Pizzorno, A. (eds.), *The Resurgence of Class Conflict in Western Europe since 1968* (London: Macmillan, 1978); Pizzorno, A., 'Identità ed interesse' in Sciolla, L. (ed.), *Identità* (Turin: Rosenberg and Sellier, 1983).
25. Diani, M. and Melucci, A., 'Searching for autonomy: the sociology of social movements in Italy', *Social Science Information*, 27 (3) 1988, 338.
26. Mouffe, C., 'The Civics Lesson', *New Statesman and Society*, 7 October 1988, 28–31.
27. Offe, C., 'New Social Movements: Challenging the Boundaries of Institutional Politics', *Social Research*, 52 (4) 1985, 830.
28. Marcil-Lacoste, L., 'The Paradoxes of Pluralism' in Mouffe, *op.cit.*; McClure, K., 'On the Subject of Rights: Pluralism, Plurality and Political Identity' in *ibid.*
29. Kaplan, G., 'Accounting for Difference: A Review of Feminism and Political Theory', *Political Theory Newsletter*, 5 (2) 1993, 140–64.
30. Gatens, M., *Feminism and Philosophy: Perspectives on Difference and Equality* (London: Polity, 1992).
31. Braidotti, R., 'Origin and development of Gender Studies in Western Europe' in *Establishing Gender Studies in Central and Eastern European Countries* (Wassenaar: Council of Europe, 1992), 23–32.
32. Eurostat, *Data for short-term economic analysis*, 6, 1994.
33. See Plamenatz, J., 'Electoral Studies and Democratic Theory', *Political Studies*, 6, 1958, 2.
34. Maddox, G. 'Contours of a Democratic Polity', *Politics*, 21 (2) 1986, 2.

35. Zincone, G., 'Women in Decision Making Arenas: Italy' in Buckley, M. and Anderson, M. (eds.), *Women, Equality and Europe* (London: Macmillan, 1988), 160–76.
36. European Women's Lobby, Press Release, Reuter, June 1994.
37. The Athens Declaration states that 'Formal and informal equality between women and men is a fundamental human right. Women represent more than half the population. Democracy requires parity in the representation and administration of Nations. Women represent half the potential talent and skills of humanity and their under-representation in decision-making is a loss for society as a whole. A balanced participation by women and men in decision-making would produce different ideas, values and styles of behaviour suited to a fairer and more balanced world for all, both women and men. The under-representation of women in decision-making prevents full account being taken of the interests and needs of the population as a whole. We proclaim the need to achieve a balanced distribution of political and public power between men and women. We demand equality of participation by women and men in public and political decision-making. We underline the need for changes to the structure of decision-making procedures in order to ensure such equality in practice.' (November 1992, Athens, conference 'Women in Power' summit meeting of women decision-makers). Signed (amongst others) by: Leono Beleza, Vice-President of the Portuguese Parliament; Melina Mercouri, former Minister of Culture of the Greek Government; Vasso Papandreou, former Member of the European Commission; Mary Robinson, President of Ireland; Rita Süssmuth, President of the German Bundestag; Simone Veil, French Minister. Source: reproduced in *Women of Europe Newsletter*, No. 43, 1994, 4
38. Cited in *Women of Europe Newsletter*, No. 39, 1993, 2–3.
39. Kaplan, *op.cit.*
40. Fabricius, F., *Human Rights and European Politics: The Legal-Political Status of Workers in The European Community* (Oxford: Providence, 1992), 6.
41. *Ibid.*
42. *Fischer Weltalmanach 94* (Frankfurt/M: Fischer Taschenbuch, 1994), 790.
43. Schunter-Kleemann, S., 'Das Demokratiedefizit der EG und die Frauenpolitik' in Biester, E., Holland-Cunz, B., Jansen, M.M., Maelck-Lewy, E., Ruf, A. and Sauer, B. (eds.), *Das unsichtbare Geschlecht Europas. Der europäische Einigungsprozeß aus feministischer Sicht* (Frankfurt/M: Campus, 1994), 20–38.
44. Page, E.C., *People Who Run Europe* (Oxford: Clarendon Press, 1997).
45. *Ibid.*, 72–3.
46. Amongst a total membership of 17, there was only one woman, Vasso Papandreou from Greece, serving in the 1989–94 legislature, and later one other woman, Christine Schrivener from France. Edith Cresson, Emma Bonnino and Monika Wulf-Mathies have served in the new Commission.
47. Elman, R. Amy (ed.), *Sexual Politics and the European Union: the New Feminist challenge* (Providence: Berghahn, 1996), 1.
48. Schunter-Kleemann, *loc.cit.*
49. Baer, S., 'Pornography and Sexual Harassment in the EU' in Elman, *op.cit.*, 51.
50. Schunter-Kleemann, *loc.cit.*, 24.
51. Quintin, O., Statement bei dem EG-Seminar 'Die institutionellen Voraussetzungen für die Gleichberechtigung von Mann und Frau in den Mitgliedsstaaten der EG' Hannover, *IFG-Dokumentation*, 1988, 43–7 and 179–88.
52. Schunter-Kleemann, *loc.cit.*
53. The tasks include: developing and submitting proposals, directives, recommendations and programs concerned with equal opportunity issues for women and men; and initiating and developing positive actions in the public and private sectors and fostering the creation of small businesses and companies, as well as local job initiatives for women. The Equal

Opportunities Unit is required to contribute to the action programs of the European Communities. The latest of these was embedded in the Third Action Program of the European Communities (1991–5), an action program for the implementation of equal opportunity strategies. The annual implementation budget runs at ECU 5 mill. (a figure that Schunter-Kleemann describes on p.40 as 'extremely modest'). Contacts with all EU networks need to be maintained. The Unit organises seminars, meetings and conferences for international exchange on issues pertaining to equal opportunity for women. The Unit runs a joint programme with the development office of the EU, adding women-specific issues. The Unit liaises with international organisations, such as the OECD, the European Council, the United Nations, and the ILO, where the equal opportunity policies of the European Communities have to be represented. (Source: Schunter-Kleemann, S., 'Das Demokratiedefizit der EG und die Verrechtlichung der Frauenfrage' in Schunter-Kleemann, S. (ed.), *Herrenhaus Europa—Geschlechterverhältnisse im Wohlfahrtsstaat* (Berlin: Edition Sigma, 1992), 40 (adapted and transl. by Kaplan).

54. *Women of Europe Newsletter*, No. 23, 1991; Schunter-Kleemann, *loc. cit.* 1994.
55. Rubery, J., 'Pay, Gender and the Social Dimension to Europe', *British Journal of Industrial Relations*, 4, 1992, 606–21.
56. Kaplan, G., *The Meagre Harvest: The Australian Women's Movement 1950s–1990s* (Sydney: Allen and Unwin, 1996).
57. Weiler, A., 'Frauenlohnpolitik in Europa' in Biester *et al.*, *op. cit.*, 39–61.
58. Hoskyns, C., *Integrating Gender. Women, Law and Politics in the European Union* (London: Verso, 1996).
59. Commission of the European Communities, *Proposal for a Council Directive amending Directive 76/207/EEC on the implementation of the principles of equal treatment for men and women as regards access to employment, vocational training and promotion, and working conditions* (Brussels, 27 March 1996), 2.
60. Hoskyns, *op.cit.*, 198.
61. Commission of the European Communities, *Proposal for a Council Decision on the fourth medium-term Community action programme on equal opportunities for women and men* (1996–2000), (COM(95) 381 final, (Brussels, 1995).
62. Martens, H. and Schumann, H., 'Die Zeit läuft davon. Europas langer Weg ins organisierte Chaos', *Spiegel Spezial: Die Erde 2000*, No.4, 1993.
63. *Ibid.*, 111.
64. *Ibid.*, 112.
65. Holland-Cunz, B., Ruf, A. and Sauer, B., 'Einleitung' in Biester *et al.*, *op. cit.*, 7–19.
66. Elman, *op.cit.*, 2.
67. Arendt, H. cited in Kaplan, G. and Kessler, C. S. (eds.), *Hannah Arendt. Thinking, Judging, Freedom* (Sydney: Allen and Unwin, 1989).
68. European Parliament (Rapporteur: J.Larive), *Report of the Committee on Women's Rights on women in the decision-making process*, 27 January 1994, A3-0035/94, Doc_EN/RR/244/244326, 6.
69. *Ibid.*, 7.
70. *Women of Europe Newsletter*, No. 70, 1997, 1 and 3.
71. Hoskyns, C., 'The European Union and the Women Within, An Overview of Women's Rights Policy' in Elman, *op. cit.*, 13–22.
72. *Women of Europe Newsletter*, No. 72, 1997, 1.
73. I wish to thank the Delegation of the European Commission in Canberra, especially Lynne Hunter from the Information Office, for the valuable assistance in providing essential parliamentary documents for this project.

6 Citizenship on the Margins: The Case of Divorce in Western Europe

LINDA HANCOCK

This chapter focuses on women and divorce in Western Europe,[1] as a means of advancing our understanding of women and citizenship within the United Europe. Analysis of the gendered effects of divorce highlights women's role as unpaid carers, and post divorce, as women independent of men, but affected by their relations to them and their children. Figures confirm the increasing feminisation of poverty,[2] to which single parent (predominantly female headed) families make a significant contribution.[3] It is also evident that high proportions of single parents are living in poverty. With increasing divorce rates in many Member States, divorced women will feature prominently amongst the poor upon retirement; whereas formerly, they would have benefited from their husbands' superannuation or jointly acquired assets.

Outcomes for divorced women with dependent children are contingent on a number of factors at the national Member State level (in addition to matters of divorce property settlement, spouse maintenance and child maintenance under national family and property laws, and variations across class and race/ethnicity).[4] Of particular relevance are the extent of state-provided child care, pensions for single parents and retirement pensions, and the extent to which such benefits are tied to worker contributions.

Whilst, to some extent, citizenship entitlements are shifting from marriage to work, both orientations raise questions for women concerning their independence, autonomy and wellbeing. Marriage has been central to women's subordination under dominant theories of citizenship. Both liberal and contract theories have in common the exclusion of women as autonomous agents, rendering women's citizenship indirect, relational and derivative. The emerging conception of the European 'citizen as worker', wherein rights to benefits are directly linked to duration and level of participation in paid work, has implications in terms of gender.

Compounding the traditional division of labour around caring functions within the family, monetarist economic policies and labour force restructuring have impacted disproportionately on women, with higher unemployment and lower full time workforce participation rates and thus less access to work-related retirement benefits. It is argued that access to work-related entitlements is further restricted for groups such as divorced women, especially single parents with dependent children. European Court of Justice rulings on sex equality have been directed primarily at women as workers, having little emphasis on the constitution of family roles.

This chapter asks what supranational[5] citizenship of the European Union, and Union institutions such as the European Court of Justice, might offer disadvantaged or marginalised groups such as divorced women, in terms of pro-active EU social justice policy and avenues for appeal against entitlements denied at the national level. EU policies and institutions could provide a means of addressing problems of indirect discrimination and structurally based inequalities. As Vogel and Moran observe, citizenship 'is concerned with the claims that persons can make on public authority'.[6] Just how far such claims might go is open to speculation.

This chapter traces the centrality of marriage to questions of women's subordination as citizen under dominant liberal and contract theories of citizenship. It discusses the marginalisation of women under emerging notions of 'citizen as worker' and examines the nexus between divorce, caring and social security in retirement for divorced women. These issues are considered against the backdrop of attempts to address the social dimension of European integration and the role of European Community institutions such as the European Court of Justice in addressing sex discrimination. In conclusion, the paper asks how a gender sensitive conceptualisation of citizenship and international or transnational feminisms might facilitate change.

Marriage, Gender, Citizenship and Work

Taking Marshall's three dimensions of civic, social and political citizenship,[7] an examination of what citizenship has meant historically for women shows that in terms of entitlements, women have been non-citizens. In the past, women have been excluded from voting, from entering into legal contracts or standing for public office, from owning property and from occupations such as the professions. This classical notion of citizenship has been a profoundly gendered site, extolling the male obligation to fight and the female obligation to procreate. Citizenship has been the 'preserve of men',[8] and women are recognised as 'second class citizens' in a system where citizenship is 'universal but hierarchically ordered'.[9] Women's low representation and often virtual absence from central decision-making societal institutions is a common feature of most Western democracies. This under-representation of women is mirrored in the persistent under-representation of women in EU institutions and decision-making positions at EU, regional, national and local levels, although this is changing.[10]

Critics such as Pateman and James argue that even in contemporary western liberal democracies, women are denied full citizenship.[11] At both community and national levels, women are in many respects on the margins of substantive citizenship. At both levels, the 'democratic deficit' refers especially to women.

The dominant discourse on women and citizenship has drawn principally on liberal and contract theories and to a lesser extent, on communitarian theories. Under liberal/democratic theories, inspired by T.H. Marshall, citizenship entails a set of rights equally enjoyed by all members of society.[12] Liberalism assumed equality and a minimum of state interference, tied to protection from harms. Criticised on various grounds, including its assumed unitary nature and evolutionary development, plus its ethnocentric bias, the main point here is to highlight the contradictions between formal political equality on the one hand, and social and economic inequality related to the market place and to private property on the other.[13]

Feminist critiques have highlighted the exclusion of women from liberal principles of freedom and equality, since women lacked the personal independence and freedom to participate equally as citizens. Held refers to the growing awareness of the inconsistency of the principle of equality with women's lives and, in particular, with motherhood.[14] Critiques of the liberal tradition's interpretation of freedom (as absence from interference) or negative liberty include the arguments that the conception of freedom as non-interference is unsatisfactory for those who lack economic, social, political and legal resources:

> ... mere non-interference can hardly provide freedom. Anyone lacking what she needs to stay alive, and lacking what she needs to act at all, is, of course, not able to act freely.[15]

Held further argues that in industrial society, 'the means to live and act'—minimum income, medical care, affordable housing, adequate child care, access to education—form the minimum pre-conditions for the extension of independence to previously excluded groups such as women, minorities and the poor.

Others have criticised the writings of liberals such as Dahl,[16] who has only in his later writings included the constraints of poverty, race and gender in considerations of the classical egalitarian ideal of the political equality of all citizens. According to Pateman and others, under liberal theory, the purportedly gender-neutral citizen is male.[17] Such conceptions render women not only invisible but dependent upon men. As Vogel observes:

As regards nationality, domicile, rights over children, taxation, pension schemes, etc., a married woman's rights and obligations remained enclosed in the ascribed subordinate status of a wife.[18]

Under both liberal and contract theories of citizenship, marriage has been central to women's subordination. Both theories have in common the exclusion of women as autonomous agents, rendering women's citizenship relational and derivative.

Under Social Contract theories, the key criticism entails the assumption of equality of the parties to the contract. In her critique, Pateman identifies the political contract as a fraternal one, between men, not men and women.[19] She argues that marriage is not entered into by free and equal individuals. Similarly, the welfare contract is predicated on ostensibly 'neutral' terms such as 'breadwinner' and 'head of household', which disguises the different ways that rights are construed for men as individuals, whereas women's rights are defined in relation to men.

Many of the rights transferred to husbands upon marriage, although now removed from the statute books, have significantly shaped the perception of women's incapacity for active citizenship. Vogel identifies the historical nexus between citizenship, security of property and certain paternity, and argues that women's subordination (through the marriage contract) was an integral part of men's citizenship.[20] The theme of the complementarity of men's privilege and women's subordination is reproduced on many different levels. Meehan criticises the presumption of equality in contract theory, in the face of disparities between men and women in practical terms.[21] How workable is the contract if differences in power advantage one party over another? This is especially evident in disputes when contracts break down, such as men's greater economic resources to fight property or custody litigation which force women to accept settlements against their future interests.

Even under the more idealised communitarian theories of citizenship (the idea that citizenship entails responsibilities for promoting the common good through participation in community life, political debate and decision-making), feminist critiques speak of a 'divided citizenship' where in practice, a woman's rights of social citizenship are in many respects still defined by her relations to others.[22] Women's rights thus stem from their ascribed status within the family as dependant (wife) or as carer. In comparison, men's entitlements to pensions, social security and unemployment benefits stem from their role as worker or breadwinner.

Communitarianism could however lay the basis for more equitable sharing of care and paid work, as has ostensibly been the case in Scandinavian countries. However, looking to whether policies based on communitarian philosophies (such as those of Scandinavian welfare states) might better accommodate women's interests, brief analysis of research on Sweden and Denmark raises some pertinent issues. As Lewis and Astrom state on Sweden:

> The central state had to secure equal treatment via labour market status before women could exercise a claim grounded in difference without suffering grave material disadvantages.[23]

Despite the high labour force participation rates for Swedish women, Lewis and Astrom's analysis highlights how women are more likely than men to work part-time; women earn 77% of men's wages; predominantly women and not men use parental leave and the option of the six hour day; access to child care is unequal and cost varies, encouraging women to take the full amount of paid leave and to plan the second child around leave entitlements. Thus, despite Sweden's active labour market policies and policies of parental leave and child care, and policies based around notions of formal equality, substantive equality is questionable when policies appear to have impacted on the lives of women but not of men. In Denmark, official schemes for accommodating the demands of family life, in the form of part-time work and family sick leave entitlements, are used more by women than men; the latter also work more overtime than women.[24]

As in other countries,[25] Swedish women are doing much more work in the public sphere, while the vast majority of men are not doing more work in the private sphere.[26] With the 1990s recessions, rising unemployment and cuts to public sector jobs have impacted disproportionately on women. As Hernes comments on both Sweden and Norway, where about half of all women employees work part-time, the choice is not between full-time and part-time work, but between part-time work and full-time home duties.[27] Hernes also claims that after twenty years of equality policies, Scandinavian women have less societal power, and most social clients are women.[28]

With the development of social policy in the EU, the emerging conception of citizenship is that of *citizen-as-worker*, wherein rights to benefits are directly linked to duration and level of participation in paid work. This has direct implications in terms of gender, as shown below.

Women's lower employment rates, greater responsibility for child care, lower levels of pay, and clustering in secondary labour market jobs or as part-time or casualised outworkers excludes them from the raft of benefits newly accorded to the citizen as worker. According to figures from the Commission of the European Communities,[29] women were earning as little as just over half and up to three-quarters of men's earnings, across what were the twelve Member States.[30] Recent Eurostat figures indicate women earn on average 20% less than their male counterparts.[31] Women's activity rate (43%) is lower than men's (69%) across the Community (the lowest is in Greece at 33%, while the highest is in Denmark at 62%). A higher percentage of women (29%) than men (4%) are in part-time employment; the majority are married women with children, earning low pay in jobs excluded until recently from retirement pensions and benefits. As we approach the end of the century, despite women's increasing participation in the labour market across the EU, the disparity between men's and women's employment opportunities, pay and working conditions remains substantial and is in some cases worsening.[32]

Women constitute a significant proportion in the informal economy, working in family businesses (especially in the Southern Member States), accruing no pension entitlements, where their input is often not perceived as 'work'.[33] As the Commission of the European Communities observed, the growth of jobs in the service sector 'reveals both new and traditional gender demarcation lines between different occupations'.[34] Averaged across the Union, women's registered unemployment (12%) is higher than men's (9%). Women constitute the majority of the long-term unemployed, and the gap between men's unemployment and women's is widening.[35]

Overwhelmingly, women have primary responsibility for childcare in Western Europe.[36] A report on *1993 and The Employment of Women* saw childcare as an 'insuperable obstacle' to growth in women's employment.[37] It noted that, with the exception of Denmark, with larger numbers in day nurseries, the employment rate of women decreases as the number of children under ten increases.[38] Drew notes the class dimension to women's labour market participation, with highly educated women experiencing continuous, less interrupted careers and those with few educational advantages discouraged from labour market participation by poverty traps.[39]

There are wide sex differences in average levels of pay for women in a sex segregated labour market. What this means is that despite equal pay for work of equal value provisions, women's employment is clustered horizontally (in a small number of poorly paid jobs) and vertically (at the bottom end of occupational hierarchies), and women are segregated in the lower grades in all sectors of employment, even in female dominated sectors.[40] The Commission of European Communities recognises that women's contribution is 'undervalued and under rewarded' because of discrimination inherent in systems relating to job classification and social security systems.[41] Land comments that it is only women with similar employment patterns to men who 'do not let family responsibilities disrupt their paid work', who receive more or less comparable benefits to men.[42]

In the context of the 1990s recession, the main growth of women's employment was in 'atypical work'; that is, part-time employment, temporary and casual work where there is less social welfare provision.[43] Some argue that recent re-organisation and restructuring of work such as contracting out, casualisation, home-based work, increased self-employment and enterprise bargaining,[44] are becoming a more significant part of women's employment patterns[45] and are occurring in areas of high female employment, such as banking, that make women particularly vulnerable to casualisation, lower pay and loss of work condition protections. There are claims that traditional forms of atypical work are back, such as piecework, disguised as self-employment.[46] The employment picture is one of increasing exclusion, marginalisation and segregation of vulnerable groups such as women from the social protection afforded to mainstream (male) full-time workers—although there have been recent attempts to extend benefits to part-time workers.

The conceptualisation of citizen-as-worker has particular relevance in the light of the Social Charter, as basically a workers' rights charter, and the issue of the exclusion of non-workers. According to the Community Charter of the Fundamental Social Rights of Workers commonly referred to as the Social Charter (1989), the scope of Community intervention is limited, and economic and social rights outlined in the Charter are linked to the exercise of an occupation. Despite the broad interpretation of 'worker' by the European Court of Justice, to include job seekers, pensioners and workers' families,[47] the focus on workers excludes those such as women and the poor who have remained in high proportions outside paid work or in the 'informal' economy.

EU provisions likely to impact on women (Community Directives and legislation on Equal Pay, Equal Treatment, Social Security, Parental Leave and Family Leave, Maternity Rights and Provisions, and Childcare) will benefit some women more than others, and will have different effects in terms of race/ethnicity and worker status. Brah points out that the current re-structuring of the labour market favouring large-scale multi-national capital over small and medium firms will disproportionately affect some regions (such as the central manufacturing area of England), some industries (textiles and the food industries), and some communities, especially black and ethnic minority women, concentrated in small to medium sized firms.[48] The trend towards 'core' workers (with status, security and civic rights) and 'others' (uncertain work, ill-paid with minimal rights) has both gender and race implications.

In her review of the role of the European Court of Justice rulings on freedom of movement, provision of professional services, social security and social advantages, equal rights for men and women at work and in social security schemes,[49] Meehan sees sex equality rulings as directed primarily at women as workers and as having very little to do with how family roles are constituted. She states that 'neither the national means of implementing social security nor the Community concepts of work and worker do much to help women to be more autonomous'.[50]

Worker status as a basis for social entitlements raises the issue of the extent to which rights are construed individualistically, as a means of enjoying individual or private liberties, rather than in relation to a solidaristic or shared moral order. McCrudden argues that Community rights for women are more about individual equality than about group justice or a new moral order based on a concept of sexual justice.[51] In any event, shifting to individual entitlements to benefits may be problematic, given the gendered distribution favouring men into protected (in terms of pension accrual) work and women into unprotected, part-time and often unpaid work. The consolidation of New Right liberal market economics, individually negotiated contracts, and the undermining of solidaristic movements such as unionism, reinforce individualism while fragmenting and dissipating group-based activism and gains.

With regard to these trends, concerns include the dominance of the market over commitments to equality[52] (although, as discussed later, this is now being recognised in Commission reports and in the Amsterdam Treaty, which explicitly reinforces equality as a fundamental right); lack of political representation of women (and women's interests) in the EP and national parliaments (perhaps with the exception of Scandinavian states, with over 30% representation of women in parliament); lack of attention to measures that will address the social, educational and economic basis for the 'gender pay gap' and measures to address the sexual division of domestic labour that affects women's access to education, training and paid work. In general, present arrangements fail to consider the gendered cost of 'caring'.

Common themes throughout the above critiques of dominant theories of citizenship are the diminution of women's rights attendant upon their greater involvement in home and caring roles compared with men; the unequal valuing of such roles in the public sphere or in civil society; exclusions based on substitution (of husbands for their wives) or women's lack of access to valued roles; and women's marginalisation in defining valued roles (principally the roles of worker and of carer) that confer basic entitlements.

The distinction between 'active' and 'passive' citizens is useful in bringing out a distinction between formal and substantive equality. Where formal entitlements exist, women have been particularly disadvantaged in terms of lack of personal independence and freedom to participate equally and actively as citizens. Historically, women exercised political rights through marriage, and the citizen was assumed to be a male head of household, acting as the 'representative of the marriage relation'.[53] Marriage, therefore, has been central to restrictions placed on wives[54] and to women's indirect citizenship and lack of agency as active citizens. Where there are state-provided benefits, these have characteristically worked via the labour market to cater for the predominantly male, regularly employed.[55] Women's rights to welfare have been indirect, based on presumed dependence on a male breadwinner and in terms of motherhood.

With this understanding of the labour market and given the centrality of marriage and women's caring roles to women's active citizenship, what then of divorce?

Divorce, Caring and Social Security in Retirement

During the 1970s and 1980s, reforms across Europe[56] mirrored those in other western nations in terms of liberalising the grounds for divorce, sex-neutral legislation presuming equity of treatment of men and women in family law concerning child custody and property settlement,[57] and, in some countries, government collection of child alimony or maintenance.[58] Between one quarter and one third of marriages across European countries end in divorce.[59] Eurostat figures show an increase in divorce from 10% of European citizens in 1945 to 20% in 1992.[60] On other figures, the rate has risen from 0.4 per 1000 in 1960 to 1.8 per 1000 in 1995, with broad differences within the Community from 3.5 per 1000 in Belgium and 2.9 per 1000 in the United Kingdom, to 0.8 per 1000 in Spain and 0.5 per 1000 in Italy.[61]

Smart argues that divorce exposes the hidden poverty of many women within marriage.[62] As the saying goes, for many women, poverty is only one divorce away. Walker and Walker, in a study of poverty and social exclusion, found that the group most at risk of poverty is lone parents, with more than half of these poor in Britain and more than a quarter in Germany, Spain and the Netherlands.[63] This not only reflects women's relatively low wages and economic dependence within marriage, but also the lack of financial support from former spouses, post-divorce; vast differences across the Community in levels of state support for single parents; and the increased costs falling on the custodial parent (usually the mother) to establish and maintain children in a new household.[64]

Divorce laws, dating from the 1970s and 1980s and based on 'formal' equality, sex-neutral legislation and a presumption of equity in property settlements, overlook substantive inequalities in the gendered division of labour (both in paid employment and in the home), the gendered anticipation of future care responsibilities, and gendered access to resources, such as training and education, that reproduce substantive inequalities. Aside from the opportunity costs of paid work and income foregone[65] during marriage, divorce exposes the hidden poverty of many women within marriage by virtue of their inability to re-enter the labour market, especially on a full-time basis, because of lack of qualifications and appropriate work experience, high levels of unemployment, and continuing child care responsibilities.

With regard to comparisons across Member States, outcomes for divorced women are contingent on state policies in a number of areas (in addition to variations related to class, ethnicity and work force participation). Foremost among these are first, the state's role in providing child care (discussed above) and secondly, single parent benefits and retirement pensions, which may or may not be tied to employee contributions; these factors differ considerably across the Community. Thirdly, Member States differ on family law, jurisprudence and court determinations in relation to property settlements, retirement, pension equity transfers upon divorce (as, for example, in the Netherlands and Germany), and the important matter of private transfers in the form of the amount and duration of spouse and child maintenance paid by non-resident parents and methods for sanctioning non-payment. Some of these points require elaboration.

First, pension levels differ vastly across the Community. Regarding single parent benefits paid independent of workers' contributions, Belgium, Denmark, France, Germany, Luxembourg and the Netherlands pay between 50% and 60% of average net earnings, whereas Ireland pays 44%, the United Kingdom 38%, Greece 32%, Italy 16%, Spain 3% and Portugal nothing.[66] With 50% of net average earnings as an accepted index of poverty, this suggests considerable hardship for pension-dependent single parents in some countries in particular. In broad comparative terms, Sweden is depicted as having come closer to solving the economic problems of single parent households through a combination of higher workforce participation and state-provided benefits, including childcare, than for example Germany, with higher economic dependence within marriage (because of lower labour force participation of women) and taxation policies favouring women staying at home during the child-rearing years.[67]

Second, in terms of retirement pensions, although there is great diversity in social protection arrangements across Member States. These include differences in the level of pensions in relation to average earnings, formulae and entitlement conditions; career breaks due to child care responsibilities affect entitlements to full retirement pensions to varying degrees across the Member States.[68]

In a Study of Social Protection in Europe, the Commission estimated that career interruptions due to illness have a marginal effect on pension entitlements; long spells of unemployment have a modest effect; spells of part-time work cause loss of pension entitlement only in a minority of countries, but 'periods of inactivity caring for children at home adversely affect pension entitlements in most Member States'.[69]

After divorce, women are, on average, materially less well off than their former spouses.[70] This finding is not confined to Western Europe, but is common to other western societies, such as the US, Australia, Canada and New Zealand.[71] Furthermore, these differences do not abate as women age. For divorced women, labour market disadvantage compounds in retirement, when shorter work history and lower earnings frequently preclude them from occupational pension schemes; this forces reliance onto (usually lower) social security retirement pensions in the 'second tier' of social assistance and welfare benefits.[72] Joshi and Davies cite an English survey by Gregory and Foster which found that half of the recently divorced men, compared with only one fifth of the women, were members of occupational pension schemes.[73] A German study found that pensions received by women in their own right were on average less than half mens'.[74] Moreover, in all Member States except Denmark and Germany, the Commission's study of 'atypical' cases (presented to reveal gaps and inadequacies in current social protection arrangements) revealed that a divorced woman with time out of the workforce due to child-rearing was the least well off at retirement age in terms of pension entitlements as a percentage of net average wages.[75]

Thus, at the time of divorce, inequities in retirement pension membership are already well established; this trend is accentuated in retirement. Women as single heads of households with dependent children are likely to have a higher propensity to poverty in old age/retirement than men, given men's propensity to remarry with greater frequency and alacrity than women, post divorce. Although re-marriage may bring new costs, it also frequently provides caring and household labour as support for men's waged employment alongside men's, on average, disproportionately higher earnings than women.[76]

On the third issue of national difference in family law and jurisprudence and financial settlements in divorce, studies of comparative family law and jurisprudence across European Member States are thin on the ground. One study analyses English family law registrars' responses in terms of three models—the 'lifelong partnership', 'individualistic' and 'insurance' models—and concludes that most decisions reflected the individualistic model, with strains of a 'clean break' approach and compensation based on either women's role as mothers or as waged workers.[77] Summing up their assessment of family law in England and Wales, Diduck and Orton argue that compensation for women's child rearing labour is at decision makers' discretion, rather than as of right.[78]

Analysing family law jurisprudence, Canadian lawyer Mahoney identifies the court's role in women's post divorce poverty, by linking the 'feminisation of poverty' to judicial misinformation and misunderstanding concerning the economic consequences of divorce for women. These include inaccurate economic assumptions about the costs of raising children, the costs of women's caring role on their own workforce participation, and unrealistic expectations about older women's abilities to earn future income, as influences on court decisions.[79] These attitudes in turn impact on the quantum of property and other settlements for women. Canadian developments in the Supreme Court judgement of Moge v Moge 1993 (on Appeal) recognised the limited ability of family court reforms to address women's poverty upon separation (because of the low level of income of many husbands) but still saw private maintenance (of wives) as a means of alleviating women's and children's poverty and important in that regard.[80] Rather than assessing women's interests as subsumed within the welfare of children, the Canadian judgement allows women to claim compensation for disadvantages accruing from their role as caregiver during the marriage. For comparative purposes, the judgement is significant for its focus on substantive equality, which, in the words of these authors:

> . . . has allowed Canadian women's organisations to go some way towards successfully challenging formal equality or same treatment principles which accept male characteristics and realities as the norm to which women must subscribe in order to achieve the social benefits men, as the more powerful group, enjoy.[81]

Further consideration of family law jurisprudence across Member States and the economic 'costs' of women's role as wife and mother is beyond the scope of this paper. Suffice it to say that, at the national level, differences attend courts' determinations on matters of property settlement, retirement pension transfers, spouse maintenance and child maintenance. These matters reside in home affairs and justice, which have only recently become a focus (albeit minor) of Community concern, with increasing prominence being given to the social dimensions of European Union.[82]

The Social Dimension and Supranational Citizenship

In 1989, the European Council affirmed the importance of social aspects of the Single European Market (SEM) being given 'the same importance as economic aspects' and accordingly being 'developed in a balanced fashion'.[83] The White Paper on European Social Policy setting out the next phase of social policy development (1995-9) sees the social dimension as an integral and significant element of the process of integration.[84] It stated that 'economic and social progress must go hand in hand' and predicted that many changes would be necessary at both national and Community levels. It described democracy, individual rights and freedoms, equality of opportunity, diversity of culture, respect for human dignity, social security and the rule of law, as uncontroversial and shared values, which need to be translated into political action by the Member States and the Union acting together. The White Paper saw jobs and employment as central to financing social policy systems across the Union and, accordingly, has placed the highest priority on job creation.[85] For nationals of Member States of the EU, citizenship is not tied exclusively to the sovereign nation-state. The European Union confers citizenship rights within a framework that co-exists with those in Member States, but which may enable nationals to claim certain economic, social and political rights from the Union.

The EP described Community citizenship as 'a concept in itself' constituting 'a genuine form of status, deriving from full recognition and protection of the human rights and fundamental freedoms of all persons, as defined in the European Convention on Human Rights, both as individuals and in social units, in particular, the family'.[86] Listed among the essential conditions of citizenship were respect for, and guarantee in the Courts of, human rights and fundamental freedoms; recognition of social, economic, political and cultural rights; and banning of all discrimination on grounds of race, creed, political views, sex, nationality or any other personal situation.[87]

Community law has established economic and social rights. Under the Maastricht European Union Treaty, a new political dimension consists in the right of EU citizens to vote in municipal elections in the Member State of residence, the right to petition and the option of lodging a complaint with the European Ombudsman.[88]

Writing on the distinctive nature of European citizenship, Meehan refers to 'citizens of the Union' and a 'transitional regime', where policies have acquired a 'life of their own' as a dimension of European citizenship, whereby 'citizens' legal status and the content of his or her rights are not determined by nationality alone'.[89] Community Directives and Regulations may give citizens rights 'irrespective of the content of national legislation'.[90] The European Parliament views the national context, at least in Europe, as too narrow for a concrete definition of citizenship.[91] The European Union is seen as a way of overcoming limits and resolving problems with which the individual state is now ill-equipped to deal.[92]

The EU is now constituted as a supranational legal order, which involves the ceding of some sovereignty by Member States to the laws of the Union, as enforceable over national laws. EU Member States are bound by equality as proclaimed in the Treaty of Amsterdam, and 'judges and administrative bodies are bound to apply the provisions and new rules laid down in the Treaty'; in addition, all multi-annual action programs will have to demonstrate compliance with the equality provisions set down in the Treaty.[93] Murray refers to the EU as 'a supranational organisation with real and binding powers'.[94] The ECJ has affirmed that policies of the Union embody entitlements for individuals in member states[95] and, of particular relevance to this paper, has recognised its duty to uphold EU citizens' rights of access to social protection and sex equality as 'fundamental rights'.[96]

The impact of EU law is shown in instances where national appeals courts have overturned cases because decisions conflicted with Community laws;[97] in relation to the Court of Justice ruling that national courts interpret national laws according to Community Directives (thus giving individuals access to remedies and damages in national courts in relation to enforceable Community rights),[98] and where the ECJ has over-ruled decisions in Member States which were in conflict with Community Law. The Treaty of Amsterdam has equality between men and women as one of its principles and a major goal of Union action.

If European citizenship confers certain social, civil and political rights, including sex equality as a 'fundamental right', then what are the consequences for women, in particular women marginalised by divorce?

Given the commitment at the Community level to equality between the sexes, what then is the potential for using Community supranational instruments and institutions like the Court of Justice, that set EU-wide standards, as a forum for pursuing claims at or from the national level? How likely is the EU to adopt pro-active policies concerning the poverty and inequalities experienced by marginalised groups such as divorced women?

The European Court of Justice and Addressing Inequality at the Community Level

Meehan observes that the ECJ has played an important role in transforming benefits into entitlements or rights.[99] ECJ rulings have confirmed the direct effect of Article 119 in national courts for public and private employees, have ensured rights for part-time workers and the right to equal pay for work that is different but of equal value. In establishing respect for personal human rights as a principle, Community law has imposed on all institutions, including national courts, a duty to impose such rights.[100] Meehan argues that the Court of Justice has gone beyond the intentions of the Member States in the meaning of 'worker' and benefits covered by Community law. In this regard rulings may entail costs that Member States did not expect to bear.

However, the optimism of these possibilities is tempered by reservations concerning Member States' lack of adherence to deadlines for the implementation of Directives; a view that social rights are unenforceable; the costs and delays of appeals to European institutions; the dominance of the market agenda over competing social rights claims; the ambiguity of gender-neutral terms and cynicism regarding benefits to women of established mechanisms of complaint and redress. On the first point, Curtin shows how few of the Directives on the single market program were incorporated into national laws on time.[101] Other commentators have remarked on the 'herculean task' of communicating Community affairs to the then twelve Member States, with their differing traditions and concerns[102] and the inevitability of delays. On the matter of transposition of Community Directives into national law, the European Parliament has expressed its concern about the time-lag between decision making and implementation.[103]

An EP report noted that the Community and the Court have 'given broad interpretation of certain guaranteed rights' but that 'economic, social and cultural rights are still, to a large extent, non-enforceable rights'.[104] Access to European institutions and avenues of redress are limited according to means, and there are long delays.[105]

Meehan cites the problem that for Community political leaders, social policy is conceptualised more in terms of economic objectives than in terms of citizens' rights'.[106] She also refers to problems not only of the slow implementation of Social Security and Equal Treatment Directives, but also the difficulties encountered with indirect discrimination. On a similar point, the Third Medium-Term Community Action Plan 1991-5 on Equal Opportunities for Women and Men observed that there should be ease of access to legal redress and remedies for individuals suffering sex discrimination, and that concepts like 'indirect discrimination' and 'equal pay for work of equal value' are complex and in need of clarification.[107]

A certain amount of well-earned cynicism might be directed at gender-neutral anti-discrimination provisions[108] under which advantaged groups such as men or whites have made claims in other jurisdictions;[109] the detrimental outcomes for women of the 'similarly situated' test[110] as compared to that of disproportionate impact; the undermining of previous entitlements for women by men's challenges for equivalent benefits; and the limitations of being locked into institutionalised means and language for defending women's equality claims.

We might therefore be sceptical about the ability of the ECJ and other institutions (nationally and supranationally) to recognise and act in relation to indirect forms of systemic sex discrimination that Mahoney identifies in the legal systems of Western democracies such as Canada and Australia.[111] Such recognition seems unlikely, given the dominance of the discourse of market crisis over that of social rights claims and widespread attempts to limit entitlements and reduce social benefits such as unemployment benefits, single parent and age pensions.

The EP's 1993 annual report from the Committee on Civil Liberties and Internal Affairs recognised that although the ECJ has extended the substance of European citizens' rights, the legal protection of citizen's rights and freedoms as outlined in the Treaties, 'lacks clarity'; a system based on case law is inadequate for informing citizens of rights and guarantees and is subject to differing interpretations 'which may weaken the protection of fundamental rights'.[112] The report identified the inherent weakness of rights and freedoms being directly or indirectly covered by Community law, arguing this is 'far from satisfactory' and did not 'offer the maximum degree of legal certainty and clarity as to the content and degree of protection required to uphold fundamental rights.[113]

There are moves within the EU to further develop an action plan on basic human rights, including social, economic, environmental and consumer rights and recognition of the need for 'clear and readily available means of redress against breaches of human rights in each member State, in advance of the establishment of a Community system for the protection of human rights'.[114] The extent to which women's rights are embodied in the concept of human rights becomes an important variable. On the hierarchy of rights, feminist critiques of human rights complain that women's rights are frequently not conceptualised on the same level (or accorded the same urgency and universality) as human rights.[115] Recent moves to include equality between men and women as a fundamental right in the Treaty of Amsterdam, and to adopt the approach of 'mainstreaming' in the use of Structural Funds, are positive moves towards addressing inequalities.[116]

The task ahead includes the construction of gender sensitive standards of citizenship that take into account the politics of motherhood and of women's caring roles[117] and that enable women to participate as fully autonomous members of society. There is a need to re-construct citizenship in ways that are sensitive to women's diversity, their lived realities and interests, including, on the same/difference dilemma, 'the capacity to say where equal treatment is appropriate and when specific treatment would be better'.[118]

Clearly, there are limits to the impact of family law reform on female and child poverty. National social protection, taxation and labour market policies are inextricably interrelated and define relationships between the state, the family and work in ways that are deeply gendered. Nevertheless, whilst aiming at transformative structural change to address systematic discrimination, reform in specific areas such as family law can be a means of securing reforms for women.

A re-definition of paid and unpaid work (as, for example, in factoring unpaid care into GDP calculations) could lay the foundations for new forms of female citizenship. Re-thinking equality in the division of labour within the family need not result in women emulating men's patterns in paid work or negating the importance of care, but could entail re-valuing the worth of domestic work as well as sharing it. Such moves may be facilitated by feminist solidarity across Member States, in the form of feminist transnational analysis and agitation, rather than being channelled vertically through national governments. By this means, rights may be consolidated and expanded as the outcome of radical struggle by transnational groups, such as European feminist movements, rather than as rights handed down by the supranational state. Feminist critiques of statism have shown the historical insensitivity of state policy (such as sex neutral and equality policies) to women's interests and to diversity amongst women. Just how successful 'mainstreaming' will be in reducing structural, gendered inequalities remains to be seen.

By looking at the centrality of marriage and work (paid and unpaid) to dominant discourses of citizenship, specific examples of women's outcomes within the intersecting areas of social security, labour policies and family law, and the potential role of supranational EU institutions in defining and upholding such rights, this paper raises other unresolved and complex questions. The challenge still remains to see the extent to which EU laws, rulings and Treaties on equality will go beyond individual treatment to establish group justice and advance substantive equality through structural change. On citizenship, is Europe moving towards supranational citizenship that will add value to national citizenship? On entitlements and the impact on marginalised groups, will there be moves to equalise benefits across member states (in, for example, social security pensions)? In harmonising the social dimension of European integration, will the lowest common denominator prevail, tempting some Member States into a deterioration of conditions under justifications of globalisation, market forces and competition? How broadly will the social agenda be implemented and will definitions of equality, justice, fairness and access to justice be framed around market concerns? Will equal treatment be aimed at achieving formal equality or be extended to substantive equality and will sex equality provisions enhance women's interests, in both the short and the long term?

Notes

1. At the outset, some of the boundaries of this paper should be noted. It does not consider issues related to potential Union membership of Central and East European countries, as regards gender, divorce and social protection. Whilst recognising diversity among women in terms of class, privilege, race/ethnicity, religion and regional and national identities, this paper operates at a general level, in reference to both gender and caring and gender and work.
2. British figures from a report on 'Households Below Average Income' by the Department of Social Security indicate that nearly one third of British children are living in poverty and that the proportion of lone parents living in poverty rose from 19% in 1979 to 59%

in 1991–2. The proportion of pensioners living below the poverty line rose from 12% to 40% over the same period. See Waterhouse, R., 'Third of UK youth in poverty', *The Age*, 16 July 1994.

3.   Sorensen, A., 'Women's Economic Risk and the Economic Position of Single Mothers', *European Sociological Review,* 10 (2) 1994, 173.

4.   Generalisations at various levels—local, national, regional, Community—mask diversity among women, especially on dimensions of class and race.

5.   Murray notes that with the Maastricht Treaty, the European Community moved from a purely intergovernmental to a supranational or federal entity. See Murray, P., *Whither— or Wither—The European Community*, Occasional Paper No.2, Melbourne Australian Institute of International Affairs (Geelong: Deakin University School of Australian and International Studies, 1993), 4.

6.   Vogel, U. and Moran, M., 'Introduction' in Vogel, U. and Moran, M., *The Frontiers of Citizenship* (London: Macmillan, 1991), xiii.

7.   Marshall, T.H., *Social Policy in the Twentieth Century* (London: Hutchinson, 1965).

8.   Vogel, U., 'Is Citizenship Gender Specific?' in Vogel and Moran, *op. cit.*, 58.

9.   Vogel, U., 'Marriage and the Boundaries of Citizenship' in Steenbergen, B., *The Condition of Citizenship* (London: Sage, 1994), 77.

10.   Five of the 25 members of the College of Commissioners were women, and the number of women parliamentarians rose from 19% to 27% after the 1994 EP elections. At the national level, although Sweden (40%) Finland (34%) and Denmark (33%) maintained high levels of women's representation in parliament, Greece and France had less than 10%. See Commission of the European Communities, *Annual Report from the Commission,* COM (96) 650 Final, 1997, 72. See also G. Kaplan's chapter in this volume.

11.   Pateman, C., *The Disorder of Women: Democracy, Feminism and Political Theory* (Cambridge: Polity Press, 1989), 210; James, S., 'The Good Enough Citizen' in Bock, G. and James, S., *Beyond Equality and Difference: Citizenship, Feminist Politics and Female Subjectivity* (London: Routledge, 1992), 48.

12.   Marshall, *op.cit.*

13.   Turner, B., 'Outline of a Theory of Citizenship.' *Sociology* 2 (4), 1990, 191.

14.   Held, V., 'Liberty and equality from a feminist perspective' in MacCormich, N. and Bankowski, Z. (eds.), *Enlightenment, Rights and Revolution* (Aberdeen: Aberdeen University Press, 1989), 216.

15.   *Ibid.*, 217.

16.   Vogel, *loc. cit.* 1991, 65.

17.   Pateman, C., *The Sexual Contract* (Cambridge: Polity, 1988).

18.   Vogel, *loc. cit.* 1991, 66.

19.   Pateman, *op. cit.* 1988.

20.   Vogel, *loc. cit.* 1991, 75.

21.   Meehan, E., *Citizenship in the European Community* (London: Sage, 1993), 105.

22.   Vogel, *loc. cit.* 1991, 77.

23.   Lewis, J. and Astrom, G., 'Equality, Difference and State Welfare: Labour Market and Family Policies in Sweden', *Feminist Studies,* 18 (1), 81.

24.   Carlson, S., *Experience from Work on the Danish Government's Action Plan for Equal Status*, European Forum, Workshop on Company Strategies, Family Strategies, Differences in Conceptualisation, Common Ground for Mutual Understanding (Florence: European University Institute, November 1994), 5.

25.   On Australian debates on gender and caring, see Bryson, L., 'The Unpaid Contributions of Women', paper presented to the 'Women and Power and Politics' International Conference for the Centenary of Women's Suffrage, 8–11 October 1994.

26.   Lewis and Astrom, *loc. cit.*, 75.

27. Hernes, H. M., *Welfare State and Woman Power: Essays in State Feminism* (Oslo: Norwegian University Press, 1987), 125.
28. *Ibid.*, 141.
29. Commission of the European Communities, *The Position of Women in the Labour Market*, No.36 (Brussels: Directorate-General for Audiovisual Information, Communication, Culture, Women's Information Service).
30. Despite some increases in labour force participation for women and increasingly egalitarian legislation, the gap between men's and women's salaries has widened in Denmark, Italy and Portugal. See European Parliament, Directorate General for Research, Citizen's Europe Series, *1993 and the Employment of Women* (Brussels and Luxembourg: 1992), 52. The Green and White Papers on European Social Policy in 1994 and 1995 both recognise the impact of structural economic change, particularly in service industries, new technology and more flexible working patterns, where women are the majority of workers, but where there is a need to guard against poor working conditions and isolation. Commission of the European Communities, *European Social Policy: a Way Forward for the Union. A White Paper*, COM (94), 27 July 1994, 42–3.
31. Commission of the European Communities, *Annual Report from the Commission, op.cit.* 1997, 34.
32. Flynn, P., 'Mainstreaming—a radical new approach to equal opportunities for future structural funds', *Women of Europe Newsletter*, March 1988.
33. Delphy, C. and Leonard, D., *Familiar Exploitation: A New Analysis of Marriage in Contemporary Western Societies* (Cambridge: Polity Press, 1992).
34. 1994, 32.
35. These statistics mask differences within and between Member States, and are open to criticism. They are presented here to illustrate women's more peripheral involvement in the sphere that confers rights and benefits. See European Parliament, Citizen's Europe Series: *1993 and the Employment of Women*, no.1, Directorate General for Research, (Brussels and Luxembourg, 1990); and Commission of the European Communities, *Annual Report from the Commission, op.cit.* 1997, 26–8.
36. This includes both looking after preschool children and supplementing state education. Enders-Dragasser writes about the impact of the '13 year morning school system' in the former GDR, with regular hours and the demands on (mainly) mothers to supervise afternoon homework and learning. See Enders-Dragasser, U., 'Childcare, Love, Work and Exploitation', *Women's International Studies Forum*, 14 (6) 1991, 551. She discusses the school's claims on mothers' unpaid labour as a 'widely accepted norm in Germany' (*ibid.*, 553), and analyses such claims as dependent on the ideology of motherhood. See also Drew, E., 'Allocation of Caring' in Drew, E., Emerek, R. and Mahon, E., *Women, Work and the Family in Europe* (London: Routledge, 1998), 33.
37. European Parliament, *1993 and the Employment . . . , op. cit.* 1992.
38. It is important to note, however, that whilst childcare leads directly to inequalities and discrimination against mothers, provisions across Europe for childcare and perceptions of child care obligations differ considerably from country to country. There are vast differences in publicly funded child care across the community. Papadopoulos points out how two clusters of countries are evident for childcare for the 0–3 age group. Those with minimum public provision (for 2–3% of children) include Austria, the former Federal Republic of Germany, Greece, Ireland, Luxembourg, Spain and the UK—with Italy offering childcare for 6% and the Netherlands for 8%. The second cluster consists of those providing childcare for over 20% of children: Finland (21%), France (23%), Belgium (30%), Sweden (33%), Denmark and the former German Democratic Republic (both 50%). See Papadopoulos, T. N., 'Greek family policy' in Drew *et al, op. cit.*, 51.
39. Drew, *loc. cit.*, 33.

40. See European Parliament, *1993 and the Employment* . . . , *op. cit.*, 9.
41. Commission of the European Communities, *The Position of Women* . . . , *op.cit.*, 6.
42. Land, H., 'Social Policies and Women in the Labour Market', in Astrom, F. and Whiting, G. (eds.), *Feminist Theories and Practical Policies* (Bristol: School for Advanced Urban Studies, 1987), 82; Drew, E. and Emerek, R., 'Employment Flexibility and Gender' in Drew *et al.*, *op. cit.*, 90.
43. European Parliament, *1993 and the Employment* . . . , *op. cit.* 1990, 2.
44. An English study of pay and gender in private and public sectors in Britain found that the devolution of pay determination, performance appraisal and merit pay, market forces and employees' use of market-rate data impacted more on women than on men, and that such reforms have widened the gender gap in pay. It also cited ignorance, complacency and prejudice on the part of personnel specialists and trade union specialists. See the Equal Opportunities Commission, *Annual Report 1992: the Equality Challenge* (London: Equal Opportunity Commission, 1992), 11.
45. See *ibid.*, 2, and Jackson, cited by Meehan, *op.cit.* 1993, 117.
46. European Parliament, Directorate General for Research, Citizen's Europe Series, *1993 and the Employment of Women*, no.1, Brussels-Luxembourg, 1992, 13.
47. Meehan, E. and Sevenhuijsen, S. (eds.), *Equality politics and gender* (London: Sage, 1991), 136. European Parliament, *Annual Report of the Committee on Civil Liberties and Internal Affairs on Respect for Human Rights in the European Community*, Session Document DOC/EN/RR/220/220877, 1993, 34.
48. Brah, A., 'Black Women and 1992' in Ward, A., Gregory, J. and Yuval-Davis, N., *Women and Citizenship in Europe: Borders, Rights and Duties* (Oakhill: Trenthan and EFSF, 1992), 21.
49. Meehan and Sevenhuijsen, *op.cit.*, 142.
50. Meehan, *op.cit.* 1993, 116.
51. McCrudden cited in *ibid.*, 102.
52. Buckley and Anderson argue that the commitment to equal pay for men and women as set out in the Treaty of Rome, Article 119, is aimed primarily at preventing unfair advantages of competition of one country over another, rather than being a serious attempt to establish equality. See Buckley, M. and Anderson, M., 'Introduction: Problems, Policies and Politics' in Buckley, M. and Anderson, M. (eds.), *Women, Equality and Europe* (London: Macmillan, 1988), 10.
53. Vogel, *loc. cit.* 1991, 59.
54. Historically, wives' legal status has been derived from their husbands' in terms of domicile, nationality, rights over children, taxation, pension schemes and government benefits. Many such discriminatory restrictions operate indirectly, and some have only recently been repealed (such as the 1988 phasing out of British tax regulations under which a married woman was treated as the chattel of her husband—*ibid.*, 66). It was only in 1983 in Greece that legislation was repealed obliging women to do domestic work in marriage and new legislation enacted giving women access to health insurance and social security independent of husbands and male guardians, and enabling women to open their own businesses.
55. Lewis and Astrom, *loc. cit.*, 63.
56. These include reforms to liberalise divorce on grounds of separation, irretrievable breakdown or no fault (England 1969-71; Italy 1970 and 1987; Netherlands 1971; France 1975; West Germany 1976; Spain 1982; Greece 1983) and moves towards a presumption of equity in property settlements. See Kaplan, G., *Contemporary Western European Feminism* (Sydney: Allen and Unwin, 1992).
57. In the United Kingdom, new legislation in 1969-70 divorce laws concerning the grounds for divorce were re-written to be gender neutral. The Family Law (Scotland) Act 1985

specified the fair sharing of matrimonial property and the fair sharing of the economic burden of childcare. See Joshi, H. and Davies, H., *The Pension Consequences of Divorce*, Discussion Paper 550 (London: Centre for Economic Policy Research, 1991).

58. In England since 1991, the Child Support Agency can assess, collect and enforce child maintenance payments. See European Observatory of National Family Policies, *National Family Policies in EC Countries in 1991*, Vols. 1 and 2 (Directorate for Employment and Industrial Relations and Social Affairs, 1993).

59. Mossuz-Lavau, J., *Women in Europe: 10 Years* (Luxembourg: Commission of the European Communities, Directorate-General for Information, Communication, Culture, Women's Information Service, 1988), 19.

60. Eurostat, *Demographic Position of the European Union*, DGV-COM (94) 595, (Luxembourg: Office of Publications, 1994), 13.

61. Eurostat, *Yearbook '97* (Luxembourg: Office for Official Publications of the European Communities, 1997), 68.

62. Smart, C., 'Justice and Divorce: The Way Forward', *Family Law*, 12, 1982.

63. Walker, A. and Walker, C., *Britain Divided* (London: Child Poverty Action Group, 1994), 56.

64. Sorensen argues that married women's economic dependency constitutes an economic risk upon divorce, and that the estimated 30% increase in costs of supporting a family split into two households falls disproportionately on women, who have less earning capacity than men to absorb such costs. See Sorenson, A., 'Women's Economic Risk and the Economic Position of Single Mothers', *European Sociological Review*, 10 (2) 1994, 177 and 185.

65. Joshi estimated that a typical married woman in the UK with two children loses about £135,000 in wages over her working life compared to a childless woman, who in turn loses the same amount of money over her working life when compared to a man. It is hard to escape a double burden interpretation of the opportunity costs of being female and caring for dependent children. Joshi 1987, cited in Millar, J., 'Cross-National Research on Women in the European Community: the case of solo women', *Women's Studies International Forum*, 15, 1992, 79.

66. Commission of the European Communities, *Social Protection in Europe* (Luxembourg: Directorate-General Employment, Industrial Relations and Social Affairs, 1993), table 14.

67. Diduck, A. and Orton, H., 'Equality and Support for Spouses', *Modern Law Review*, 57 (5) 1994.

68. The loss of pension is greatest in the Netherlands (24% of full pension) followed by Denmark and Italy (20% to 21% of full pension) and Belgium (10%). In other countries such as Luxembourg, France and Ireland, the loss is between 2% and 6% of the full pension and in Greece, Ireland, Portugal, Spain, and the UK, voluntary contributions while not working can compensate the loss (although such payments are difficult and unlikely, being required at a time when household income is limited by women's lack of paid work—see Commission of the European Communities, *Social Protection . . .* , *op.cit.* 1993, 126).

69. *Ibid.*, 129.

70. Smart, C., 'Marriage, Divorce and Women's Economic Dependency', in Freeman M.D.A., *State, Law and the Family* (London: Tavistock, 1984); Smart, C., *The Ties That Bind: Law, Marriage and the Reproduction of Patriarchal Relations* (London: Routledge and Kegan Paul, 1984); Joshi and Davies, *op.cit.*; Pateman, C., 'Equality, Difference, Subordination: the Politics of Motherhood and Women's Citizenship' in Bock and James, *op. cit.*, 1992.

71. See Edwards, A. and Magarey, S., *Women in a Restructuring Australia: Work and Welfare*

(St. Leonards: Allen and Unwin, 1995).

72. Scheiwe, K., *Male and Female Times*, Ph.D. thesis (Florence: European University Institute, 1991), 119.
73. Joshi and Davies, *op.cit.*, 10.
74. Scheiwe, *op.cit.*, 134.
75. Commission of the European Communities, *Social Protection . . .* , *op.cit.*, 123–9.
76. Millar, J., 'Cross-national Research on Women in the European Community: The Case of Solo Women', *Women's Studies International Forum*, 15, 1992, 77.
77. Eeekelaar J. M., 'Equality and the Purpose of Maintenance', *Journal of Legal Studies*, 15 (2) 1988.
78. Diduck and Orton, *loc. cit.*, 681.
79. Mahoney, K. E., 'Gender Bias in Judicial Decisions', Lecture at the Supreme Court of Western Australia, Perth, 1992, unpublished paper, 9.
80. *Ibid.*
81. *Ibid.*
82. Lodge, J., 'Social Europe: Fostering a Peoples' Europe?' in Lodge J. (ed.), *The European Community and the Challenge of the Future* (London: Pinter, 1989); Lo Faro, A., 'EC Social Policy and 1993: The Dark Side of European Integration', *Comparative Law Journal*, 14 (1) 1992, 1-32.
83. Communique of the European Council, Madrid, June 1989, 3 cited in Hughes, J., *The Social Charter and the Single European Market*, (London: European Labor Forum, 1991).
84. Commission of the European Communities, *European Social Policy, op. cit.* 1994.
85. *Ibid.*, 11.
86. European Parliament, *Interim Report of the Committee on Institutional Affairs on Union Citizenship*, Rapporteur Mrs. Rosaria Bindi, 23 May 1991, DOC EN/RR/110451, 5.
87. Commission of the European Communities, *European Social Policy, op. cit.* 1994, 5.
88. *Ibid.*
89. Meehan, *op. cit.* 1993, 9.
90. *Ibid.*, 11.
91. European Parliament, *Interim Report of the Committee on Institutional Affairs on Union Citizenship, op.cit.*, 9.
92. *Ibid.*, 9.
93. Freixes Sanjuán, T., 'Women in the New European Society', *Women of Europe Newsletter*, 1998, 3.
94. Murray, *op. cit.*, 15.
95. Meehan, *op. cit.* 1993; Curtin, D., 'Directives: The Effectiveness of Judicial Protection of Individual Rights' in Snyder, F. (ed.), *European Community Law Vol. 1*, (Aldershot: Dartmouth, 1992), 395-426.
96. Meehan, E., 'European citizenship and Social Policies' in Vogel and Moran, *op. cit.*, 125.
97. In England, in the case of Mrs. Thomas and Other v. Secretary of State for Social Security, the woman's treatment was declared unlawful as a contravention of Directive 79/7/EEC (Equal Opportunity Commission, *Annual Report 1992, op. cit.*, 9). In another English case, Miss Marshall established that dismissal because of age contravened sex discrimination Provisions under Article 5 of Directive 76/207 (*European Law Review*, Editorial, 18 (5) 1993).
98. The Frankovich ruling reinforced states' liability in damages to ensure that individuals do not suffer unduly through the non-compliance of Member States. See Coppel, J., 'Individual Enforcement of Community Law: the future of the Frankovich Remedy', *EUI Working Paper*, No.93/6 (Florence: European University Institute, 1993).
99. Meehan, *op.cit.* 1993, 81.
100. *Ibid.*, 111.

101. Curtin, *loc. cit.*, 396.
102. *European Law Review*, Editorial, 18 (5) 1993, 366.
103. European Parliament, Session Document, *Report drawn on behalf of the Committee on Legal affairs and Citizen's Rights,* Luxembourg, COM (89) 411 final—Doc. C 3-133/89, 1990, 6.
104. European Parliament, Session Document, *Annual Report of the Committee on Civil Liberties and Internal Affairs on Respect for Human Rights in the European Community*, DOC/EN/RR/220/220877, 1993, 31, 33.
105. Wistrich, E., *After 1992: The United States of Europe* (London: Routledge, 1989), 81.
106. Meehan, *loc. cit.*, 125.
107. Commission of the European Communities, *Equal Opportunities for Women and Men: The Third Medium-term Community Action Program 1991-1995*, No. 34 (Brussels: Directorate General for Audiovisual, Information, Communication, Culture, Women's Information Service, 1992).
108. See Mackinnon, C., 'Reflections on Sex Equality in Law', *Yale Law Journal*, 14 (1) 1991, 1–32.
109. An assessment of claims under the Canadian Charter of Rights found that 35 out of the 44 claims made under the equality guarantee were made by or on behalf of men and only 66 out of 591 cases were made by persons 'disadvantaged'. Bacchi, C. and Marquis, V., 'Women and the Republic: "Rights" and Wrongs', *Australian Feminist Studies*, 19, 1994, 99.
110. In a Canadian challenge in 1989 which replaced the similarly situated test in preference to discrimination according to disadvantage, Mahoney comments that under the latter, judges would need to view women in their real-world context in order 'to confront the reality that the systematic abuse and deprivation of power women experience is because of their place in the sexual hierarchy' in Mahoney, *loc. cit.*, 123. Commenting similarly on Canada, More refers to the Supreme Court of Canada's emphasis on disproportionate impact, a concept recognised by the ECJ since 1981 and reflected in a line of judgements concerning indirect discrimination again women in pay, pension rights, severance pay and eligibility for seniority pay between full-time and part-time workers. See More, G.C., 'Equal Treatment of the Sexes in European Community Law: what does "equal" mean?' *Feminist Legal Studies*, 1 (1) 1993, 69.
111. Mahoney, *loc. cit.*
112. European Parliament, *Annual Report of the Committee on Civil Liberties* . . . , *op. cit.*, 22.
113. *Ibid.*, 23.
114. *Ibid.*, 5–6.
115. Charlesworth, H., 'Women and International Law', *Australian Feminist Studies*, 19, 1992, 115-28.
116. Under mainstreaming, Structural Funds applications will need to demonstrate how they intend to promote equality between men and women. Flynn, *loc. cit.*, 7.
117. Pateman, *loc. cit.*
118. Meehan, *op.cit.* 1993, 107.

7 Exclusion and Inclusion in Central and Eastern Europe

LESLIE HOLMES

While some have been claiming that Western Europe is moving towards[1] or is already in a postnationalist era,[2] for many the salient negative feature of post-communism in Central and East Europe (hereafter CEE)[3] is nationalism and ethnic politics, which in some cases has become highly aggressive (e.g. racism-related violence). Although there are many other negative social and political aspects of post-communism—the position of women, for instance, has deteriorated in several countries[4]—the nationalism/racism issue is potentially the most serious; clearly, it has already *actually* been the most dangerous in parts of the former Yugoslavia and former Soviet Union (hereafter FSU). In this chapter, the primary focus is on the various manifestations of nationalism and ethnic politics in CEE. One major objective is to explore the variety of its forms in post-communist Europe (here meaning those countries of Europe that were formerly under communist control[5]), as part of an examination of exclusionary and inclusionary phenomena in the region. There will also be a very brief consideration of less obvious forms of exclusion and inclusion.

Marx and Lenin are just two of a number of analysts who have argued that nationalism can in some cases be a desirable, positive phenomenon.[6] Certainly, many twentieth-century Marxists would accept that counter-hegemonic nationalism that seeks to liberate one group from oppression by, or even the imperialism of, another is often justifiable (though Marx himself condemned this particular form in many cases[7]). From this perspective, the rejection of external domination (by the USSR in the case of most of Eastern Europe; by Russia in the case of most of the non-Russian republics of the USSR; by Serbia in the case of most of the republics of the SFRY) that was a major feature of the 1989–91 revolutions can be interpreted as both an understandable and justifiable reason for nationalism in the late-communist and early post-communist eras. In a 1997 book,[8] I proposed a 14-point descriptive model of early post-communism, the *first* component of which is the assertion of sovereignty and the rise of nationalism; this relates directly to the rejection of domination.

One of the potential problems of justifying and accepting what can be identified as a first type of exclusion, foreign domination, is that it almost necessarily justifies the notions of both 'otherness' (including, in its extreme form, the identification of enemies) and community, the 'them' and 'us' syndrome. This coupled pair, otherness and community, is invariably linked with notions of exclusion and inclusion, and can thus be seen as a source of divisiveness in today's Europe. In order to understand this point, it is useful to examine the logic of nationalism in post-communist Europe.

As just argued, an important dimension of the 1989–91 revolutions was the rejection of what was perceived to be foreign domination. There were many reasons for this perception. In the *economic* sphere, the Council for Mutual Economic Assistance (CMEA) had since the early-1960s made various attempts to impose a division of labour on the Soviet bloc. Moreover, since 1975 (under the Bucharest formula), the previous trading regime—which had in general been advantageous to the East European states, disadvantageous to the USSR—had been replaced by one in which prices for raw materials were tagged to world prices, while prices for manufactured goods were not in any direct sense. This led to a deterioration in the trading position of many East European countries, and an improvement in the USSR's. Within Yugoslavia, the wealthier republics such as Slovenia and Croatia had since at least the early-1970s complained on various occasions that they were being compelled by a Serb-dominated system to subsidise a rise in living-standards for those inhabiting the poorer parts of the federation, notably Macedonia and Kosovo.

The perception of domination was at least as marked in the *military* sphere. Although Romania and Bulgaria did not have Soviet troops stationed in them on a long-term basis—unlike Czechoslovakia, the GDR, Hungary and Poland—both they and their communist neighbours to the north-west were subject to pressure from the Warsaw Treaty Organisation (WTO). Even Romania, which had enjoyed a reputation since the early-1960s as a 'maverick' within the Soviet camp, fell into line vis-à-vis the WTO in 1969, following the invasion of Czechoslovakia in August 1968; Nicolae Ceauşescu came to appreciate that what had occurred in Prague *could* happen in Bucharest.

Political domination of the East European states was arguably more subtle than the economic and military forms, yet was no less significant. For instance, if an East European leader appeared to be obstructing Soviet interests, he (*sic*) might well be removed, even if he had long had a reputation for being a loyal communist; Walter Ulbricht (who was removed as East German leader in May 1971) is a prime example.

A nagging problem faced by some East European communist leaderships over the decades was the public's perception that they were being too sycophantic towards Moscow. Even the usually very stable and peaceful Bulgaria experienced an attempted coup d'état in 1965, initiated by a group of senior (mostly military) officials who considered that Todor Zhivkov was being too obsequious towards the Soviets at the expense of Bulgarian interests. This was an example of double ignominy; citizens were indignant not merely about foreign domination, but also about the sycophancy and complicity of their own elites vis-à-vis the hegemonists.

Some of the official nationalism of post-communist governments, like so much else in post-communism, is a direct reaction to the hypocrisy of the communist power system. During the communist era, there was much talk of proletarian or socialist internationalism. But this was uttered in the same breath as governments proclaimed their own versions of 'socialism in one country' and, in the case of the USSR, the basically imperialistic tenets of Stalinism or the Brezhnev Doctrine (from 1968 until well into the Gorbachev era).[9] Many post-communist politicians prefer to be open and unambiguous about their nationalism.

All this helps to explain not only the nationalism aspect of the 1989–91 revolutions, but also the nationalism of post-communist governments. In their endeavours to distance themselves from their communist predecessors, many post-communist politicians have emphasised their patriotism; Vladimir Mečiar in Slovakia is a good example. On one level, this can be seen as part of official nationalism—a rejuvenated form of *nation-state building* in countries that in several cases were, as of 1989, still relatively new. Thus Poland had become a sovereign state again only in 1918, at much the same time as both Czechoslovakia and Yugoslavia came into existence. The newest state in communist Europe was the GDR, which in a sense celebrated its 40th birthday in October 1989 by ousting Erich Honecker. And, of course, the disintegration *since* 1989 of Czecho-Slovakia,[10] Yugoslavia and the USSR has meant that there are many far newer states (albeit in some cases resurrected ones), all of which are either finding or reasserting a national identity. In fact, of the 27 European and FSU sovereign states usually identified as 'post-communist', no fewer than 22 have come into existence or been reconstituted since 1991.

But on another level, the official nationalism of post-communist governments is symptomatic of the highly problematic nature of post-communism itself. While a comprehensive elaboration of these problems is beyond the scope of this chapter, some consideration is vital here if nationalism, and hence a major aspect of the inclusion/exclusion dimension of contemporary CEE, is to be understood. For the purposes of this paper, four problems—some with numerous ramifications—will be examined.

First, the rejection of a totalising and teleological ideology has left what virtually amounts to an ideological vacuum in the post-communist world. Although many politicians and citizens advocated democracy and a market economy as communist power was overthrown, few had a firm grasp of what these concepts meant in practice (for instance, in terms of all the insecurities that a pure form of the latter implies), let alone of how they could be achieved. There was no solid tradition or understanding of liberalism, social democracy or conservatism. More fundamentally, the very notion of political ideology was anathema to many, for whom grand theories of any kind had been completely discredited for the foreseeable future.

One implication of this ideological deficit is that there is less of the social adhesive to bind a community than there might otherwise be. Marxism-Leninism claimed to provide not merely a *telos*, but also an ethical framework for society. Hence, its discrediting has left a serious moral vacuum, which is hardly conducive to the development of greater tolerance in society. Finally, the vacuum has left many with a personal as well as collective identity crisis. The turn to ethnicity and nationalism—and to the notion of being included in a defined and recognisable community at the same time as one distinguishes that group from 'others'—in so much of the post-communist world must be understood partly in terms of the collapse of long-established parameters. It does appear that recent forms of nationalism, or what Michael Walzer has called 'the new tribalism',[11] can provide a sense of stability and continuity in periods of high levels of instability, insecurity and anxiety.[12]

Second, the widespread absence of a deep understanding and direct experience of systems other than a communist one also meant that there was little tradition of compromise and consensus-seeking in the political sphere. If the popular cynicism about political institutions—yet another legacy of communist power—is added to this, it becomes obvious why the creation of a stable, democratic political culture in the post-communist world will be a prolonged and difficult task.

A third problem is the economic condition of post-communist countries. In the early-1990s, following their double-rejective revolutions, all of the post-communist states experienced serious economic crises, with substantial declines in GDP and real living standards; most also suffered from high unemployment and severe inflation. Given that living standards were by West European standards unimpressive to start with, the potential social implications of these crises begin to become obvious. By 1993, only Poland, Romania and Slovenia (and possibly Albania, although there are doubts about the reliability of some of its official data[13]) had moved into positive economic growth for the first time since the anti-communist revolutions. Although the situation had improved by 1996, with all countries except parts of the former Yugoslavia and FSU having experienced positive growth, this was in every case from such a low base that it will be many years yet before the post-communist countries look 'comfortable' by Western standards. Indeed, as of 1996, Poland was apparently the only post-communist state to have surpassed the best output figures of the communist period.[14]

There are many reasons for this sorry economic situation. A major one is the communist legacy: this includes excessive skewing, here referring to the sectoral imbalance in the economy that resulted from decades of privileging the producer over the consumer; relatively low levels of investment in several countries over a prolonged period, resulting in outdated and inefficient plant; the problems associated with the attempts to manage increasingly complex economies through a central planning agency; the numerous disincentives to initiative; etc.

A second was the timing of the 1989–91 revolutions. It was in one sense unfortunate that so many countries removed the communist power system over such a short period, since even the affluent West could not afford to bail them all out simultaneously to the requisite extent. The situation was further exacerbated once the West itself began to enter a recession at the end of the 1980s and beginning of the 1990s. One indication of the enormity of the required bail-out is provided by the data on West German aid of all kinds to the former German Democratic Republic (GDR). In the single year 1992, the German government provided more funds in real terms (i.e. allowing for inflation, etc.) to the 'five new Länder' than the USA poured into *all* the European recipient countries of Marshall Aid in the *five*-year period 1947-1952.[15] If it is borne in mind that the GDR had by many criteria the most developed economy in Eastern Europe, the magnitude of the scale of assistance required throughout the post-communist world comes into focus. If the EC's preoccupation with its own future in 1992 (i.e. Maastricht, the imminent accession of three or four new Member States, etc.), and the priority the West placed on assisting Russia (largely for legitimate strategic reasons) are added to this, it becomes obvious why the CEE states were unlucky in terms of the international context in which their anti-communist revolutions occurred.

The fourth problem identified here is directly related to the second and third factors. There is a tragic irony in the fact that what began as an abstract desire for 'democracy' was soon either coexisting with or being replaced by growing cynicism about not only political institutions but also 'the market'.[16] Indeed, the severity of the economic and social problems of early post-communism suggest the need for strong leadership and strong political institutions.[17] In the absence of consensus on institutions and their optimal relationships, both the likelihood of, and perceived need for, a charismatic strong *individual* leader, who could develop dictatorial qualities, increases. All of this relates to nationalism, ethnic politics, exclusion and inclusion, since these are factors often exploited by charismatic leaders in troubled times.

To no small extent, the kinds of problems identified above are all linked to what is arguably the most fundamental problem of early post-communism, legitimation. Given that I have explored this issue at length elsewhere,[18] and that to do so properly here would require more space than is available, suffice it to say that since early post-communism cannot yet legitimate itself on the basis of performance (eudaemonism), legal-rationality, or in most cases even goal-rationality (teleologism), its next best hope is official nationalism. Many aspects of exclusion and inclusion in contemporary CEE can be partly explained in terms of this.

Before developing this argument, it is worth identifying some of the major forms of exclusion in post-communist Europe, following which is a brief section on inclusion.

Examples of Exclusion

Although the distinction between the state and society is even more tenuous in today's CEE than elsewhere,[19] it is worth drawing a distinction for analytical and heuristic purposes between official (state-sanctioned) and unofficial (citizen-based) forms of exclusion.

One of the most widely-reported dimensions of official exclusion is the narrow approach adopted by some post-communist governments towards citizenship. The Estonian, notably, introduced legislation in November 1991, February and April 1992 that defined citizenship in relatively exclusive terms and in practice appeared to sanction the disenfranchisement of ethnic minorities. This was widely perceived as being directed primarily against Russians living in Estonia.[20] Despite protests from the Russian and other governments, this policy was taken even further in June 1993, when the Estonian parliament passed legislation requiring the country's half-million 'foreigners' (i.e. non-Estonian former Soviet citizens still resident in the country) to submit a formal application for a residence-permit or face deportation. The Estonian president, Lennart Meri, deferred signing the legislation into force until he had had an opportunity to consult with international bodies. He finally signed a revised version of the legislation in July 1993, which, unlike the original version, did not require regular re-application for residency permits or that residents apply for citizenship. Nevertheless, permanent residents would have voting rights only in local elections, not national ones.[21]

This was not the end of the story. Although it was symbolically significant that the post-communist Estonian parliament admitted its first ethnic Russian in March 1994, Moscow continued to protest about the treatment of Russians in Estonia; in May 1994, Russian defence minister Pavel Grachev even went as far as to accuse the Estonian authorities of conducting a policy of apartheid. Not everyone was as critical; while human rights organisations and many of the media in the West were condemning Estonian policy, the High Commissioner for National Minorities attached to the Conference on Security and Cooperation in Europe, Max van der Stoel, explicitly declared in September 1994 that the Estonian authorities had *not* violated residents' human rights, despite the claims of both the Russians and these Western critics. It should also be noted that the Estonian authorities permitted the establishment of two political parties in October 1994 that were explicitly intended to attract the Russian constituency.

However, the Estonian authorities continued to pursue contradictory policies. In January 1995, the parliament adopted a new citizenship law, according to which it was to become more difficult for residents to become citizens; instead of the previous two years (plus one year waiting period) minimum, those seeking naturalisation would in future need to have resided in Estonia at least five years (and then wait a further year). It also adopted a language law that sought to raise and formalise the requirements of Estonian language competency among public servants. Predictably, the Russian authorities protested. In an apparent attempt to placate Moscow, President Meri then (in February) proposed dropping Estonia's territorial claims against Russia. Despite opposition from many Estonians, the Tallinn government announced in November 1995 that it would recognise the existing boundaries between Russia and Estonia on a *de facto* basis; although the Russians would have preferred a *de jure* recognition, this move reduced the level of tension between Moscow and Tallinn. Yet tensions within the Estonian government continued to simmer during 1996. In August, the Estonian Minister without Portfolio responsible for European affairs resigned on the grounds that his country was being too liberal in its treatment of Russians and in its relations with Russia.[22] Prime Minister Vahi then announced that the existing regulations on visas between Russia and Estonia—which constituted one of the reasons for the minister's resignation—would be tightened. In a sense, they were. Thus, the Estonian authorities announced in May 1997 that passports issued by the former USSR would no longer be recognised, which invalidated the travel documents of many people living in Estonia who were not Estonian citizens. One implication of this was that such people would either have to apply for non-citizens' passports or else formally apply for citizenship of another state; either way, they would be made to feel even more like outsiders within Estonia.

But, as already hinted at, non-Estonians within Estonia have had a leading politician to champion their cause, at least some of the time. That person is President Meri, who has generally been a liberal in terms of citizenship laws. It was thus encouraging that Meri was re-elected Estonian president in September 1996, beating the more nationalistic and hard-line Arnold Ruutel. Indeed, one analyst has argued that Estonia was in a number of ways treating the Russian minority (just under 30% of the population) better during 1996, and that even a Russian fact-finding mission that visited Estonia in December 1996 acknowledged this.[23] However, Meri has had to continue his struggle with the more exclusionary members of the Estonian parliament. At the time of writing, the most recent major example of this was that Meri refused to sign the amended version of the 1995 language law that was agreed by parliament in November 1997, and which would have considerably increased the restrictions on officials, especially elected deputies, whose mother tongue was not Estonian. Meri referred the issue to the Constitutional Review Chamber of the National Court, which in February 1998 ruled that the new version of the language law was unconstitutional. It remains to be seen what the next step will be in the battle between the more liberal president and the more exclusionary parliament. Overall, while the situation as of early 1998 had clearly improved since the early-1990s, there were still tensions between the Estonian authorities and Russians living in Estonia (particularly former members of the Russian military).

Given both the events in and since 1940 (when the USSR forcibly incorporated Estonia), and the substantial numbers of Russians still living in Estonia, the reasons for the somewhat exclusionary—though generally improving—Estonian policy on citizenship are not entirely surprising. Nor is it unusual for a multi-ethnic country to insist on the predominance of the language of the largest ethnic group, largely for practical reasons. Yet the fact is that many of the Russian residents were born in Estonia, with many being third or even fourth generation. Moreover, many are older people who were not required to study Estonian to any advanced level, if at all, in the past, and many of whom would experience problems at this stage of their lives in achieving a reasonably high level of competency in a relatively difficult language. Any desire among Estonians for retribution for Soviet domination and oppression in the past should surely be sought against the Russian *state* rather than ordinary Russian people. This could be in the form of claims for damages, demands for preferential trading terms, etc. That Russians and others born in Estonia are distinguished from ethnic Estonians can be seen as a form of official racism. While Estonian citizenship laws are still not as exclusionary as German, for instance, since they are not ultimately based on *jus sanguinis*, nor are they as open as in many countries of the region. Although, as Stephen Castles argues elsewhere in this volume, citizenship based on *jus soli* is not without problems either, a conception of citizenship that granted people full rights on the basis of either ancestry *or* place of birth would represent a step forward, in that it could not then be interpreted as racist.[24]

The above all said, it must be acknowledged that none of the post-communist countries had had much experience with the liberal, individual-oriented conception of citizenship and civil rights that allegedly forms the basis of policy on citizenship in most Western countries.[25] For T. H. Marshall, full citizenship rights include protection by the state in the form of welfare provisions.[26] One form of official exclusion in the post-communist world that relates to this is a differential approach to state-provided welfare benefits on the basis of ethnicity. Once again, Estonia provides a good example of this issue. In the June 1993 legislation on aliens passed by parliament, it was unclear that non-Estonian residents would be eligible for all social security benefits. Only following international pressure (including from the Council of Europe) was this guaranteed, in the revised version of the legislation signed by President Meri in July.[27] Another example of this welfare-related form of exclusion is Slovak policy towards Romanies. It is alleged that Slovak prime minister Mečiar suggested publicly in early September 1993 that family welfare payments to large Romany families be reduced.[28]

Related to the question of rights other than voting and welfare ones, mention should be made of the differential approach towards private ownership adopted by some post-communist governments—what might be called citizens' economic and property rights. In March 1993, the Czech government sought to prevent Slovaks from participating in the privatisation process in Czechia, even where they had purchased privatisation vouchers *before* the dissolution of Czecho-Slovakia at the end of 1992. This ban was short-lived, however, being lifted in May 1993. A more enduring tension is that between the Czech government and both Jews and Germans who have sought restitution of property they or their ancestors owned in the pre-communist era.[29]

A third form of exclusion is a desire to separate a given territory that is generally perceived to be the home of one or more ethnic groups from a larger territory in which those ethnic groups have co-existed with others in recent times. It is clear in the Czecho-Slovak case that the Czech and Slovak governments initiated and implemented the dissolution of Czecho-Slovakia in the face of widespread opposition from both Czechs and Slovaks.[30] The dissolution of the USSR was similarly opposed by many Soviet citizens, whose views were overridden by various nationalist elites. Official separatism/secessionism has also been a salient feature of politics in former Yugoslavia,[31] although, with the exception of Serbia and Montenegro, it is much less clear that this break-up occurred against the wishes of a majority of citizens in the various republics.

An interesting form of 'exclusion', largely because it highlights the problems of equating nationalism with all forms of ethnically-based inclusion and exclusion, is where the dominant ethnic group in one political unit might *a priori* be expected to seek integration with members of what is widely perceived to be the same ethnic group in another political unit, but does not do so. This constitutes a case of anticipated irredentism and inclusionary policy not materialising.[32] Thus, there is little evidence that either the authorities or most of the citizens within Hungary are actively seeking to link up with their co-ethnics in Vojvodina, Transylvania, Ukraine or Slovakia. The Hungarian government does protest against the treatment of the Hungarian minorities in other countries.[33] But this is often as a result of pressure from Hungarians outside of Hungary, and is in any case quite different from making demands for unification. Indeed, current official policy states that Hungary has no territorial/border disputes with its neighbours, even though its 'three pillar' approach to foreign policy does on occasion bring it into conflict with neighbours in which there are Hungarian minorities.[34] Similarly, the Moldovans have confounded some Western predictions of a push to unify Moldova and Romania. The Moldovan president until December 1996, Mircea Snegur, used to emphasise his opposition to proposals for such a merger (even though he attempted to have the official name of the country's language changed from Moldovan to Romanian), while his successor, Petru Lucinschi, has indicated that he is more interested in a closer relationship with Russia than with Romania. Finally, the reluctance of the Russian government during the early 1990s to lend too much support to the demands of some Crimean Russians that their region (formally an Autonomous Republic) be permitted to transfer from Ukraine to Russia was yet another example of exclusion of co-ethnics.[35] Here, then, are examples of nations that either seek to exclude fellow-ethnics, or at least are not enthusiastic to include them.

A fourth form of official exclusion is anti-immigration policies. In the case of most post-communist states, the problem has been less one of keeping potential migrants out than of keeping citizens and residents in; many of the latter have sought better lives in Western Europe, for instance. Since the former GDR is now part of Germany, however, it follows that it is party to the marked clampdown on asylum-seeking and other forms of migration that became effective 1 July 1993. This clampdown has had implications for some of the other CEE states. Thus, Poland, Hungary and Czechia have become more attractive to Croats, Romanians, Russians, etc. than they previously were, as access to Germany and the EU more generally has become increasingly difficult. This has resulted in tougher entry laws and/or immigration policies in some cases. By way of a very early example, it is claimed that Hungary rejected some 900,000 entry applications in the 12-month period October 1991–October 1992.[36] Most of those refused entry were from Romania and the FSU. This 'policy' was based largely on police interpretations of who should and should not be admitted, since Hungary had no clear legislation at that time on entry requirements.

Much of this official exclusion is based on the perceived costs of migrants, and thus relates to the economic problems of early post-communism. Where there is high unemployment (or merely the potential for it, as in Czechia), a shortage of accommodation—exacerbated by uncertainties about property ownership—and an underfunded social welfare system, it is partly understandable that many governments tighten up on immigration; this phenomenon is familiar enough to Australians and many other Westerners. Where this practice deserves greater criticism is where the exclusionary policies appear to be targetted at some ethnic groups more than others, which begins to look like official racism. Like so many ethical questions of this nature, however, the situation is not always as clear-cut as it might initially appear to be. Thus, Czechia introduced legislation effective July 1993 that required citizens of the most troubled parts of the post-communist world (viz. Armenia, Azerbaijan, Bosnia-Hercegovina, Georgia, Tajikistan and Yugoslavia) to obtain visas before attempting to enter the country. Clearly, this constitutes an unequal policy, in that some groups would find it more difficult to enter Czechia than others. On the other hand, the reason those groups were singled out was not clearly based on racism. Rather, and fairly obviously, it was based on the assumption that there was *a priori* a relatively greater probability that citizens of those war-torn areas would apply not only to enter but also to settle in Czechia than were citizens from elsewhere.

Fifth, there have been attempts to suppress the languages of ethnic minorities. Thus in 1991, Serbia passed a law that not only made Serbian the sole official language in Vojvodina but also expressly forbade the use of Hungarian in business. In March 1992, the Latvians passed legislation that all but removed Russian from the entire educational system; hitherto, education had often been offered in both Latvian and Russian. At an early stage of the Estonian citizenship debate, it appeared as if many residents would never be eligible to apply for citizenship unless they had a relatively good command of the Estonian language.[37] And in November 1995, the Slovak parliament passed a law that restricted the use in public of languages other than Slovak—despite the fact that the Slovak premier, Mečiar, had signed a friendship treaty with Hungary in March that, *inter alia*, committed his country to recognise that it had a responsibility to protect and even foster the language identity of minorities. Slovak president Michal Kovač only signed this law on the understanding that a bill on minority languages be submitted in the near future, which both prime minister Mečiar and chair of the parliament Ivan Gašparovič promised would happen. The Slovak parliament did eventually ratify the friendship treaty with Hungary in March 1996, and thus, in principle, committed itself to the same responsibilities for protecting and fostering minority languages as Mečiar had done a year before. Yet the promised bill on minority languages had still not even been drafted one year after the November 1995 legislation, and the Slovak Constitutional Court was deliberating on whether or not the 1995 law was compatible with Article 34 of the Slovak Constitution.[38] Eventually, in September 1997, the Constitutional Court ruled that it was unconstitutional to require all Slovak citizens to use exclusively the Slovak language when interacting with official agencies, but upheld several other aspects of the controversial law. It did this largely on the grounds that most of the challenges against these were made and submitted in technically incorrect ways. Many believed that this was a political move by the Court, however, rather than a purely legalistic judgement.

No discussion of the exclusionary dimension of language policy in CEE would be complete without reference to the redesignation of what was once seen as one language—albeit written in two alphabets—as *three*; what used to be called Serbo-Croat has now been reclassified as Serbian, Croatian and Bosnian.

Finally, as the sixth form, reference must be made to what is the most ethically-reprehensible form of official exclusionary policy in contemporary eastern Europe, ethnic cleansing. This has been defined as -

> . . . the expulsion of an 'undesirable' population from a given territory due to religious or ethnic discrimination, political, strategic or ideological considerations, or a combination of these.[39]

It is by no means a new phenomenon, having been traced back to the Assyrians in the eighth century BC.[40] During the twentieth century, both fascist and communist dictators such as Hitler and Stalin have engaged in it. But it appears particularly unacceptable in late twentieth century Europe— an area that, as the starting arena for two world wars, should have learnt better than anywhere else the lessons of history vis-à-vis aggressive nationalism and extreme levels of exclusion. While the world's media have justifiably concentrated during the 1990s on ethnic cleansing in Bosnia-Herzegovina, it should not be overlooked that serious allegations have also been made about other post-communist states, including Georgia.[41] As a final and bitterly ironic twist, Christopher Hann has argued that examples of ethnic cleansing earlier this century (he focuses on the case of Eastern Poland in the 1940s) indicate that such actions do not achieve their perpetrators' evil objectives anyway.[42]

Citizen-based forms of exclusion are also numerous. In addition to popular support for official policies, there are forms of nationalism and ethnic politics among the citizenry that assume a force of their own. Overt racism, of a kind rarely found being explicitly pursued by states, is rampant throughout the formerly communist world, for instance.[43] Romanies are a particularly popular target in many countries of the region.[44] Their treatment is a complex form of exclusion, in that it demonstrates that two or more ethnic groups who are citizens of a given state can join forces to exclude—treat as 'outsiders'—a third group that is seeking equal status and treatment in that state, and which might have been living there long-term, but which these others believe does not deserve full rights. In other words, this constitutes an example of exclusion that combines restrictive notions of what is sometimes, if not unproblematically, called civic nationalism with more blatantly ethnic nationalism.

Separatism by citizen groups, as distinct from the state, can also be found in the post-communist world. Although this might well be led by local elites, including people who are or were politicians, and may eventually result in a new internationally recognised state, this is still conceptually distinct from current official state policy. Well-known examples in the post-communist world include the Abkhaz in Georgia and the Chechens in Russia. Autonomist unofficial nationalism can also be found in post-communist Europe; examples include the various Moravian and Silesian nationalists who have advocated a federal arrangement for the Czech Republic, and those Hungarians in Vojvodina and Albanians in Kosovo who have demanded greater autonomy within Serbia/ new Yugoslavia. It is also possible that some Hungarians in Slovakia will make overtly autonomist demands in the future.[45]

Having considered examples of various forms of exclusion in the post-communist world that are based on ethnicity, nations and states, it is important to note that there are other significant forms of exclusion. One that was briefly alluded to earlier is gender-based exclusion. While this falls outside the scope of the present chapter, it is worth noting the comparative data on female representation in CEE presented by Einhorn,[46] which reveal the extent to which women appear to be being squeezed out of—or, at least, not positively encouraged into (included in)—the formal political institutions and processes. Another basis of exclusion is ideological. Thus many communist parties have been banned (e.g. in Russia in late-1991; in Albania in 1992; in Latvia in 1993).[47]

Examples of Inclusion

Like exclusion, inclusion assumes several forms in contemporary CEE, and only the outlines can be sketched in an analysis of this scale.

In terms of inclusion by governments, moves towards cooperation and integration are a useful starting point. Currently, probably the best-known and most developed example of post-communist economic cooperation is CEFTA (the Central European Free Trade Agreement), established in December 1992 on the basis of the Visegrad Four (Czechia, Hungary, Poland and Slovakia);[48] Slovenia and Romania subsequently also joined, in January 1996 and July 1997 respectively. Many other examples include countries that were not under communist rule (e.g. the Council of Baltic States, now incorporating eleven states in the Baltic region, including Poland and the post-communist

Baltic states, but also Germany and Denmark).[49] Perhaps the most difficult example of all to interpret is the Commonwealth of Independent States (CIS). Persuasive arguments can be made to the effect both that this organisation represents Russian neo-imperialism and that the establishment and continued existence of this huge unit provides reason for *guarded* optimism about the possibilities for cooperation, at a time when so much of what is happening in the post-communist world highlights the difficulties of this.

One problematical aspect of integrationist moves concerns official attitudes towards the West. In their endeavours to be accepted as Europeans and to improve their economic prospects, both of which relate to legitimation, several post-communist governments have sought membership of Western organisations (see below). This attempt to be included, however, can be perceived by some citizens and politicians as new forms of traditional regime sycophancy towards powerful foreign states, which is usually delegitimising. It can encourage a rise in citizen patriotism, which can in turn lead to other forms of both official and unofficial exclusionary nationalism. Once again, the complex relationship between inclusion and exclusion comes sharply into focus.

Second, most new citizenship laws in the post-communist world are less exclusionary or less clearly formulated than the Estonian and Latvian; it is precisely because of the exceptionality of these two Baltic states' approaches that their laws have attracted so much attention in the West. Various analysts have noted the far more inclusive citizenship policies not only of big countries like Russia and Ukraine, but also of the third post-communist Baltic state, Lithuania, for instance.[50] Interestingly, one of the reasons for tensions during the 1990s between Moldova and Romania is precisely that Moldova has moved away from the notion of being a second Romanian state and towards the idea of multi-ethnicity.[51] Poland, too, has recently demonstrated a more inclusive approach towards one group in particular. In early-1998, President Kwásniewski announced that Jews who had been forced by the anti-Semitic communist regime of the time to leave Poland in 1968 would be permitted not only to return to Poland and have their full citizenship rights reinstated, but also to retain the citizenship of the country they were leaving. This acceptance by the Polish authorities of dual citizenship is exceptional, and can be interpreted as an encouragement to Jews outside Poland to return to their former homeland and experience it, without having to risk the possibility of not being able to return to their recent home state with full citizenship rights.

Likewise, access to social welfare systems in most countries is not as exclusionary as those in Estonia appeared at one stage likely to be (the cynic will point out that most of these systems are so badly underfunded that it is not clear that access to them is much of an advantage!).[52]

Fourth, there are irredentist moves in some parts of the post-communist world that contrast sharply with the apparent lack of interest among Hungarians in Hungary to link up with their fellow-ethnics. In addition to the interest of *some* Hungarians outside Hungary to leave Slovakia and other countries, and of some Crimean Russians to join Russia, there are several cases of aggressive irredentism in which a given ethnic group has made territorial claims largely on the basis of wanting to link up with fellow-ethnics living in those territories. Among the best-known examples to have surfaced in the post-communist world are the South Ossetians in Georgia (with North Ossetians in Russia); Armenians in Nagorno-Karabakh/Azerbaijan (with Armenians in Armenia); Serbs and Croats with fellow-ethnics in Bosnia-Herzegovina. The irony of making this observation is that it reveals that inclusionary ambitions can in some circumstances be as dangerous and morally questionable as exclusionary stances. Considered from a different perspective, it reveals that irredentism can be as exclusionary, even if sub-consciously, as inclusionary.

In terms of accepting diverse political orientations, post-communism is far more inclusionary than was its predecessor. While the ideological position of many political parties is blurred, for reasons that include the rejection of teleologism referred to above, there is a range of competing viewpoints on offer to the electorate in the vast majority of CEE states. This is in marked contrast to most of the communist period, when the official commitment to the Leninist vanguard concept of the communist party excluded the possibility of real political competition.

Official Nationalism and Legitimation

Having provided an overview of various kinds and examples of exclusion and inclusion in Central and Eastern Europe, it is appropriate to return to the argument about legitimation.

Given the profound economic and social problems of early post-communism, plus—in light of both these problems and the fate of their communist predecessors—the sense of insecurity some politicians themselves experience in the fragile politics of most CEE countries, such people often 'play to the gallery' even more than do their counterparts in more consolidated and legitimate systems. If playing the nationalist card is considered necessary to win elections and stay in power, then it is likely to be played. In this sense, the political inexperience of most post-communist populations, which can be attributed largely to the paternalistic approach of the communists, is a major factor encouraging official nationalism. More self-legitimate regimes would not perceive such a need to play populist cards as do so many post-communist ones.

But this official nationalism suffers from two major drawbacks. First, like any official nationalism, it is insufficient in itself to act as a regime and system legitimator in the medium-to-long term; as Max Weber and many others since have argued, a modern state *system* ultimately has to be legitimated in terms of legal-rationality (although it is maintained here that a particular *regime* may succeed or fail more on the basis of eudaemonism). Ethnic nationalism can undermine and be in contradiction with the notion of equal human rights that is a cornerstone of liberal democracy and hence legal-rationality.

Second, and to some extent developing out of the last point, official nationalism can trigger unofficial nationalism, which may in some circumstances serve to undermine a given regime and even system. This is obvious in the case of secessionism/separatism. But if official nationalism encourages unofficial unitarism and/or racism and ethnic conflict, this can in turn destabilise an already fragile arrangement.

Thus, while it is possible to appreciate some of the reasons for official nationalism and exclusionary policies by post-communist governments and politicians, these institutions and officials will have to learn rapidly that many of their own citizens soon come to understand both the limitations and the drawbacks of these. Evidence of the growing public awareness and rejection of nationalist and exclusionary approaches in some CEE states include the parliamentary election results in Lithuania in 1992, Kuchma's victory over Kravchuk in the 1994 Ukrainian presidential elections, and the public demonstrations against President Slobodan Milošević of Serbia from late-1996.[53] Over time, many citizens come to realise that politicians often use nationalism and ethnic politics as a diversionary tactic, to find scapegoats for, or to direct attention away from, fundamental economic problems.

Of course, official nationalism is only one of many factors that encourage unofficial nationalism and ethnic tensions; since I have elsewhere elaborated ten factors explaining the rise of nationalistic sentiments and politics, it would be inappropriate to rehearse that argument again here.[54]

Conclusions

It is easy to exaggerate the levels of ethnic tension and exclusionary politics in CEE; as writers such as Stephen Holmes have pointed out, there has been far *less* extremism and aggressive exclusion in the region than might *a priori* have been expected.[55] This chapter has considered some of the many positive inclusionary moves that have—unceremoniously—been taken in many countries of the region in recent years, as well as some of the negative developments that have *not* occurred.

Nevertheless, the emphasis here has deliberately been on *exclusionary* aspects, since these often constitute actual or potential problems that need to be addressed. The focus so far has also been on domestic and CEE regional factors, problems and policies. But if the issues identified are to be properly contextualised and resolved, some consideration of the situation in, and the role of, the West is vital.

Despite the claims in some of the sources cited at the beginning of this chapter that nationalism and related phenomena are now being superseded in Western Europe, it is quite clear that racism, nationalism and other forms of exclusionary politics have in the 1990s been thriving there too. Indeed, in the context of the increase in population movements, economic problems, and public resistance to deepening EU integration in so many West European countries, exclusionary phenomena were increasing right across the continent during much of the decade.[56] Such developments are undesirable and of concern, and the West should set a better example than it often does in dealing with them; acting as a role-model in its handling of its own exclusionary extremists is one indirect way in which it can assist the CEE countries. Unfortunately, while Germany has in recent years taken concrete measures to outlaw various symbols and acts of racist extremism,[57] governments in Austria, France, Italy and elsewhere do not invariably demonstrate the resolve they should in dealing with such elements within their own societies. Moreover, even Germany— as well as countries such as Italy—was by 1997 adopting a rather exclusionary policy vis-à-vis Bosnian and Albanian refugees.[58] And whereas the Schengen agreement has virtually eliminated the borders between the participating EU countries, the external boundaries of the Schengen area have in many ways become even more difficult for outsiders, especially non-EU citizens, to cross. There is still plenty of scope for more inclusive policies on both citizenship and residency in Western Europe.

Although exclusionary extremism is a serious problem in Western Europe, its potential implications are even worse in most CEE states, given their still fragile nature and that economic and economy-related problems (e.g. the inadequate welfare provisions) are so much more severe than in, for instance, EU Member States. This means that the likelihood of such phenomena destabilising and delegitimising the nascent democracies is greater in most CEE countries than in most West European ones. If fragile democracies are replaced by populist dictatorships, the problems of exclusion will be greatly exacerbated; and if exclusionary attitudes lead to civil wars, as happened in the former Yugoslavia, the results will be disastrous.

Such a grave scenario is not a necessary one, however, and there are ways in which the West can play a more direct and useful role, if CEE countries want this. Western international and supranational organisations can exert a positive influence on CEE states not only through conditionality (which is sometimes questionable anyway), but, importantly and ultimately more effectively, through setting an example of inclusion at the international level.

Countries such as Estonia, Hungary, Romania and even Slovakia, to name but four, have proven willing to reach agreement with neighbours on borders and citizenship when they have believed that, by doing so, they would *inter alia* enhance their chances of being integrated into the West. The endorsement of the Hungarian-Slovak treaty is a prime example. The West, via agencies such as the Council of Europe and the EU, should continue to encourage such agreements. But it must also reward those countries that are prepared to pursue conciliatory policies. At an earlier point in this analysis, it was argued that excessive sycophancy towards the West by CEE governments can encourage xenophobia and various forms of nationalism. However, there is a greater danger that xenophobic nationalism within individual CEE countries will be fuelled if those countries continue to be excluded from Western military and economic blocs, notably NATO and the EU.[59] It is understandable that the West was cautious not to assume prematurely that the old power systems in CEE really had been dismantled in the period 1989-91. But it is now several years since the collapse of communism in these countries, and, given growing doubts in several CEE states about Western commitment, the West must continue to make it clear that countries that make concerted and successful efforts to meet the criteria NATO and the EU themselves laid down in 1995[60] will not continue to be excluded from Western 'clubs'.

Several positive developments have occurred lately. Czechia, Hungary and Poland were all admitted to the OECD (Organisation for Economic Cooperation and Development) during 1996, for example, which was symbolically important to them. NATO had until recently been hesitant about moving too rapidly on the integration of CEE states. There were good reasons for this, notably a number of technical problems of compatibility and Russia's objections since late-1993. But neither of these factors should serve as a block indefinitely. The former is being overcome anyway as time passes. Regarding the latter, the West has made strenuous efforts to address many of Moscow's concerns about NATO's expansion eastwards, and to consult with Moscow whenever possible. One major symbolic advance in this area was the signing of the 'Founding Act on Mutual Relations, Cooperation and Security' by President Yeltsin and the heads of government of the 16 NATO member-states in Paris in May 1997. While this did not signify that Russia would have any veto-rights over NATO decisions, it did constitute a formalisation of the notion that NATO would consult with Moscow on issues that could be perceived as being of direct relevance to Russia, including NATO's eastward expansion. But to have made further concessions would not have been in the West's interest. Russia is still a volatile country, and its elite is deeply divided, including on its attitudes towards cooperation with the West. Its domestic tensions could last for many years yet, and it is conceivable that an aggressive nationalist with expansionist policies will come to power in the future; given that Russia remains a major nuclear power, the potential ramifications of such a development are clear. Meanwhile, many of the CEE countries are seeking assistance from and closer relations with NATO, and the recent momentum must be maintained.[61]

It would be naïve to assume that many of the CEE countries did not view NATO's Partnership for Peace program formally proposed in January 1994, and subsequently agreed to by most of the post-communist states (including even Russia, in June 1994), as, if not a sop, little more than a symbolic starting point.[62] The measures taken by NATO since late-1995 are encouraging, however. It was decided in December 1995 to commence a series of one-year long dialogues with the eleven CEE countries (Albania, Czechia, Estonia, Republic of Macedonia, Hungary, Latvia, Lithuania, Poland, Romania, Slovakia and Slovenia) that had expressed a firm interest in engaging in such an exercise; one year later, NATO ministers agreed to convene a summit to discuss the outcome of these dialogues and decide which countries would be invited to begin accession talks.[63] That summit took place in Madrid in July 1997, and NATO agreed formally to invite three CEE countries (Czechia, Hungary and Poland) to join its ranks. As had been predicted by many observers, NATO Secretary-General Javier Solana proposed April 1999 as the most suitable date for accession; this will be the 50th anniversary of the signing of the document that formally established NATO. It was disappointing to the other CEE applicants that they were not included in this first tranche. However, if these other countries can see for themselves that CEE states will indeed be admitted once they meet NATO's own specified criteria, this should act as a further spur to the consolidation of more democratic and tolerant systems in them.[64]

Czechia, Hungary and Poland look set to be among the first countries to be admitted to the EU too. Poland had been planning to be ready for admission by 2000.[65] Unfortunately, when European Commission President Jacques Santer introduced the Agenda 2000 project to the European Parliament in July 1997, it was made clear that the earliest date for any EU enlargement would be 2002. This can be explained largely in terms of the EU's own internal problems, particularly the preparation for the Economic and Monetary Union (EMU), the introduction of a common currency, and the need to reform some of the political arrangements, rather than a conscious desire to exclude CEE countries. Nevertheless, there was some sense of disappointment in Poland and the other applicant countries. On the other hand, it was *five* CEE countries (Czechia, Estonia, Hungary, Poland and Slovenia), not just three, that were invited to commence admission negotiations in July 1997;[66] these negotiations formally began in early 1998. This development could be seen to be excluding other CEE applicants. As with the NATO situation, however, the fact that some CEE countries are apparently about to be included in the EU might act as a further incentive to the so-called 'laggards' to accelerate their economic and political reforms.[67] It is important that the EU does not appear to be indifferent towards—excluding—those CEE states that work hard to meet its entry requirements. If it is accepted that the incorporation of Greece into the EC in 1981, and then of Spain and Portugal in 1986, helped consolidate democratic and more tolerant cultures in those countries after the collapse of their dictatorships, this argument becomes even more persuasive.[68]

In an ideal world, people would not seek to exclude others. But we do not live in an ideal world, nor will we. Exclusivity cannot simply be wished away. The psychological need for identity and belonging to a group—whether it be based on ethnicity, gender, sexuality, age, religion, class or some other social construct (or a mixture of these)—appears to be a fact of life for most people. As soon as individuals start to identify with one group, they demarcate themselves from others. In this sense, exclusion and inclusion constitute necessarily related and mutually interactive concepts; there cannot be one without the other. Yet they can manifest themselves in quite different ways. In metaphorical terms, the boundaries between groups can be painted lines on the ground—which are easy enough to cross and are not *per se* threatening—or high barbed-wire fences. Both state authorities and civil societies must work towards painted lines.

Notes

1. Touraine, A., 'European countries in a post-national era' in Rootes, C. and Davis, H. (eds.), *Social Change and Political Transformation* (London: UCL Press, 1994), 13–26.
2. Dogan, M., 'The Decline of Nationalisms within Western Europe', *Comparative Politics*, 26 (3) 1994, 281–305; it should be noted that Dogan's claim is based on a very narrow definition of nationalism, so that it is less preposterous than it initially appears.
3. For the purposes of this chapter, CEE includes the European Soviet successor states.
4. See e.g. Corrin, C. (ed.), *Superwomen and the Double Burden* (London: Scarlet Press, 1992); Einhorn, B., *Cinderella Goes to Market* (London: Verso, 1993); Funk, N. and Mueller, M. (eds.), *Gender Politics and Post-Communism* (New York: Routledge, 1993); Rueschemeyer, M. (ed.), *Women in the Politics of Postcommunist Eastern Europe* (Armonk, NY: Sharpe, 1994); the various articles in *Women's Studies International Forum*, 17 (2-3) 1994, 267–314; the articles in *Transition*, 1 (16) 1995, 2–28; Renne, T. (ed.), *Ana's Land* (Boulder CO: Westview, 1997); and the articles in *Transitions*, 5 (1) 1998, 14–79.
5. There are at least two other meanings of post-communism currently in use. The first is popular among citizens of the CEE countries, and refers to the communist successor parties. The second refers to the post-communist and post-Cold War era generally, and

is therefore a phenomenon that, in its ramifications, embraces the whole of Europe (and beyond).

6. See Zwick, P., *National Communism* (Boulder: Westview, 1983), 15–31.
7. *Ibid.*, 23–8.
8. Holmes, L., *Post-Communism* (Cambridge: Polity, 1997), 15–21.
9. On the Brezhnev Doctrine, according to which the USSR claimed both the right and the duty to interfere in the domestic affairs of countries within its orbit if 'socialist internationalism' appeared to be under threat, see Light, M., *The Soviet Theory of International Relations* (Brighton: Harvester Wheatsheaf, 1988), 194–200.
10. The term Czechoslovakia is used here to refer to the period up to late-1989; Czecho-Slovakia, conversely, refers to the period from the collapse of communist power until the dissolution of the country on 31 December 1992.
11. Walzer, M., 'The New Tribalism', *Dissent*, Spring 1992, 164–71; also in *Esprit*, November 1992—as cited in Rupnik, J., 'The Reawakening of European Nationalisms', *Social Research*, 63 (1) 1996, 42 (this entire issue of *Social Research* is devoted to nationalism in CEE).
12. For a subtle analysis of the relationship between nationalism and the ideological vacuum see Hall, J., 'After the Vacuum: Post-Communism in the Light of Tocqueville' in Crawford, B. (ed.), *Markets, States and Democracy* (Boulder: Westview, 1995), esp. 86–8.
13. See Zanga, L., 'Albanian Statistics: Filling the Information Void', *RFE/RL Research Report*, 3 (10) 1994, esp. 36.
14. The term 'apparently' is used here to highlight the fact that, since we now have proof that at least some communist states manipulated economic performance data, we shall never know for certain how accurate official statistics from the communist era were. For growth rates in individual CEE states see the EIU *Country Report* for the particular country.
15. For details of the transfers to eastern Germany for each year 1992 through 1995 see Flockton, C., 'Economic Management and the Challenge of Reunification' in Smith, G., Paterson, W. and Padgett, S. (eds.), *Developments in German Politics 2* (London: Macmillan, 1996), 218–20.
16. See e.g. Rhodes, M., 'The Former Soviet Union and the Future: Facing Uncertainty', *RFE/RL Research Report*, 2 (24) 1993, 52–5; Shafir, M., 'Romanians and the Transition to Democracy', *RFE/RL Research Report*, 2 (18) 1993, 42–8; Rose, R. and Haerpfer, C., 'Mass Response to Transformation in Post-Communist Societies', *Europe-Asia Studies*, 46 (1) 1994, 3–28.
17. For an elaboration of this argument see Holmes, L., 'The Democratic State or State Democracy? Problems of Post-Communist Transition', *Jean Monnet Chair Papers*, No.48 (Florence: European University Institute, 1998).
18. Holmes, *op. cit.* 1997, 42–58 and 337–43; Holmes, L., *The End of Communist Power* (Cambridge: Polity Press, 1993), 8–44 and 274–91; Holmes, L., 'Normalisation and Legitimation in Postcommunist Russia' in White, S., Pravda, A. and Gitelman, Z. (eds.), *Developments in Russian and Post-Soviet Politics* (London: Macmillan, 1994), 323–30.
19. In addition to the fragility of the state's institutions, its frequent inability to deal satisfactorily with major issues, and its difficulties in exercising power on the basis of either popular legitimacy or coercion, the fact that so many borders in CEE and the CIS are still being contested means that the territorial integrity of several states is in question. Unfortunately, the huge question of 'what is the state?' in the post-communist world is beyond the scope of this chapter.
20. For details and an explanation see Kionka, R., 'Estonian Political Struggle Centres on Voting Rights', *RFE/RL Research Report*, 1 (24) 1992, esp. 15–16.
21. This is in fact the same situation as in Australia, the EU member states, and many other Western states—which should therefore be wary about 'throwing stones'!
22. This portfolio was abolished in May 1997, allegedly because the new prime minister,

Mart Siiman, wanted to handle Estonia's relations with Western Europe himself. Conversely, a Ministry for Ethnic Relations was established at that time.

23. Taht, J., 'Estonia Proves Itself', *Transition*, 3 (2) 1997, 25.
24. Conceptions that are based on a plurality of criteria, such as ancestry or place of birth or merely expressed commitment to a state (as in Australia or the United States), represent a yet more inclusive approach to citizenship. Although it is true that even these broader approaches involve exclusionary aspects (for instance, in excluding people who are not prepared to swear allegiance to a particular kind of socio-political system), they are not inherently racist. Ultimately, *all* conceptions of citizenship of a particular state are more or less exclusionary, in that there will always be people seeking such citizenship who will be denied it. The only ways of overcoming exclusivity would be to introduce a single world (universal) citizenship or else to abolish citizenship altogether!
25. For an elaboration of this argument see Schöpflin, G., *Politics in Eastern Europe* (Oxford: Blackwell, 1993), esp. 281–4.
26. Marshall, T.H., *Class, Citizenship and Social Development* (New York: Doubleday Anchor, 1965), esp. 71–134. For a recent analysis of Marshall's ideas and their relationship to contemporary developments see Bulmer, M. and Rees, A.M. (eds.), *Citizenship Today* (London: UCL Press, 1996).
27. For a more favourable interpretation of Estonia's position on citizenship from that presented here, written by an Estonian, see Park, A., 'Ethnicity and Independence: The Case of Estonia in Comparative Perspective', *Europe-Asia Studies*, 46 (1) 1994, 69–87. It should in fairness be noted that Park acknowledges on p.85 that his article addresses the situation only to June 1993, and that he was aware that a new phase might be about to begin.
28. Fisher, S., 'Romanies in Slovakia', *RFE/RL Research Report*, 2 (42) 1993, esp. 57–8.
29. See e.g. *Warsaw Voice*, Nos. 5 (2 February) and 6 (9 February), 1997.
30. See Pehe, J., 'Czechs and Slovaks Prepare to Part', *RFE/RL Research Report*, 1 (37) 1992, esp. 12. Detailed survey results on Czech and Slovak attitudes towards division up to July 1992 are presented in tabular form in Wolchik, S., 'The Politics of Transition and the Break-Up of Czechoslovakia' in Musil, J. (ed.), *The End of Czechoslovakia* (Budapest: Central European University Press, 1995), 233 and 235.
31. See Aleksandar Pavkovic's chapter in the present volume.
32. One example of where this expectation *has* been met is the unification of Germany in 1990.
33. See e.g. Ionescu, D. and Reisch, A., 'Still No Breakthrough in Romanian-Hungarian Relations', *RFE/RL Research Report*, 2 (42) 1993, 26–32; Oltay, E., 'Hungarians under Political Pressure in Vojvodina', *RFE/RL Research Report*, 2 (48) 1993, 43–8.
34. Reisch, A., 'Slovakia's Minority Policy under International Scrutiny', *RFE/RL Research Report*, 2 (49) 1993, 35 and Szilagyi, Z., 'Hungarian Minority Summit Causes Uproar in the Region', *Transition*, 2 (18) 1996, 45–8. The 'three pillars', according to Szilagyi (p.45), are integration into Western political and security organisations; the establishment or maintenance of good relations with all neighbouring states; and protection of the rights of Hungarian minorities in other countries.
35. On various aspects of developments in Crimea during the 1990s see Wilson, A., 'Crimea's Political Cauldron', *RFE/RL Research Report*, 2 (45) 1993, 1–8; Solchanyk, R., 'Crimea's Presidential Election', *RFE/RL Research Report*, 3 (11) 1994, 1–4; Solchanyk, R., 'The Politics of State-Building: Centre-Periphery Relations in Post-Soviet Ukraine', *Europe-Asia Studies*, 46 (1) 1994, esp. 50–9. For a more up-to-date analysis, which, while not being overly optimistic, does highlight and explain a number of recent improvements in both Russo-Ukrainian relations and relations between Sevastopol and Kyiv see Sasse, G., 'The Crimean Issue', *Journal of Communist Studies and Transition Politics*, 12 (1) 1996,

83–100. It should be noted that while the Russian *government* has tended to downplay the differences between Moscow and Kyiv, many Russian parliamentarians and high-profile politicians, such as Moscow mayor Yurii Luzhkov, have attempted to exacerbate them by playing a Russian nationalist and populist card; these people have frequently and very publicly argued that Sevastopol is part of Russia, and should be treated as such.

36. Hockenos, P., *Free to Hate* (New York: Routledge, 1993), 148.
37. See above for other aspects of Estonian language laws.
38. See Fisher, S., 'Making Slovakia more 'Slovak'', *Transition*, 2 (24) 1996, 14–17. This entire issue of *Transition* (29 November 1996) is devoted to the question of language and identity in various post-communist states.
39. Bell-Fialkoff, A., 'A Brief History of Ethnic Cleansing', *Foreign Affairs*, 72 (3) 1993, 110.
40. *Ibid.*, 111.
41. For an argument that recent developments in the mass media permit ethnic cleansing to play a vital role in influencing mass perceptions of other cultures in a way that was not feasible in the past see Ahmed, A., ''Ethnic Cleansing': a metaphor for our time', *Ethnic and Racial Studies*, 18 (1) 1995, 1–25.
42. Hann, C., 'Ethnic cleansing in Eastern Europe: Poles and Ukrainians beside the Curzon Line', *Nations and Nationalism*, 2 (3) 1996, 389–406.
43. For a book-length single-authored study of the extreme right and racism in post-communist Europe see Hockenos, *op. cit.* For book-length multi-author analyses of political extremism throughout the post-communist world, that include much on the more unsavoury forms of nationalism and exclusion, see Held, J. (ed.), *Democracy and Right-Wing Politics in Eastern Europe in the 1990s* (New York: Columbia University Press, 1993), and the entire issue of *RFE/RL Research Report*, 3 (16) 1994. A more recent collection of articles can be found in *Transitions*, 5 (7) 1998, 18–47. For a relatively recent analysis of the situation in both CEE and Western Europe see Cheles, L. *et al.* (eds.), *The Far Right in Western and Eastern Europe* (London: Longman, 1995), while even broader geographical coverage can be found in Braun, A. and Scheinberg, S. (eds.), *The Extreme Right* (Boulder, CO: Westview, 1997) and Merkl, P. and Weinberg, L. (eds.), *The Revival of Right-Wing Extremism in the Nineties* (London: Cass, 1997).
44. In July 1995, for example, skinheads attacked a group of Romanies in Ziar Nad Hronom (Slovakia), killing one of them by setting him alight. Two skinheads were later charged with murder, and President Kovač expressed his outrage at the attack. But not all public figures were as unambiguously condemnatory. Notably, the leader of the junior partner in the ruling coalition, Jan Slota of the Slovak National Party, while expressing regret over the incident, also implicitly suggested that he 'understood' the motives for it when he stated publicly that crime rates in Slovakia were particularly high where there were concentrations of Romanies. Given all this, it is hardly surprising that a coalition of several small Romany organisations—the Union of Romany Political Parties in Slovakia—was formed in September 1995, with the specific objective of defending and promoting Romany interests. On the situation of Romanies generally in the post-communist countries see Barany, Z., 'Living on the Edge: The East European Roma in Postcommunist Politics and Societies', *Slavic Review*, 53 (2) 1994, 321–44, while a much fuller analysis of their history in the region is provided in Crowe, D., *A History of the Gypsies of Eastern Europe and Russia* (New York: St. Martin's, 1995).
45. There were few signs of this up to 1994—see Fisher, S., 'Meeting of Slovakia's Hungarians Causes Stir', *RFE/RL Research Report*, 3 (4) 1994, 42–7. Some Hungarians in Slovakia were disappointed by the initial reactions of the Slovak parliament to the March 1995 treaty between Hungary and Slovakia, however, while a number of indications since Mečiar's return to power in late-1994 that Slovakia might be moving away from democracy has

made many Hungarians there apprehensive; this *could* trigger more overt autonomism or even irredentism in the future if local Hungarian elites believe they would benefit from this.

46. Einhorn, *op .cit.*, esp. 148–81; for more up-to-date figures—many from May 1996—see Holmes, *op. cit.* 1997, 258–61.

47. It should be noted that communist parties can reappear, often in almost identical guise, following a ruling of the particular country's constitutional court; the clearest example of this is in Russia. The Czech government was apparently considering banning the Communist Party of Bohemia and Moravia (as well as the ultra-right Republican Party) in early 1997—see Gomez, V., 'Banning Extremists', *Transition*, 3 (4) 1997, 3—although President Havel advised against this.

48. See Vachudova, M., 'The Visegrad Four: No Alternative to Cooperation?', *RFE/RL Research Report*, 2 (34) 1993, 38–47.

49. For early analyses of the various new formations see Bakos, G., 'After COMECON: A Free Trade Area in Central Europe?', *Europe-Asia Studies*, 45 (6) 1993, 1025–44; Clarke, D.L., 'Europe's Changing Constellations', *RFE/RL Research Report*, 2 (37) 1993, 13–15; Reisch, A., 'The Central European Initiative: To Be or Not To Be?', *RFE/RL Research Report*, 2 (34) 1993, 30–7.

50. Barrington, L., 'The Domestic and International Consequences of Citizenship in the Soviet Successor States', *Europe-Asia Studies*, 47 (5) 1995, 731–63 and Resler, T., 'Dilemmas of Democratisation: Safeguarding Minorities in Russia, Ukraine and Lithuania', *Europe-Asia Studies*, 49 (1) 1997, 89–106. Barrington argues that Russia's 'liberal' policy, including its acceptance of dual citizenship, might have a darker side, in that it could be used to pressure other states to emulate Moscow's approach, and even to justify interference in other countries' affairs if Russians are perceived to be receiving poor treatment. In the social sciences, there are almost always at least two ways of interpreting anything.

51. Socor, V., 'Moldova: Democracy Advances, Independence at Risk', *RFE/RL Research Report*, 3 (1) 1994, esp. 48–9.

52. For analyses of the problems of numerous dimensions of the welfare systems in the post-communist states see the various articles in *RFE/RL Research Report*, 2 (17) 1993, 1–23 and 2 (40) 1993, 31–62; Gedeon, P., 'Hungary: Social Policy in Transition', *East European Politics and Societies*, 9 (3) 1995, 433–58; Mikhalev, V., 'Social Security in Russia under Economic Transformation', *Europe-Asia Studies*, 48 (1) 1996, 5–25; and Snavely, K., 'The Welfare State and the Emerging Non-profit Sector in Bulgaria', *Europe-Asia Studies*, 48 (4) 1996, 647–62.

53. In some ways, Yeltsin's victory over Zyuganov in the Russian presidential elections of mid-1996 could also be seen as a victory over exclusionary and inward-looking nationalism, since Zyuganov emphasised his nationalist leanings far more than his communist values in the later stages of the electoral campaign. However, it needs to be remembered that Yeltsin originally came to power on one level as a secessionist nationalist, arguing for Russian interests and identity over Soviet. Moreover, he made much during the 1996 campaign of Belarus' April 1996 treaty with Russia, suggesting that this might serve as a model for other CIS states and that something akin to the FSU could eventually re-emerge (which conflicts somewhat with his earlier position and reflects the Russian president's unpredictability). For Russian accusations that Yeltsin was responsible for the break-up of the USSR see Dunlop, J., 'Russia: in search of an identity?' in Bremmer, I. and Taras, R. (eds.), *New States, New Politics* (Cambridge: Cambridge University Press, 1997), 39; see too Laba, R., 'How Yeltsin's Exploitation of Ethnic Nationalism Brought Down an Empire', *Transition*, 2 (1) 1996, 5–13.

54. See Holmes, L., 'Nationalism and Ethnic Politics in Contemporary Europe—With Particular Reference to Germany', *European Studies Journal*, 10 (1-2) 1993, 175–97; Holmes, *op. cit.* 1997, 296–8.

55. Holmes, S., 'Cultural Legacies or State Collapse? Probing the Postcommunist Dilemma' in Mandelbaum, M. (ed.), *Postcommunism: Four Perspectives* (New York: Council on Foreign Relations, 1996), esp. 35–42.
56. For a useful review article that summarises and critically assesses some of the recent literature on both post-war migration to Western Europe (including during the 1990s) and the relationships between this and racist politics see Messina, A., 'The Not So Silent Revolution', *World Politics*, 49 (1) 1996, 130–54. Two of the better books among the numerous studies of nationalism in Europe, East and West, to have been published in recent years are Kupchan, C. (ed.), *Nationalism and Nationalities in the New Europe* (Ithaca: Cornell University Press, 1995) and Brubaker, R., *Nationalism Reframed* (Cambridge: Cambridge University Press, 1996). For detailed information on ethnic groups in CEE and the actual or potential conflicts between them see Brunner, G., *Nationality Problems and Minority Conflicts in Eastern Europe* (Gütersloh: Bertelsmann Foundation, 1996).
57. Unfortunately, with less success than had been hoped for. The number of recorded racist attacks in Germany increased in 1997, after having been in decline for several years.
58. In 1998, moreover, the German province of Bavaria created a precedent by ordering the deportation of a Turkish couple who had lived in Germany for three decades, on the grounds that their 13-year old son—who was born in Germany—had committed a crime. It remains to be seen whether this is an isolated example of blatant state exclusionism or whether the German authorities really are becoming more overtly racist and exclusionary.
59. For an early analysis of CEE attempts to join NATO see Reisch, A., 'Central and East Europe's Quest for NATO membership', *RFE/RL Research Report*, 2 (28) 1993, 33–47. For a more recent analysis see Clarke, D., 'Uncomfortable Partners', *Transition*, 1 (2) 1995, 27–31.
60. In NATO's case in its *Study on NATO Enlargement* published in September; in the EU's case in its May White Paper on the criteria for membership, *Preparation of the Associated Countries of Central and Eastern Europe for Integration into the Internal Market of the Union.*
61. Ideally, Russia itself would move closer to and eventually join NATO. If the West is serious about promoting peace, this scenario should be actively pursued. For an argument in favour of more engagement with Russia see Pierre, A. and Trenin, D., 'Developing NATO-Russian Relations', *Survival*, 39 (1) 1997, 5–18. It should be noted that many Western analysts have been highly critical of NATO's expansion. Some have argued that the enlargement is being poorly implemented, while others criticise the very notion of expansion. For examples of the former argument see Eyal, J., 'NATO's enlargement: anatomy of a decision', *International Affairs* (London), 73 (4) 1997, 695–719; Perlmutter, A. and Carpenter, T., 'NATO's Expensive Trip East', *Foreign Affairs*, 77 (1) 1998, 2–6. For the more radical position see Brown, M., 'The flawed logic of NATO expansion', *Survival*, 37 (1) 1995, 34–52; Gaddis, J.L., 'History, Grand Strategy and NATO Enlargement', *Survival*, 40 (1) 1998, 145–51.
62. For the Czech president making this point, complaining about the reticence of the West, and warning of the dangers of such an exclusionary approach see Havel, V., 'A Call for Sacrifice', *Foreign Affairs*, 73 (2) 1994, 2–7. For an early analysis of the Partnership for Peace Program see Borawski, J., 'Partnership for Peace and beyond', *International Affairs* (London), 71 (2) 1995, 233–46.
63. For details on all this, plus the official US administration's position, see US Department of State, *Report to the Congress on the Enlargement of the North Atlantic Treaty Organisation: Rationale, Benefits, Costs and Implications* (Washington DC: 24 February 1997).
64. It is worth noting that France pushed to have at least two other CEE countries, Romania and Slovenia, admitted in this first wave, but that this was resisted by, in particular, the USA and the UK. Nevertheless, Solana indicated at the Madrid summit that the second

wave of admissions was likely to include not only Romania and Slovenia, but also Estonia, Latvia and Lithuania.

65. *Warsaw Voice*, No.5 (2 February), 1997.
66. In addition to the five CEE countries, Cyprus was also invited to begin accession negotiations.
67. In February 1998, the EU released details of the individual targets ('accession partnerships') it was setting for each potential new Member State. In the cases of Estonia, Latvia and Slovakia, for example, it was emphasised that they would have to adopt more tolerant policies towards ethnic minorities and their languages.
68. It is acknowledged here that incorporation is now a considerably more complicated task than it was in the 1980s; the EU itself has both expanded and become more integrated, and the number of CEE countries is far higher than the three Southern European 'consolidating' democracies. But the present problems are not insurmountable, and the potentially destabilising effects on the rest of Europe of extremist regimes coming to power in CEE countries should help to focus the minds of those responsible for EU development. For recent analyses of various dimensions of the proposed EU expansion see *Transitions*, 5 (4) 1998, 18–83, while a more detailed technical analysis of the economic impact on enlargement, esp. on the CEE states, can be found in Gabrisch, H., 'Eastern Enlargement of the European Union: Macroeconomic Effects in New Member States', *Europe-Asia Studies*, 49 (4) 1997, 567–90.

8 Yugoslavism: A National Identity That Failed?

ALEKSANDAR PAVKOVIC

Introduction[1]

The second disintegration of the Yugoslav state in 1991, fifty years after the first disintegration, appears to signal the futility and failure of the national idea on which the state was founded—the Yugoslav idea. Yet this appearance, like many others in that part of the world, is deceptive. The state which disintegrated in 1991 and the Kingdom of Yugoslavia which was carved up by the victorious Axis in 1941 resembled little the state which the creators of the Yugoslav idea dreamed about in the 19th century. Their dreams of a common state were based on their firm belief that the South Slav—Yugoslav— peoples or, as they put it, tribes, constitute one and the same nation. The Socialist Federal Republic of Yugoslavia which ended in 1991 with the secession of two of its six federal units was not based on any such belief. On the contrary, from its inception in 1943 to its end, the state never officially recognised the existence of a Yugoslav nation. As a consequence, this state never officially recognised Yugoslavism as a separate national identity. In spite of this, in the 1981 census there were 1.2 million Yugoslavs (around 6% of the population in Yugoslavia), the only group of people in Yugoslavia whose national identity was effectively denied.

One of the many paradoxes the disintegration of Yugoslavia presents is this: as federal Yugoslavia disintegrated into a bloody civil war, those who were most loyal to it, the self-declared Yugoslavs, lost very little. The state which disintegrated never recognised their national identity nor their allegiance. Upon the disintegration of Yugoslavia, the self-declared Yugoslavs were left with their only true possession—the imaginary homeland of their own which no civil power can ever destroy.

This paper attempts to explore the origins of this paradox. The exploration need not be motivated solely by an antiquarian curiosity. The paradox points to a failure to forge a single, politically effective, national identity in a state of nationally divided loyalties. This failure may offer a lesson or two to the dreamers of the United Europe populated by a growing nation of Europeans.

Yugoslavism: The Origins

Like many national ideas in Eastern Europe, the Yugoslav idea is much older than the state which it helped to create. Its intellectual origins, like the origins of many national ideas in this part of Europe, are to be found in the Herderian view of a nation defined by its language and folk customs, the two expressions of its national soul. In 1830 a young Croat student of law Ljudevit Gaj (1809-1872), inspired by this Herderian view, discovered the oral poetry of the South Slavs and their dialects and started a national awakening movement similar to the Czech and, later, Hungarian movements. But unlike other national awakening movements, he lacked a native name for the nation which he was rediscovering. Using the term popularised by the short-lived Napoleonic administration of the South Slav lands, he called this nation Illyrians. The term, intended for all South Slavs, was rejected by most Serb intellectuals of the time; the term 'Illyrian' was replaced by many of Gaj's followers with the native term Croat, which was intended to refer to mainly Roman Catholic inhabitants of the long-lost medieval Triune Kingdom of Croatia, Slavonia and Dalmatia. The idea of a single South Slav nation reappeared, under its native name of Yugoslavism, only in the 1860s, once again among Croat intellectuals. While Gaj's primary goal was to introduce a standard language for this nation and reconstruct its literary traditions, two Roman Catholic clerics, Bishop Josip Juraj Strossmayer (1815-1905) and Canon Franjo Racki (1828-1894), had much wider aims. They wanted to forge a national identity of Yugoslavs on the basis of a common history, literature and scholarship. In addition, they aimed at the political unification of all South Slavs, initially in the Habsburg monarchy and later, when this failed, of the Habsburg South Slavs with those of the semi-independent Principality of Serbia and of the Ottoman lands. Unlike some later proponents of the Yugoslav idea, Strossmayer and Racki could not conceive a Yugoslav state without a Yugoslav national identity. The most urgent task, the historian Racki emphasised in his speeches and writings, was to research the history of the South Slavs, divided as they were into different states, to discover their common but forgotten past. In addition, a common literature and scholarship needed to be created among them.

These two tasks were not tasks of discovery but of construction and creation. One had to construct a non-existent common past and to create from scratch a common literature. As he undertook almost single-handedly to do the former,

Racki was fully aware of how daunting these two tasks were. In one of his public speeches, he noted that even when the Croats and Serbs were living in independent states, in the 10th and 11th century AD, there was no contact between them. The Ottoman conquest of the Serbian lands in the 15th century cut off the latter from the Croatian and Slovene lands under the Habsburgs. Racki here appeared to argue that it was just an accident or misfortune of history that these three nations and other South Slavs had had so little contact in the past. The study of their history would disclose, he hoped, at least one feature in common: the long and unwanted rule of foreign powers and the persistent struggle of South Slavs for liberation from this rule. This feature, he implied, provided a sufficient basis for their feeling of common kinship and a common historical destiny.

As for common literature, Racki was convinced that it would inevitably arise on the basis of the neoštokavian standard language accepted by Croat and Serb linguists in their agreement in Vienna in 1850. A common literature and a common sense of past rule, he had no doubt, would forge the new sense of Yugoslav national identity.

Thus the creators of the Yugoslav idea had to put their trust into the future: in the near future, they hoped, historical and ethnographic scholarship as well as common literature would forge the desired sense of common national identity among the educated. In this respect, we now have to admit, the future failed them badly. Most educated Serbs and Croats have never developed the sense of common national identity overriding their primary national identities, although some of them tried hard to follow the ideals of Strossmayer and Racki.

The Failure to Create a Common National Identity

The reasons why the educated, the intellectuals, failed to develop a common national identity are complex and as yet unexplored. To grasp the magnitude of their failure, it may be sufficient to list a few well known differences between the Serb and Croat cultures in 1918, the year which saw the creation of their first common state, the Kingdom of Serbs, Croats and Slovenes.

The hopes that the standard neoštokavian based on the east Hercegovina *ijekavian* sub-dialect would provide a basis for a common literature were dashed a few decades after its adoption. The prevalent dialect in Serbian literature became the Vojvodina/Šumadija *ekavski* subdialect which most Serbian intellectuals spoke. Although Croat intellectuals gradually abandoned the Zagreb kajkavian dialect and other non-štokavian dialects and adopted the *ijekavian* neoštokavian standard, their literary standard expanded its vocabulary in a way quite unlike the Serb standard. Following the Czech linguistic model, Zagreb linguists resisted the intrusion of foreign (e.g. German) borrowings, preferring to create calques. An equal resistance was shown to the use of Serb words even when they were of Slav origin. In contrast, Serb men of letters took to foreign borrowing, mainly from the French, preferring them to the Croat Slavic calques. Each of the literary standards retained their alphabet (Cyrillic for the Serbian, Latin for the Croatian), in spite of attempts by some Serb men of letters to introduce the Latin alphabet as a sign of broad-minded Yugoslavism. In 1918 there were thus two distinct but mutually fully comprehensible literary standards based on two different sub-dialects and with a differing everyday as well as technical vocabulary, using two different alphabets.

Apart from differing literary models (the Serbs went to Paris while the Croats went to Vienna and Germany), only a few enthusiastic Croat writers and poets who lived in Belgrade participated in Serbian literary life and spread the Yugoslav idea in literature. No Serbian writer of any note participated in the literary life of Zagreb before 1914. This absence of contact and mutual recognition of influence was deplored with a sad regularity.

During and immediately after World War I, a Yugoslav literary journal appeared in Zagreb, the creation of the then avantgarde and anti-establishment writers and poets from the South Slav lands of Austro-Hungary. Among its early contributors we find the names of the greatest Serb and Yugoslav writers, Miloš Crnjanski and Ivo Andric. But the journal floundered in the early 1920s as its original contributors became part of their respective cultural establishments; no Yugoslav literary journal has ever appeared since without state subsidies and encouragement.

By 1918, the historical research into the common past had not advanced much further than in Racki's time. With a few exceptions, Croat historians would restrict their research to Croatia and Serb historians to the Serbs. After 1918 the situation appeared to have changed: the most distinguished Serb and Croat historians, such as Vladimir Corovic (1885-1941) and Ferdo Šišic (1869-1940), were those who actively propagated the Yugoslav idea and wrote histories of Yugoslav peoples and of the Yugoslav idea. But their approaches often betrayed their national origins. The Serb historians would often see Yugoslav history as a road to full assimilation of Yugoslav peoples into one single and indivisible nation; the Serb armed struggle and their victory in World War I loomed very large in this process. The Croat historians would not only see more diversity in this process but would eschew any suggestion of assimilation. In spite of the towering presence of the pro-Yugoslav historians, many less distinguished historians showed no interest in Yugoslav history.

There were, it is argued here, three distinct but related reasons why these efforts of small groups of intellectuals to create a common past, literature and language met with so little success. First, by 1918, the three main national groups in the Kingdom—Serbs, Croats and Slovenes—already had flourishing if somewhat parochial cultures of their own. The cultural life of these nations was concentrated in their capital cities, where small but fairly hierarchical intellectual elites were firmly in control. For most of the members of these elites, as well as for their constituency (the provincial intelligentsia), the creation of a new unified culture represented a threat both to their current position and to their identity. To put it rather crudely, these intellectuals did not see a safe place for themselves in this grand new Yugoslav edifice comparable to the relatively safe place which they had occupied until then.

Second, the few grand *intellos* who were pushing the Yugoslav line and continued doing so after 1918 disagreed among themselves about the form the new culture and the new identity should take. The Serb intellectuals mostly but not exclusively pushed the assimilationist or unitarist line: all national distinct characteristics should be fused into one new identity based on a rather mythical past of the struggle for liberation. The Croat and Slovene intellectuals wanted the national varieties preserved and the new unity to be created in diversity. All of them appeared to have very vague ideas as to the actual content of the new concept of identity; the only thing they were able to agree on was that the new identity should be liberating from the oppression of the past prejudice. It appeared more of a wish and a hope than a concept of identity.

Third, the new and liberating identity had little basis in the past or in the present practice. There simply was no Yugoslav common past, as Racki had long ago noted. The persistent disagreement from 1917-18 onwards between the Serb and Croat political elites over the constitutional structure of the new Kingdom of Serbs, Croats and Slovenes (Croat political leaders demanding a federal or confederal structure, while most Serb leaders preferred a unitary state) not only revealed the absence of a common sense of national identity but clearly impeded the development of any such identity among the political elites or their constituencies.

Unitary Yugoslavism from the Top Down

The royal *coup d'état* in January 1929 was not triggered by the crisis of Yugoslavism but by a severe political crisis following the shooting, in June 1928 in the Yugoslav parliament, of several deputies of the Croat Peasant party, including its leader Stjepan Radic, by a Serb deputy. In dissolving the parliament and embarking on a personal rule, King Aleksandar Karadjordjevic (1888-1934) attempted to change the very foundation of his kingdom. Instead of the three separate tribes of the South Slavs, he sought to forge a new nation of Yugoslavs. One of his measures was rather ominously linguistic: he changed the name of the country to Yugoslavia, the country of the South Slavs. The other measures were political and coercive. He banned all political and cultural organisations based on national or religious affiliation and replaced them with pan-Yugoslav mainly secular organisations, charged with carrying out Yugoslav propaganda. He and his advisers hoped to instill a unitary Yugoslav national identity, an identity which simply denied separate national identities, by systematic state organised propaganda and coercion, if necessary.

As would have been expected, the opposition to this was formidable: it embraced most political parties of all nations, including the Serbs, most of the national intelligentsias as well as the Roman Catholic Church (but not the Serbian Orthodox). The royal ban on political parties based on national affiliation, plus dictatorship, drove several politicians, both Serbs and Croats, into exile. Among them was Ante Pavelic, who in 1929 founded the Croat Ustasha[2] movement, a terrorist and racist organisation whose goal was the independence of Croatia and its 'cleansing' of inferior races such as Serbs and Jews. King Aleksandar's unitary Yugoslavism failed to take root not only among the politicians with well-established national constituencies but also among the ordinary people from all national groups.

In fact, King Aleksandar's coercive measures carried out by his newly converted Yugoslav administrators dealt a death blow to this conception of Yugoslavism. From then on Yugoslavism which denied separate national identities and sought to replace them with a new unitary Yugoslavism was associated with coercion and dictatorship. This conception is still the bogeyman of all opponents of Yugoslavism: all that Yugoslavism does, they argue, is to coerce people into abandoning their cherished national traditions for the sake of some non-existing identity which means nothing to anyone, even its proponents.

Soon after King Aleksandar's assassination in 1934 by a Macedonian terrorist on the orders of the Croat Ustashe, his successors abandoned the ideology of unitary Yugoslavism without finding any replacement for it. The Kingdom of Yugoslavia survived on the basis of a political compromise of Croat and Serb leaders until 1941 when, after a quick defeat of the Yugoslav Royal Army, the Axis powers carved up the country into various units, among them an Ustashe-ruled 'Independent State of Croatia'. Yugoslavism thus appeared to have died before the state which it helped to create.

Yugoslavism in the Service of a Communist Party

It was the communists who resurrected both Yugoslavism and the Yugoslav state. Unlike the unitarist model, the communist model of the Yugoslav idea preserved, nay emphasised, the distinctiveness of the South Slav nations, elevating to the rank of constituent Yugoslav nations Macedonians, Montenegrins and, later, Muslims: nations which were not recognised before. The Communist Party of Yugoslavia, the victor of a multi-faceted civil war, in 1946 officially divided Yugoslavia up into six federal units called republics—Bosnia-Hercegovina, Croatia, Macedonia, Montenegro, Serbia and Slovenia—and an autonomous province and an autonomous region in Serbia. The population was divided into five (from 1968, six) constituent nations and numerous national minorities (later called 'nationalities'). Each of the six constituent nations—Croats, Macedonians, Montenegrins, Serbs, Slovenes and, from 1968 on, Muslims—and some of the larger nationalities (e.g. Albanians again from 1968 on) was entitled to its own glorious past and literature, its Academy of Sciences, its universities, intellectuals and cultures. In spite of the distinctness, these, the communists argued, were not only equal but also brotherly nations living in unity. This implied that these nations were related by blood and that their relations were governed by reciprocity and mutual support, characteristic of a family. More importantly, according to the communist party dogma, they had irrevocably decided to live in a single state—hence their political unity.

According to the communist version of Yugoslavism, in order to be a Yugoslav one need not shed one's previous—some would say 'inborn'—national identity. One needed only to recognise this higher bond uniting all the officially recognised nations and nationalities together. The bond was forged in the great National Liberation Struggle from 1941 to 1945 in which all the nations and national minorities of Yugoslavia, led by the Communist Party, fought the Axis and their Yugoslav servants (such as the Ustashe).

Yugoslavism as a supra-national identity thus became a political identity: a political statement endorsing the communist arrangement of brotherly peoples living in a single state. This political identity, tailored to fit the communist elite and its rank-and-file, was to subordinate and control but not to replace the existing national identities. It required no elaborate national myths, no national culture in common, nor a Yugoslav intellectual elite to propagate it. The main and only national myth was that of a communist-led National Liberation Struggle in which the brotherly Yugoslav peoples freed themselves not only of their occupiers but of the past national prejudices and hatreds instilled by the native bourgeoisies and their foreign helpers. To inoculate this new sense of identity, it was often thought, nothing more was needed than for all children and adults to study the seven enemy offensives—the legendary Axis offensives against the numerically inferior, poorly armed but ultimately victorious communist-led Partisans.

Although the Yugoslav Communist Party never acknowledged the existence of a distinct nation of Yugoslavs, in the period from 1953 to 1964 the Party toyed with the idea of building a common Yugoslav national consciousness, which was called Yugoslav socialist patriotism. According to the Program of the League of Communists of Yugoslavia of 1958, socialist Yugoslavism was an aspect of both socialist internationalism and democratic national consciousness which, in socialist Yugoslavia, were being developed in unison. This socialist Yugoslavism was not to lead to the creation of a new nation to replace the old ones but was rather a process of organic growth and strengthening of the existing socialist community. According to the 1958 program, this process would involve the creation of a common Yugoslav culture—this unfulfilled dream of all Yugoslavs from Racki onwards. The first stages of this process involved forging closer links among Yugoslav 'cultural workers'—scientists, writers, scholars and teachers—as well as introducing the same school curriculum (at least in literature and history) in all Yugoslav schools. (Until then each of the six federal units—republics—in Yugoslavia had separate school and university curricula, each emphasising the achievements of the nations of the republic in question.)

The new policy of closer links among national and republics' intelligentsias was implemented primarily through frequent exchange of visits by their members organised in the newly founded Yugoslav professional associations of teachers, philosophers, historians, etc. But apart from large collections of papers and speeches (and memorably lavish state-subsidised banquets), these exchanges produced nothing. No common Yugoslav school textbooks nor curriculum were ever introduced. In spite of the lavish banquets, the idea of a common Yugoslav cultural space or framework came under sustained attack by Slovene and Croat writers and officials who argued that those who promoted this idea of common Yugoslavism were in fact promoting the interests of the central bureaucracy. The mainly Serb promoters of the Yugoslav idea argued, in turn, that their critics were promoting the interests of bureaucracies of the republics from which they came.

Indeed, it was these republics' bureaucracies and their communist elites which defeated the central communist apparatus in 1964, when the Yugoslav communist party dropped the project of building a common socialist Yugoslavism from its Party program. The final defeat of Yugoslavism came in 1966 when the vice-president of Yugoslavia and the effective head of the Yugoslav security apparatus, Aleksandar Rankovic, was expelled, through coordinated action of the communist national elites, from the Yugoslav communist party. As Rankovic was a Serb, Yugoslavism—which he was alleged to have promoted—was conveniently unmasked as a species of Greater Serbian nationalism.

This was the end of the politically promoted Yugoslavism but not the end of a non-political Yugoslavism. The shock came with the 1981 census: 1.2 million citizens of Yugoslavia (out of the total of around 22 million) declared themselves to be Yugoslavs; in the 1961 census there were only 317,000 Yugoslavs and they appeared to be a dying breed.[3] Yugoslav communist party ideologues were at loss how to explain this surge. The easiest explanation was to view it as a result of the increase in mixed marriages in the post-war era. The resultant progeny of these marriages had no nation to go to and so they chose to declare themselves as Yugoslavs. Their choice of Yugoslavism was then not a result of an ideologically deviant nationalist view but of mixed marriage. As a personal choice, the Party ideologues claimed, it was not ideologically or politically deviant because it did not even express a desire or longing for the creation of a separate nation of Yugoslavs. Their choice of Yugoslavism, the Party apologists argued, was a non-political and non-ideological declaration of non-national belonging.

But why did the million odd people have to express their non-national belonging in this particular way? After all, clause 170 of the Yugoslav Constitution of 1974 gave every Yugoslav citizen a legal right to *decline* to declare his/her nationality. In the 1981 census, 47,000 people availed themselves of this clause and refused to declare their nationality. If more than a million Yugoslavs did not have a nation to go to, why did they not simply decline to declare any nationality? The official, somewhat implausible explanations, summarised above, could not hide two rather awkward facts. The younger generation of mainly better educated people were refusing to accept the official ideology according to which there was no Yugoslav nationality; by declaring themselves members of the officially non-existent nationality, they were in effect rejecting the official ideological explanations. It was, in short, a muted form of opposition. Second, the official ideology proved to be unable to accommodate what appeared to be a wave of the future, the children of mixed marriages. The official ideology, however dynamic and future-oriented it presented itself to be, was simply not that.

It appears that the failure of official communist national ideology to accommodate the new Yugoslavs stemmed from the use to which national identities were put in communist Yugoslavia. These official national identities were primarily mobilisational. Patriotic Yugoslavism as a supranational identity was promoted in order to broaden the base of loyalty to the regime and to exhort the citizens to sacrifice in the construction and defence of their country. Once the need for this mobilisation decreased—with the introduction of material incentives and consumerism in the early 1960s and the disappearance of the threat of invasion by the USSR—patriotic Yugoslavism had no further role to play. The resurgence of separate national ideologies—of Croat, Slovene, Macedonian, Muslim and Albanian national groups—was once again a mobilisation and legitimising tool of republics' and provincial communist elites which, in the early 1960s, were in the process of consolidating their grip on power. To them any appeal to Yugoslavism was a direct threat to their national power base: for these rising national communist elites, Yugoslavism thus became a nationalistic deviation.

All in all, national identities—whether those of separate nations or of the no longer recognised supranational Yugoslavs—were viewed by communist elites as instruments of legitimation and mobilisation. Apart from these two roles, national identity had no other political role to play. Naturally, citizens of Yugoslavia were not or could not be prohibited from choosing any national identity they wished to have as long as their choice did not threaten the established political elites.

After 1966 a citizen of Yugoslavia who publicly declared himself/herself a Yugoslav would be automatically excluded from any political participation except from voting in non-contested one-party elections. A self-declared Yugoslav had no right to be elected to any posts in a republic or the Yugoslav federation or to be appointed to any middle- or upper-level office in any administration, whether of the communist party or government. All of those posts were specifically reserved for those who belonged to the officially recognised separate nations and nationalities. Yugoslavism thus became a private and anti-political choice. Its non-recognition only signalled the breakdown between citizens' freely chosen national identity and their political participation. Thus self-declared Yugoslavs were effectively disenfranchised long before their putative state disintegrated.

Who Failed?

The history of Yugoslavism as presented here is a history of three failures. First, the South Slav intellectuals failed to produce the standard language and culture as well as a shared historical past in which a distinct Yugoslav national identity could be anchored. Second, King Aleksandar and his coterie quite predictably failed to impose this national identity by political will and coercive suppression of competing separate national identities. Third, the communists failed to develop the Yugoslav patriotism which they initially promoted into a distinct national identity and reverted to the politics of national rivalry which characterised pre-World War II Yugoslavia.

Therefore, it is not Yugoslavism as a national identity that failed but the intellectuals and politicians who undertook to promote it. The 1.28 million citizens who in 1981 freely chose to be Yugoslavs and to be effectively disenfranchised, remain as a silent *witness* to the power of an old ideal and a warning to those intellectuals and politicians who are trying to forge new national identities. They warn, first, that the new national identity which citizens are free to choose needs to have a specific content. One needs to know what it is to be a Yugoslav or European. Second, in order to make the new identity politically or culturally relevant, those who choose the new identity need to be given a political voice. In short, one has to enable those who choose to pursue new ideals to pursue them in a political and cultural arena. In Yugoslavia's case, giving self-declared Yugoslavs a political voice would have seriously destabilised national communist elites. In the case of Europe, the political and cultural organisations of new Europeans would probably be equally destabilising of the entrenched national elites in Europe. But until such organisations are established and flourishing there can be little room for optimism about the brave new United Europe.

Notes

1. An earlier version of this essay entitled 'The Yugoslav Idea: A Short History of a Failure' was published in Perkins, J. and Tampke, J. (eds.) *Europe: Retrospects and Prospects*, (Manly: Southern Highlands Publishers, 1995).
2. 'Ustaša' (transliterated here as 'Ustasha', and 'Ustashe' in the plural) in Croatian means 'insurgent': the term is meant to portray the movement as a national liberation movement—the movement for the liberation of Croats from the domination and exploitation of the Serbs.
3. The 1991 census—the census completed just as the Yugoslav federation was about to dissolve into war in July 1991—showed that there were still 710,000 self-declared Yugoslavs left, approximately 3 per cent of the population of the state which was about to disappear.

Index

marginalisation 56–57, 59, 61–62,
  69, 103, 104, 110
marriage 97–113
Marshall Aid Program 125
Marshall case 118
Marshall, T. H. 8–9, 55, 98, 99, 128
Martens, H. 90
Marx, K. 121
Marxism-Leninism 124
masculinism 5
McCrudden, C. 104
Mečiar, V. 123, 129, 131, 143
media, mass 7
Meehan, E. 10, 14, 100, 103, 109,
  110, 111
Mercouri, M. 82, 94
Meri, L. 126–128, 129
migrants 2, 12–13, 15–16, 55–70
military dictatorship 74
Milošević, S. 136
Minorities Policy 67
mobilisation 155–156
Moge v. Moge case 108
Moldova 130, 134
Montenegrins 153
Montenegro 129, 153
Moran, M. 98
Moravians 133
Moroccans 63, 65
*Movimiento Democrático das
  Mulheres* 77
Movimiento Democrático de Mujeres
  77
Mujeres Libres 77
multiculturalism 7, 13, 57, 61, 64, 66,
  67–70
Murray, P. 109
Muslims 153, 156

Nagorno-Karabakh 135
Napoleonic empire 26
National Liberation Struggle 153
National socialism 74–75

nationalism 121–157
  autonomist 133, 144
  civic 133
  irredentist 5, 129–130, 134–135,
    144
  official 123, 126, 129, 135–136
  secessionist 129, 136, 144
  separatist 5, 129, 133, 136
  unitarist 136, 151–152
  unofficial 132–133, 136
nationality 17–18
nation-state, problems with the term
  19
naturalisation 60, 63, 66, 68
Nazism – *see* National socialism
neo-liberalism – *see* economic
  rationalism
neo-Nazis 60
neoštokavian language 148
Netherlands, the 67–68, 77, 85, 105,
  106, 116, 117
New Right 104
new social movements 9, 79–80
'new tribalism' 124
New Zealand 107
Newman, M. 9
Niederlassungsbewilligung 58
Noi Donne 93
North Atlantic Treaty Organisation
  138–139, 145
Northern League 5
Norway 2, 101

Oberndörfer, D. 61
Offe, C. 80
Organisation for Economic
  Cooperation and Development
  95, 138
Orton, H. 107
Ossetians 135
Ostalgie 12
Ottoman lands 148